Hong Kong Babylon

Hong Kong Babylon

An Insider's Guide to the Hollywood of the East

Fredric Dannen and Barry Long

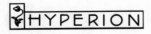 

NEW YORK

Published in Great Britain by Faber and Faber Limited.

The chapter "Hong Kong Babylon" originally appeared, in condensed form, in *The New Yorker*.

Library of Congress Cataloging-in-Publication Data

Dannen, Fredric.
Hong Kong Babylon: An Insider's Guide to the Hollywood of the East — 1st. ed.
p.   cm.
"Miramax Books"
Includes filmographies

ISBN 0–7868–6267–X

1. Motion pictures — Hong Kong — Catalogs.   2. Motion picture producers and directors — Hong Kong — Interviews.   3. Motion pictures actors and actresses — Hong Kong — Interviews.   I. Title
PN1993.5.H6D36   1997
016.79143'75'095125 — DC21   97–11201
                                          CIP

FIRST EDITION

10 9 8 7 6 5 4 3 2 1

Contents

Acknowledgments

Fredric Dannen: This book would not exist without John Bennet, my esteemed editor at *The New Yorker*, who oversaw the original article on which it is based; or Lynn Hirschberg, who encouraged me to write the book; or Jeffrey Ressner, who encouraged me not to write it.

At Miramax Books, I was very fortunate to have, in Susan Dalsimer, another top-flight editor; thanks also to Kristin Powers, who provided much valuable assistance, and to Paul Schnee; to Walter Donohue and Justine Willett of Faber and Faber; to Kristin Kliemann of Hyperion; and to Scott Greenstein and John Hughes, of Miramax, for their support.

My thanks to all the critics who agreed to contribute to Chapter 4.

My co-author and I both wish to gratefully acknowledge Art Black for proofreading the book, and making numerous helpful suggestions.

In Hong Kong, Christina Nathanail worked tirelessly to get me interviews with at least a dozen key people, for no reason apart from generosity. Norman Wang was also instrumental in getting me access to people, and, in some cases, serving as translator.

Thanks, also, to Sam Pinkus, my hardworking agent; to *New Yorker* fact-checkers Aaron Retica and Blake Eskin; and to Peter J. Boyer, Alison Dakota-Gee, Joseph M. Fierro, Greg Girard, Nicki Gostin, Kim Heron, Rick Hertzberg, Stacy Mosher, Gerald Posner, David Remnick, Shawn Sites, Gavin Smith, Edward Stancik, Dorothy Wickenden, and Jaime Wolf. And, especially, to Tina Brown.

Barry Long: My thanks to Ruth and Warren Long, Diep Derstine, Rob Price, Hector Rodriguez, Eliot Tong, and George Wu, and especially to Steve Puchalski at Shock Cinema, for encouraging me to write, and to Joe, for putting up with me.

For the use of the photographs, the publishers wish to acknowledge Christopher Doyle, who has provided photographs of Leslie Cheung, Willie Chan, Ann Hui, Stanley Kwan, Sammo Hung, and from *Days of Being Wild* and *Ashes of Time*; and PhotoFest for photographs of Chow Yun-fat, Tony Leung Ka-fai, and from *Bullet in the Head*, *A Better Tomorrow*, *The Killer*, and *Hard-Boiled*. Photographs from *Boat People* and *Full Contact* courtesy of BFI Posters, Stills and Designs.

Stills courtesy of BFI Stills, Posters and Designs, Photofest, Christopher Doyle, Miramax, Media Asia, Made in Hong Kong, Tai Seng, and from the individual film-makers: Clara Law, Eddie Fong, Josephine Siao, Stanley Tong, Tsui Hark, John Woo.

Copyright for the photos in this book is held by the following: Golden Princess Film Production Ltd. (*Bullet in the Head* and *Hard-Boiled*); Cinema City Company Ltd. (*A Better Tomorrow*); United Filmmakers Organization (Peter Chan) Miramax (*Chungking Express, Drunken Master II, Project A*, and portraits of Michelle Yeoh and Jet Li); Christopher Doyle (self-portrait, as well as portraits of Peter Chan, Leslie Cheung, Tony Leung Ka-fai, Wong Kar-wai, Willie Chan, Stanley Kwan, Ann Hui, and the stills from *Days of Being Wild* and *Ashes of Time*); Media Asia Group, copyright Star TV (*Peking Opera Blues, Center Stage, Rouge, A Chinese Ghost Story, Police Story*); MGM/UA (*Warriors of Virtue*, portrait of Ronny Yu); Peter Chow International (*Swordsman II*) Made in Hong Kong (Simon Yam); Electric Pictures/Polygram Film (*Fallen Angels*); Columbia Pictures and Mandalay Entertainment (Tsui Hark on the set of *Double Team*); Circle Films (*The Killer*); BoB & Partners Co. (Anthony Wong); City Entertainment (Sylvia Chang); UFO Concept Ltd. (*The Spooky Bunch*).

A Note on Access

The purpose of this book is to provide a broad overview of the modern Hong Kong cinema, and what it has to offer the Western viewer; and, if this book is at all successful, the reader will be motivated to see any number of the movies described herein. Home viewing has become an increasingly easy option. Though to date only a small handful of Hong Kong films – such as John Woo's *The Killer* and the Jackie Chan vehicle *Rumble in the Bronx* – are available at the typical video outlets, many cities in North America have cult-video stores that carry a larger selection of titles. Readers who live near a Chinatown are guaranteed to find a large number of the Hong Kong films they seek, either on video cassette or laser disk, at video stores in the neighborhood. Though the majority of Hong Kong movies have alternative English titles – and, most importantly, English subtitles – the proprietors of Chinatown establishments often do not recognize the English titles. For that reason, we have provided the Chinese titles for the more than three hundred movies in the Plot Summaries section that begins on page 169.

Mail-order rental is another option. In North America the best outlet for that purpose is Facets Rentals-by-Mail (address: 1517 West Fullerton Avenue, Chicago, IL 60614; tel: 800-532-2377; e-mail: rental@facets.org); the cost is $10 per movie, shipping included. Tai Seng offers a large selection of Hong Kong videos for sale (address: 170 South Spruce Avenue, Suite 200, South San Francisco, CA 94080; tel: 888-668-8338; e-mail: vidinfo@taiseng.com; World Wide Web: http://www.taiseng.com). Though Tai Seng charges about $40 per cassette, for some unfortunate reason, many of its selections span two tapes, even when the total running time is less than two hours.

Screenings of Hong Kong movies, apart from those that regularly occur at Chinatown cinemas, have also become increasingly common in North America. Meanwhile, on cable television, the International Channel presents its *Cantonese Movie Theater* every Saturday at 4 p.m. Pacific Standard Time and 7 p.m. Eastern Standard Time. A programming schedule can be found on the World Wide Web at http://i-channel.com/program/schedules/cantonese.html.

In London, key players in the area of Hong Kong movies are Eastern Heroes Label and Shops (96 Shaftesbury Ave., London W1V 7DH; 3A Buck Street, Camden, London NW1 8NJ), Made in Hong Kong (231 Portobello Road, London W11 1LT; tel: 0171 792 9791; fax: 0171 792 9871; e-mail: mink@ballgag.demon.co.uk), and MIA Video (2nd Floor, 70 Baker Street, London W1M 1DJ; tel: 0171 935 9225; fax: 0171 935 9565).

All readers with Web access are urged to visit the Hong Kong Cinema homepage at http://egret0.stanford.edu/hk/ for links to a comprehensive data base on movies and film personalities, as well as a frequently updated schedule of screenings in various regions of North America. Meanwhile, the homepage at http://www.mdstud.chalmers.se/hkmovie/ is a gateway to directories of video outlets around the world that rent and sell Hong Kong movies.

A Note on Names

The Chinese names that appear in this book have been rendered, with few exceptions, in the form deemed most accessible to the English-speaking reader. Hong Kong movie personalities tend to make this easy, since many of them have dual English and Chinese names. The top actress Anita Mui, for example, is actually Mui Yim-fong. Sometimes the personality's English name, which is usually of the owner's devising, is fanciful (the director Lam Ling-tung chooses to be called Ringo Lam); or obscure (the actor Chow Yun-fat was briefly known as Amon Chow, though he hasn't used that name for years, and neither do we); or unfortunate (the actress Cheng Yu-ling is called Do Do Cheng, but also Carol Cheng; we opt for Carol).

When no commonly used English name is available, we provide a transliterated Cantonese name. It is important to remember that the Chinese customarily put their family names first. The director Tsui Hark, for example, is Mr. Tsui, not Mr. Hark. The rule is not immutable, however – the director's wife, Nansun Shi, is properly addressed as Ms. Shi.

1 Hong Kong Babylon

A Reporter Looks at the Hollywood of the East

Fredric Dannen

The Cantonese Cinema: An Introduction

Jackie Chan, the most popular film actor in the world, stepped out onto the ledge of a clock tower. More than fifty feet below, in a town square, a group of onlookers waited anxiously to see him jump. They had been waiting for days. The onlookers were the cast and crew of *Project A*, an adventure movie about pirates on the China Sea in turn-of-the-century Hong Kong. In reality, the time was 1982, and Jackie Chan was the new king of the Hong Kong cinema, the territory's biggest draw since Bruce Lee had died, a decade earlier. Chan, like Lee, had once been a kung-fu artist, but now he was something different – a comedy-action star who did his own stunts. The scene in the town square called for Chan, who has been cornered by pirates, to dangle Harold Lloyd-style from the clock's minute hand, then plummet through two cloth awnings and hit the ground – all in one take, to make it clear that Chan was not using a safety mat. The crew had pre-tested the stunt, in a manner of speaking, by tossing a sack of topsoil off the ledge, but the test was not terribly scientific, and Chan could not be certain that the fall wouldn't kill him. "I just don't want to go down," Chan recalls thinking. "Scared." So the entire production of *Project A* came to a halt for more than a week while he stood on the ledge every day, steeling himself. Finally, he announced that he was ready, let go of the clockface, and, as planned, tore through the first awning. But instead of tearing through the second awning, he inadvertently bounced off it, was flipped upside down, and hit the ground head first. By some miracle of Hong Kong luck, he was not seriously injured. A few days later, he tried the stunt again. This time, it went perfectly.

When I first met Chan one morning a few years ago, at his office building on the Kowloon side of Hong Kong, he had recently broken his ankle jumping from a bridge onto a hovercraft for his new movie, *Rumble in the Bronx*. I got there early and waited for him downstairs, expecting him to arrive with an entourage. Instead, he walked in unaccompanied and, as if I might not recognize him, said, in a quiet voice, "I am Jackie." He was dressed in black pants, a matching vest, and a white shirt, and carried a cellular phone. Chan is about five feet nine, lean and muscular, with a Beatles haircut, and a handsome face offset by a pug nose. The nose, which he has broken three times, gives him an underdog look, which is central to his screen persona. He escorted me upstairs, moving slowly and stiffly. Chan is in his forties, and more than two decades of stunt work have wrought permanent skeletal damage. His most serious accident occurred in Yugoslavia in 1986, during the filming of *Armour of God*, an Indiana Jones-style adventure. He walked away unharmed from the film's most dangerous stunt, for which he was dropped onto a floating hot air balloon, but while he was performing a relatively easy leap onto a tree he turned to make sure the camera would catch his face, missed a branch, fell forty feet, and hit his head on a rock. He required brain surgery, and still has a hole in his skull.

Chan's office was furnished like a living room, and was empty of books and papers – for reasons to be explained later, he can't read or write. He can't sit still, either. By my third or fourth question, he was out of his chair, demonstrating kung-fu, complete with sound effects ("tong! tong! tong! tong! tong!"). Every fifteen minutes, a jet took off from Kai Tak airport, which was just nearby, and appeared as though it would crash through Chan's window. Hong Kong is one of the most densely populated places in the world: about six and a half million people live on a land mass smaller than Providence, Rhode Island; and in the central urban areas, Hong Kong Island and Kowloon, the density tops 65,000 people per square mile. The cramped living conditions are often offered as a reason why the people of Hong Kong love to go to the movies. The city produces more than 200 motion pictures a year, and is the second-largest exporter of films in the world, after the United States. Hong Kong is the movie factory for all Asia. Its movies fill the cinemas in Taiwan, Singapore, Malaysia, Thailand, the

Philippines and Indonesia, and are immensely popular in South Korea and Japan. In mainland China, until recently, most Hong Kong movies were officially banned – and pirated like mad. When Chan went to Manchuria in 1993 to film his acclaimed *Drunken Master II*, he discovered that everyone he met had seen his movies.

Indeed, in sheer numbers, Jackie Chan is surely the most recognized movie star on the planet. "In Asia," he says, "I am *Jurassic Park*. I am *E.T.*" A personal appearance by Chan in Seoul or Taipei or Tokyo can cause a riot. Japanese girls, for some reason, are among his most obsessively loyal fans, and, largely for fear of upsetting them, he keeps quiet about his many romantic involvements, and about the existence of his teenage son, Jackson, the product of a long-dissolved marriage to the Taiwanese movie actress Lum Fang-gew. When, a few years ago, it was falsely reported that Chan planned to remarry, one Japanese girl swallowed poison in front of his office building, and was narrowly rescued; another jumped in front of a train, and was killed. "This makes me a lot of trouble," Chan said, adding that other female fans have stalked him. "Some of these girl, they scare the shit out of you."

At the time of our first meeting, Chan, for all his fame in the East, remained a mere cult figure in the West. Outside of its Chinatowns, he could pass by unrecognized on any street in the United States or Great Britain. He was not happy about this. He once said he wanted to be as well known to Western moviegoers as the Teenage Mutant Ninja Turtles, another star act from his Hong Kong-based film studio, Golden Harvest. More likely, Chan's true basis of comparison was a different Golden Harvest star, the late Bruce Lee. Lee, who was born in San Francisco, was still the only Hong Kong movie actor to have achieved celebrity in the United States.[1] Chan had tried to follow in Lee's footsteps by taking the lead role in two Hollywood action movies. In 1980, he was featured opposite José Ferrer in *The Big Brawl*, and, five years later, played Danny Aiello's cop partner in *The Protector*. Both movies were failures. In between, he was cast as a Japanese racing-car driver in the comedy

---

1 Notwithstanding the brief renown of Nancy Kwan, who had the title role in the hit 1960 movie *The World of Suzie Wong*.

The Cannonball Run and its sequel, and got lost amid the large cast, which included Burt Reynolds.

I asked Chan whether *Rumble in the Bronx*, which was produced by Golden Harvest, and filmed primarily in Vancouver, was another go at appealing to a mainstream American audience. He denied entertaining any such hopes. "I know being Oriental very difficult to get in American market," he said, sighing. Another jet took off from Kai Tak and rattled the windows of his office.

Chan's pessimism was understandable, but his time was finally at hand. In February, 1996, New Line Cinema released a dubbed and re-edited version of *Rumble in the Bronx* to 1,500 theatres in the United States, and by the end of its opening weekend, it was the No. 1 movie in America. Within a year's time, two other recent Chan movies – *Supercop* and *First Strike* – played successfully in the United States. In the interim, Chan was a presenter at the Oscars, and, as further proof of his American conquest, starred on national television in a Mountain Dew commercial.

Chan's change of fortune did not occur in a vacuum. As it happened, the movie that *Rumble in the Bronx* knocked down to No. 2 was *Broken Arrow*, directed by John Woo, another Hong Kong movie personality. Meanwhile, several other Hong Kong directors – among them, Ringo Lam, Tsui Hark, Stanley Tong, Kirk Wong, and Ronny Yu – were courted by Hollywood studios. The actor Chow Yun-fat, who is often called the Cary Grant of Hong Kong, moved to Los Angeles; the action queen Michelle Yeoh,[1] a female counterpart to Jackie Chan, and his co-star in *Supercop*, was cast by MGM as the heroine in a James Bond movie. One might say that the Hong Kong cinema itself has come to America.

There is a fundamental reason behind the migration of talent: after a prolonged creative and financial boom, spanning the 1980s and early 1990s, the Hong Kong movie industry is undergoing an uneasy transition. A down cycle set in around 1993, with a marked decline in domestic theater attendance, affecting all but the biggest box-office stars, such as Jackie Chan and Chow Yun-fat. Though downturns are to be expected in the movie business, this one has

1 Also known as Michelle Khan.

come at a time when Hong Kong is anxious about its very future, because of Hong Kong's reunification with China, after a century and a half of British colonial rule, imminently to occur as this book went to print. No one in the movie industry knows what to expect. Hong Kong directors who have filmed in China complain that they have encountered censorship, bureaucracy and corruption. Many more industry leaders are expected to emigrate, and quite a few are likely to come to the United States.

The melding of Hong Kong and Hollywood is not only well timed from a political standpoint, but logical from a commercial one. The two movie capitals have a great deal in common; in fact, Hong Kong is often called *Dongfang Haolaiwu*, the Hollywood of the East. Hong Kong, for the time being at least, is expected to remain a major money center, with more Rolls-Royces per capita than anywhere else on earth; accordingly, its film studios, like those in Hollywood, put their emphasis on mass-appeal entertainment, particularly action films and comedies. Hong Kong movies may also lack high-mindedness for another reason, not financial, but linguistic. Natives of Hong Kong speak Cantonese, the dialect of south China, a lingo that is profanity-rich and demotic. Cantonese is rather less refined than Mandarin, the dialect of mainland China and Taiwan, where the films tend to be more highbrow, such as *Raise the Red Lantern* by China's Zhang Yimou, and *A City of Sadness*, by Taiwan's Hou Hsiao-hsien.[1]

Refinement is not a characteristic of the Cantonese movie. Perhaps the best way to describe the Hong Kong genre is to speak of its comic-book aesthetic: it is a cinema of incessant action, eye-popping effects, and cartoon-like violence. I think, for instance, of the tree-devil serpent in *A Chinese Ghost Story* (1987) who saps the life of its victims with a mile-long tongue, and whose human form is an aging drag queen; the climactic shootout in *Full Contact* (1992) which is filmed from the bullets' point of view; the martial-arts star Jet Li in *Once upon a Time in China* (1991) fighting on a ladder suspended high above the ground like a seesaw; the psychotically evil male and female Siamese twins in *The Bride*

1 Ang Lee, who made the transition to Hollywood by directing *Sense and Sensibility*, is also Taiwanese.

with White Hair (1993) who kill with a look; and Jackie Chan in *Police Story* (1985) hanging from a speeding bus by an umbrella.

Chan, it should be noted, is unique to the industry in a number of respects, including his insistence on making what he terms family pictures – movies, he says, with "no sex, no dirty joke, no make-love scene. I know my movie a lot of children see it." Generally speaking, the level of sex and gore in the Hong Kong cinema is peerless. Hong Kong has a three-tiered ratings system, but even Category III, which is equivalent to Hollywood's X or NC-17, carries no comparable stigma. Popular, mainstream films shock the viewer in ways that no Hollywood studio would ever attempt. The gangster film *The Big Heat* (1988) opens with a shot of a power drill piercing a man's hand. In *The Heroic Trio* (1993) three of the top actresses in Hong Kong – Michelle Yeoh, Anita Mui, and Maggie Cheung – are costumed superheroines doing battle with a subterranean villain who is kidnapping babies he plans to train as his netherworld army; in one scene, two of the heroines encounter a group of five-year-old boys who already show signs of training – so they blow them up. In *Run and Kill* (1993) a man incinerates his enemy's twelve-year-old daughter into charcoal, sets her corpse at the enemy's feet, and mimics the girl's voice, saying, "Daddy, I am so dark, can you still recognize me?"

The one taboo is overt political content; Hong Kong movies are free of it. Though hordes of Hong Kongers did take to the streets to protest the Tiananmen Square Massacre, the film industry does not like to dwell on politics – it is considered too uncommercial a subject, and, in light of the reunification with China, may be dangerous as well. When a Hong Kong director does touch on a political theme, "You have to hide it," says the director Eddie Fong, whose *Private Eye Blues* is filled with veiled references to the Chinese takeover. Fong complains, in fact, that it is difficult to make a movie in Hong Kong about any serious topic. "The audience for Hong Kong films, they're really low," he says. "They just want cheap entertainment." In despair, he and his wife, the noted art-film director Clara Law (*Autumn Moon*), have moved to Australia.

The Cantonese art film does exist, but almost apologetically. The leading art-house director of the moment, Wong Kar-wai, tends to work in popular genres, such as the martial-arts movie (*Ashes of Time*) and the gangster film (*Fallen Angels*), though he does turn those genres on their head. Another art-house favorite, Ann Hui, who in 1995 directed *Summer Snow*, an award-winning film concerning a man with Alzheimer's disease, says that film-makers such as herself are viewed as misfits in Hong Kong. For a period in the early 1990s, most of the offers she received from producers were to direct Category III pornography and swordfighting epics. She declined all those offers, and says she will continue to make movies her way. "One thing I appreciate about the Hong Kong film industry is that people acknowledge good quality, and you always get a chance to work if you try hard," she says.

Then again, Hong Kong movies tend to be made so quickly and cheaply that it's difficult even for box-office flops to lose much money. Budgets are minuscule by Hollywood standards: $1 million is average, and $5 million is big.[1] Film companies are able to churn out features from start to finish in seven or eight weeks, and sometimes less: a recent girls-in-the-gang movie called *Sexy and Dangerous*, adapted from a popular comic book, went from conception to completion in twenty days. Movies are edited as they are being shot, and post-production time is astonishingly brief; I was told of one major film for which the shooting ended four days before the sneak preview. Production values are frequently spotty, and such niceties as an original film score and a director of photography are often dispensed with. (On the other hand, the credits often include a person lacking in Hollywood productions: a separate director just for the action sequences.) The vast majority of Hong Kong movies are filmed without synchronized sound, and the entire soundtrack is created afterwards in a recording studio. It's cheaper that way. Often, top stars don't even bother to dub in their own voices, but instead use voice doubles.

Hong Kong films usually are subtitled in Chinese and English – the former because written Chinese is the same for all the different spoken dialects, and the latter simply by tradition. Similarly, the movies have dual Cantonese and English titles, though those titles

---

1 All monetary figures used in this chapter are in United States dollars, not Hong Kong dollars.

seldom match up. (For example, the crime drama *Soul* is known to Cantonese speakers as *Lo Neung Gau So*, or *Old Married Woman Dog Disturbance*.) The use of English greatly assists the American or British fan, though the haste and economy with which the subtitles are prepared often shows. ("After seeing Kitty . . . . I had priapism!") Occasionally, even the English titles appear careless – one popular Jackie Chan movie is entitled *Wheels on Meals*.

The movies' low budgets help explain why so much emphasis is placed on stunt work. The definitive moment in *Stone Age Warriors* (1990), a medium-budget shocker filmed in New Guinea among aboriginal headhunters, comes as the movie's two heroines plunge over a hundred-foot waterfall; and the way the director, Stanley Tong, filmed the scene is a perfect illustration of the difference between Hollywood and Hong Kong. When Harrison Ford appears to dive over the raging waters of a dam in *The Fugitive*, it is an illusion created by means of a computer matting technique known as blue screen. Hong Kong directors cannot afford the blue screen, so Tong and his stunt assistant dressed up as the two heroines, tied themselves to some trees with wire, and went over the falls.

The Hong Kong community of male and female actors in leading roles is rather small, and it does not take long for the same twenty or thirty faces to become familiar. When Hong Kong movie stars are on a hot streak, they can work at a pace that Western film actors would find incomprehensible. For example, over the past decade, Andy Lau, who, like many top actors, is also a Cantonese pop recording star, has appeared in more than seventy films. At his peak, in 1991, he averaged a movie a month, and during one stretch he was acting in four different movies a day, at as many locations, and sleeping in his car.

The overexposure of certain top names has to do with the unique economics of the film industry in Hong Kong. The theater chains of Asia are so eager for new Hong Kong pictures that a movie company can pre-sell an as yet unproduced film, for a considerable sum, all around the Asian circuit. The only thing that matters is the cast. Indeed, many Hong Kong films are shot without a script. Anyone – literally anyone – who can persuade a popular performer or two to appear in his movie can make the movie with little or no investment of his own. As a result, some of the most active movie producers in the city during the past decade have been the triads – Hong Kong and Taiwanese organized crime figures – whose powers of persuasion compensate for their ignorance of film technique.

It isn't only faces that recur in Hong Kong movies – so do plots. Hong Kong is sequel-happy. The hit horror-comedy *Mr. Vampire* was released in 1985; by 1987, there was already a *Mr. Vampire IV*, followed by *New Mr. Vampire* and a *Mr. Vampire 1992*. Hong Kong producers do not often acquire the rights to novels, because Hong Kong is not known for novelists – it's an effort finding a bookstore in the territory. Plots of Hollywood films are ripped off shamelessly. For example, *The Bodyguard* was remade as *Bodyguard from Beijing*, with Jet Li in the role originated by Kevin Costner. Hong Kong audiences have traditionally preferred even an inferior all-Chinese remake of a Hollywood production to the original.[1] Many movie industry people, including Jackie Chan, were dismayed when, in 1993, for the first time in decades, a Hollywood film, *Jurassic Park*, was the top-grossing picture of the year in Hong Kong; it happened again in 1994 with *Speed*. To the industry, the second-place showing represented a serious loss of face. Now, the triumphs of Chan and John Woo in the United States have more than made up for it.

From Shanghai to Hong Kong: The Shaw Brothers, Golden Harvest, and Bruce Lee

Whatever its feelings of rivalry toward Hollywood, the Hong Kong cinema is unmistakably its heir and descendant; on the set of any Hong Kong movie, the director always yells "Action!" and "Cut!" even if he speaks no other words of English. Indeed, the first known Hong Kong movie was financed by an American theater owner, one Benjamin Polaski. It was called *To Steal a Roasted Duck*, and was made in 1909 with a director and cast from Shanghai. Until the

1 When Caucasian actors are cast at all in Hong Kong movies, they tend to play villains. Despite a century and a half of colonization, less than 2 per cent of the population of Hong Kong is white, and the Cantonese word for Caucasian is *gweilo*, which translates roughly as "white ghost."

early 1950s, both Shanghai and Hong Kong were major movie towns, and talent regularly flowed between them. But Shanghai, which produced Mandarin-language films, not Hong Kong, was considered the movie capital of Asia. During the Japanese occupation of Hong Kong between 1941 and 1945, all existing Cantonese-language films were melted down for the silver, and production of new ones was banned, but, for some reason, Mandarin films were permitted. The defeat of the Japanese, followed by the nationalization of Shanghai's private studios by the Communists, left Hong Kong's movie industry pre-eminent.

Nevertheless, having secured a foothold, Mandarin films continued to flourish in Hong Kong. During the 1950s, they were regarded as the high-quality, cosmopolitan features, while Cantonese movies were seen as the low-budget, hastily produced B pictures. A large percentage of the Mandarin films were musicals. The Cantonese cinema aspired to nothing so lavish; instead, in 1949, it gave birth to the modern martial-arts movie – or, as some fans prefer, the "chop-socky" – when Kwan Tak-hing, a former performer of the Peking Opera, played the title role in *The True Story of Wong Fei-hung*. (Wong Fei-hung was a south China patriot and martial-arts master who died in 1924; he has been called, somewhat inappropriately, the Cantonese Robin Hood, for having championed the downtrodden.) Kwan went on to repeat the role in around one hundred subsequent movies, all in black and white, up until 1970, no doubt setting a record for the longest-running movie serial in history.

Hong Kong's biggest movie studio from the early 1960s until the early 1980s was Shaw Brothers, and its head man, Run Run Shaw, was the city's most powerful movie mogul. He was the second of four brothers from Shanghai who changed their family name to Shaw from Shiao when they began producing and exhibiting films in China in the 1920s, because their father, a wealthy textile manufacturer, did not approve. By 1939, the Shaws owned more than a hundred theaters all over Southeast Asia, but the theaters were confiscated by the Japanese during the war, and Run Run was imprisoned for subversion. Luckily, the Shaws had had the foresight to bury a chest full of gold and precious stones, and when the war ended, they were still rich.

In 1958, Run Run moved the Shaw Brothers operation to Hong

Kong, and three years later he oversaw the completion of Movie Town, the largest studio complex ever built in Asia, on a forty-six-acre lot in Hong Kong's Clearwater Bay. The lot included dormitories for actors, dubbing rooms, processing laboratories, sound stages, and a replica of a Qing Dynasty town familiar to fans of badly dubbed martial-arts movies on late-night American television. ("He insulted our school, Master!") Shaw Brothers turned out such films by the score, though along with the run-of-the-mill productions were several that are considered classics – King Hu's *Come Drink with Me* (1966), a swordplay picture set in medieval China, for one. Unfortunately, a disagreement with the Shaws over the film's ending caused Hu to quit the studio and produce his own movies out of Taiwan. (His subsequent efforts included the 1967 classic *Dragon Gate Inn*, and 1971's *A Touch of Zen*, the only movie by a Hong Kong director to win a top prize at Cannes until this year.) The Shaws had better luck holding on to another standout director, Chang Cheh, who had begun his movie career in Shanghai writing scripts for Shaw's biggest competitor, the Cathay Production Company. His best-known film is probably *The One-Armed Swordsman* (1967), though he went on to direct many other enduring pictures, and, in the process, helped train an eager young assistant director at Shaw Brothers: John Woo.

For reasons that remain obscure, Shaw Brothers and Cathay made the majority of their movies in the Mandarin dialect, including the martial-arts films. Cantonese movies continued to be produced by other studios, and one of the most popular stars of the 1950s and 1960s was a child actress from Shanghai named Josephine Siao, known to the Cantonese as Siao Fong-fong, or Little Bird. By the time she was twenty-one, she had acted in some two hundred movies, from swordplay films to musicals, both in Cantonese and Mandarin. "We didn't have labor laws for children then," she told me.[1] It was odd enough that so many films in a foreign dialect had been produced in Hong Kong for so long, but what occurred after 1963 may have no parallel in any other culture – movies in Hong Kong's native tongue began to disappear

---

1 Siao continues to act; for her role in Ann Hui's 1995 drama *Summer Snow*, she was awarded Best Actress at the Berlin Film Festival. An interview with Siao appears on page 120.

altogether. By the early 1970s, the Cantonese-language cinema was virtually nonexistent in Hong Kong; according to the film historian Paul Fonoroff, only two Cantonese features were produced between 1971 and 1973. It was not until 1977 that the trend reversed itself, and the contemporary Cantonese cinema came into existence.

The year Shaw Brothers relocated to Hong Kong, Run Run hired thirty-one-year-old Raymond Chow, a former journalist and the son of the chairman of the Bank of China, as head of advertising and publicity. Before long, Chow had moved up to head of production, a position he held for eleven years. "We were very close, but our relationship was strictly business," Chow says of Run Run. "I was never really a partner of Shaw Brothers. Had I been one, I probably would never have set up my own corporation."

The company that Chow founded – in 1970, along with Leonard Ho, who had been his right hand at Shaw Brothers – was Golden Harvest. Run Run scoffed, but Golden Harvest has gone on to become the biggest movie conglomerate in Hong Kong, while by 1986, Shaw Brothers had all but withdrawn from movies to concentrate on television. (In the meantime, Run Run was knighted by Queen Elizabeth and became Sir Run Run.) Golden Harvest resolutely rode out the financial slump of the mid-1990s, as one film production company after another deserted the business – or became a Golden Harvest acquisition. Chow, who is now in his late sixties, is a shy, slight, balding man with glasses. He was so fragile as a boy, he says, that his father used his influence to get him kung-fu lessons with an instructor whose own master was Wong Fei-hung, the Cantonese Robin Hood.

Chow's appreciation of the martial arts proved fortunate. One evening in 1970, when Golden Harvest was a new and struggling enterprise, Chow turned on his television and was riveted by a live kickboxing demonstration. The kickboxer was Bruce Lee, a dual Hong Kong and American citizen, who had been born in San Francisco in 1940 because his father, a Cantonese opera star, was on tour there. Lee spent his childhood in Hong Kong, learning to fight and frequently getting into trouble with the law as a member

of a violent, anti-British youth gang. His parents shipped him to
America in 1959. Two years later, he enrolled at the University of
Washington in Seattle, and met an American student, Linda Emery,
whom he married. Lee dropped out of college, opened a kung-fu
academy in Oakland, and came to the attention of the producer
William Dozier, who cast him as Kato in the television series *The
Green Hornet*, in 1966. When the series was canceled a year later,
Lee continued to seek acting jobs, while giving kung-fu lessons to
the likes of Steve McQueen and James Coburn. The demonstration
of Lee's fighting skills that Raymond Chow saw on television took
place during a brief visit to Hong Kong.

"It must have been fate that I was watching that program,"
Chow told me. "Bruce was showing so much power that evening,
it was unbelievable. He started his routine by putting cardboard
in front of the MC and three other men; then he kicked them,
and the whole team just collapsed. After that, he kicked a
wooden board suspended from a string, and broke it. That's so
much more difficult than if someone is holding the board. It takes
perfect timing and a tremendous amount of force. Then he said,
'I'll try to do something that is even more difficult. I'll toss a
board and see if I can break it in mid-air.' And he did that! I was
so amazed.

"After that TV show, I had one of our people try to contact the
station, but he had already left to go back to America. A few weeks
later, one of his friends told us that he was talking to Shaw
Brothers, but he was unhappy with the offer. So I called him up.
That was the first time I ever talked to him. I said, 'How about
coming back and working for us? It's time you did something for
the Chinese movies.' He said, 'OK, I'd like to try that.' And we
signed a contract for three pictures . . . .

"Whatever Bruce did, he did it with such intensity, it was scary.
He had films of all the famous fights, and he would study them
frame by frame – how to avoid being hurt, and how you can hurt
most. An extremely intense man."

Golden Harvest flew Bruce Lee to Bangkok to shoot his first
feature film, *The Big Boss*, in which he plays a young Chinese man
working in a Thailand ice factory. *The Big Boss* was crudely and
inexpensively made, on a budget of only $50,000, and, like

virtually every Hong Kong picture of the time, it was produced in Mandarin, requiring Lee to use a voice double. Upon its release in 1971, it smashed all previous box-office records in Asia, and netted Golden Harvest a return of 500 times its investment. Lee's next two films, *Fist of Fury* and *The Way of the Dragon*, both released in 1972, were even bigger hits.[1] Lee's last completed movie, *Enter the Dragon* – an English-language film, shot in Hong Kong, with an American director, Robert Clouse, and an international cast – was co-produced by Golden Harvest and Warner Bros.

Bruce Lee did not live to attend the opening of *Enter the Dragon*. On July 20, 1973, while visiting the home of the actress Betty Ting Pei in Hong Kong, he complained of a severe headache, and, after Ting gave him a dose of Equagesic, a painkiller that had been prescribed for her, he lay down to take a nap. Two months earlier, during a dubbing session, Lee had collapsed and was found to have excess fluid around the brain. At a Japanese restaurant not far from Ting's home, Raymond Chow and the Australian actor George Lazenby waited for Lee to arrive, to discuss Lee's forthcoming movie, *Game of Death*. At around seven o'clock, Ting called Chow at the restaurant in a panic – she could not wake Lee even with a slap on the face. Lee was taken to the emergency ward of Queen Elizabeth Hospital, where doctors spent forty-five minutes attempting unsuccessfully to revive him.

Lee's sudden death at age thirty-two was instantly controversial. In response to rumors of foul play, the Hong Kong government ordered a coroner's inquest, and a specialist was flown in from London. He concluded that the drug Ting gave Lee had caused an edema in Lee's brain; to this day conspiracy theorists remain unconvinced.[2] "It was a very simple though extremely technical accident," Raymond Chow says. "Nobody wants to believe it."

1 The English titles of Lee's first three movies were altered for their release in the United States. *The Big Boss* was renamed *Fist of Fury*; *Fist of Fury* became *The Chinese Connection*; and *The Way of the Dragon* was called *Return of the Dragon*.
2 The conspiracy buffs were given further ammunition on April 1, 1993, when Lee's only son, Brandon, was shot dead on the set of the American film *The Crow*, in a careless accident involving a dummy bullet.

Stunt Men, Stunt Woman: Jackie Chan, Stanley Tong, and Michelle Yeoh

Though Raymond Chow says he was devastated by Bruce Lee's death, Golden Harvest did not take long to bounce back. With it rebounded the Cantonese-language cinema. "I always believed that films in Hong Kong should be in Cantonese, which is spoken by 95 percent of the population," Chow says. Golden Harvest's first Cantonese-language superstar was Michael Hui, a former TV game-show host turned movie comedian, who teamed up with his brothers Sam and Ricky in hit comedies such as *The Private Eyes* (1976), about an inept detective agency. Hui paved the way for Golden Harvest's next Cantonese-language superstar, Jackie Chan. Today, Chan is so much a bulwark of Golden Harvest that he has a seat on the board, and profit-sharing in his own films, an incentive used in Hollywood, but otherwise unheard of in Hong Kong. (He makes an estimated $20 million per movie, four or five times as much as his nearest competitor.) Chan says of Raymond Chow: "He treats me like a son."

Chow echoes that sentiment, though, he adds, Chan is a rather profligate son. Chan, who has directed nearly half of his films for Golden Harvest, is a perfectionist, and his productions are the antithesis of Hong Kong's rapid, assembly-line approach to film-making. He took four months apiece to shoot the climactic action sequences of *Operation Condor* (1991) and *Drunken Master II* (1994); and for *Dragon Lord* (1982) he filmed a two-second segment, in which he kicks a shuttlecock a certain way, 1600 times, until he got it right. "With a Jackie Chan movie, there is no schedule and no budget," says his long-time manager, Willie Chan, who is no relation.

Chan often speaks of Buster Keaton, who also performed stunts of considerable bravado, as his idol and inspiration. (In Chan's *Project A II*, the 1987 sequel to *Project A*, the façade of a building collapses on him, but he passes safely through a window – a sight gag borrowed from Keaton's *Steamboat Bill Jr.*) While Keaton grew up in vaudeville, Chan grew up in a kind of traveling circus.

He was born Chen Gang-shen, in Hong Kong, on April 7, 1954, and was an only child. His parents were so poor that his father seriously considered an offer to sell him to the British doctor who delivered him. His infant home was the servants' quarters of the Australian embassy in Hong Kong, where his father worked as a cook, and his mother as a maid. When Chan was seven, his parents abandoned him to a boarding school in Hong Kong called the China Drama Academy. There, Yu Chan-yuan, a feared taskmaster, trained about fifty boys and girls in the art of Peking Opera – an entertainment in which acrobatics, mime, martial arts, and sword-play are as important as singing. The school was free, but Master Yu was entitled to whatever his students earned from their performances. Too young to understand his enrollment contract, Chan selected the longest possible term of indentured servitude – ten years.

Chan quickly came to regret his decision, but he was unable to run away, as several other children at the academy did, because his parents moved to Australia, where they live to this day. (He remains on good terms with them.) The daily routine at the school was beyond grueling. Chan and his fellow students were awakened every morning at a quarter past five and put through their paces until midnight. They learned to sing by screaming in front of a brick wall, and to perform somersaults and back flips like Olympians. They learned to apply face paint. They learned to punch and kick, and to handle more than a dozen weapons, including the spear and the broadsword. Only about an hour a day was spent on formal education, which is why Chan is essentially illiterate.

Master Yu was a tyrant of Dickensian proportions. He served no breakfast to his students, and the boys and girls were kept in a state of constant hunger. Chan's endurance for pain clearly stems from his training exercises at the school; if he was unable to complete a routine, he was stretched by force. Master Yu beat his students mercilessly with a wooden cane for the slightest infraction, or simply because he had lost at horse racing. Chan got his first flogging on his sixth day at the school after accidentally dropping a walnut. The day I met Chan, he acted out one of his beatings, and seemed to relive it: "When he hit me with the big wood, if I show it

in my face, it doesn't count. Do it over. If I'm making a sound –
Uhh! – do it over. If I go like this" – he jerked his body – "Bom! Do
it over. If my tears coming down – Pow! – it doesn't count, do it
over . . . ."

Chan slept under a stairwell at the school with a group of other
boys, and fought them for scarce blankets. One of his bunkmates
was a chubby boy four years Chan's senior named Sammo Hung.
He would grow up to be a major Hong Kong movie personality,
both in his own right, and as Jackie Chan's sometime director and
co-star.[1] Hung's stock character is a fatty with improbable martial-
arts skills – one of his movies is called *Enter the Fat Dragon* – but
he is also a capable dramatic actor, and in 1988 he played Master
Yu in *Painted Faces*, a biographical movie depicting Hung's own
childhood. Hung told me that Yu, now living in San Francisco and
suffering from Alzheimer's, had complained at the time that the
portrayal was "too severe." In fact, the movie considerably
underplays Yu's brutality, and Jackie Chan, who is also portrayed
in the movie, has debunked it; the scenes of child torture in the
mainland Chinese movie *Farewell My Concubine*, which depicts a
Peking Opera academy, are more to the point.[2]

When Chan graduated at seventeen, in 1971, the Peking Opera
was dying in Hong Kong, and he discovered that his training best
suited him for the movies. He got menial work as an extra in
martial-arts films produced by Shaw Brothers. His speciality was
playing dead. Within a year, he had moved up to stunt man, and
Golden Harvest employed him as a stunt double for Mr. Suzuki, the
central villain in Bruce Lee's *Fist of Fury*. Chan says Lee took a
liking to him when he managed to complete a scene even though
Lee had accidentally kicked him in the temple. Chan, for his part,
idolized the kung-fu star. On one occasion, Lee accompanied Chan

1 Two of Chan's other fellow students at the China Drama Academy also made it
big in the movies: Yuen Biao, an action star, who appears with both Chan and
Sammo Hung in several films, including *Project A*; and Corey Yuen, a director of
action films.
2 Chen Kaige, the director of *Farewell My Concubine*, offered Jackie Chan the
second male lead in that movie, opposite another Hong Kong film star, Leslie
Cheung, but Chan was forced to turn it down. "Golden Harvest did not think
Jackie was suitable for that role, because there was some homosexuality
involved," Cheung told me. "They did not want to ruin the hero."

to a bowling alley, silently watched him play a few matches, and left. "The whole bowling alley knows I bring Bruce Lee with me," Chan recalls. "Oh! For a couple of days, I'm so happy!"

Yearning to become a star like Lee, Chan won the lead role in a 1973 movie called *The Little Tiger of Canton*. It went unreleased, and Chan, discouraged and broke, moved to Australia to live with his parents. He worked during the day as a mason and house painter, and at night as a dishwasher and cook. "But after six months, I'm feeling very boring," he says. Chan lied to his father, telling him he had been called back to Hong Kong to star in a movie. Instead, he was relegated back to stunt man. By 1975, he had managed to land a few supporting roles, including a part in *Hand of Death*, a chop-socky of little distinction, except that it was directed by a young John Woo. Resolved at last to abandon his movie dreams, Chan returned to Australia, he believed, for good.

Then he got a telegram from Willie Chan, who ran a production company for Lo Wei, the director of the late Bruce Lee's first two movies. Lo Wei was casting about for a "new" Bruce Lee, and Willie had advanced Jackie's name. (Willie was playing a hunch, since he barely knew Jackie; they'd met when Jackie handled crowd control at a movie star's wedding.) Bruce Lee was called Siu Lung, or Little Dragon, so Jackie Chan was rechristened Sing Lung, or Completed Dragon – the name by which he is still known throughout Asia. Unfortunately, Bruce Lee imitation was already on its way to becoming a small industry.[1] Between 1977 and 1978, Chan made seven kung-fu quickies for Lo Wei – all flops.

Chan parted company with Lo Wei, and had an epiphany. "The audience like Bruce Lee and doesn't like me," he recalls thinking. "Why? Bruce Lee kick fast; at that time I kick also fast. His punch is power; my punch also very power. But he is the legend. So how can I get rid of the Bruce Lee shadow and be Jackie Chan? Then I look at Bruce Lee all the film. OK. When Bruce Lee kick high, I kick low.

1 Ric Meyers, co-author of *The Encyclopedia of Martial-Arts Movies* (Scarecrow Press: 1995), has counted more than a dozen impersonators. A few called themselves Bruce Li; there was also a Bruce Le, a Bruce Rhe, a Bruce Leong, a Dragon Lee, a Conan Lee, a Rocky Lee, a Bronson Lee, a Tarzen Lee – even, eventually, a Bluce Ree.

When Bruce Lee punch, he is the superhero; when I punch, ahh!" –
he shakes his hand. "It hurts." By combining kung-fu with comedy
– and Cantonese – Chan was reborn a star. In *Drunken Master*, the
1978 movie that made him famous throughout Asia, Chan plays
Wong Fei-hung, the Cantonese Robin Hood, and plays him for
laughs, as a disrespectful young man who is taught how to fight by
an old wino of an uncle.

Chan joined Golden Harvest in 1979, and the following year,
with Raymond Chow's support, he began a two-year residency in
Los Angeles and enrolled in a language school in Beverly Hills to
work on his English. After returning to Hong Kong, having failed
to crack the American market, he decided that he would no longer
make historical kung-fu films.[1] He moved his stories into urban
settings, and his new style of picture, beginning with *Project A*,
probably has no better analogue than the action-filled comedies of
the American silent movie era. He also began a tradition of
showing out-takes of flubbed stunts during the closing credits of his
movies; at the end of *Project A*, for example, one can see him
landing on his head after bouncing off the second awning of the
clock tower. No one leaves a Jackie Chan movie during the closing
credits.

With each new movie, Chan tried to outdo the outlandish stunts
of the previous one. Before long, he was unable to get insurance. It
was also becoming difficult for Golden Harvest to recruit stunt
men who were willing to act with him – "Everybody knows Jackie
Chan is crazy," he says – and soon he found it necessary to
assemble his own stunt team, and pay their frequent hospital bills.
During the filming of *Police Story*, a 1985 movie about a maverick
Hong Kong cop, two stunt men crashed through the upper deck of
a double-decker bus and hit the pavement, instead of landing on
the car roof that was supposed to have cushioned their fall. As
usual, though, Chan left the most hair-raising moments for
himself; in the last reel of *Police Story* he jumps off a railing
in the atrium of a department store, slides down a seventy-foot
string of exploding Christmas lights, and crashes through a

1 The one exception to date has been *Drunken Master II*, Chan's 1994 sequel to
his breakthrough hit of 1978.

glass ceiling. Because of a misunderstanding, the prop man used house current instead of a low-voltage car battery to light the bulbs, and Chan could have been electrocuted. Luckily, he suffered no permanent injuries, although, he says, "All the skin peel off my hands."

Around the time Jackie Chan started making his urban action-comedies, a man named Stanley Tong was attempting to eke out a living the way Chan had begun, as an anonymous stunt man. Tong, who was born in Hong Kong six years to the day after Chan, is baby-faced and slender, and talks with a slight lisp. As a teen, his parents sent him to school in Winnipeg, where he excelled as a track-and-field star, taught martial arts, which he'd learned as a boy, and, on weekends, drove a souped-up Trans Am way over the speed limit.

Tong returned to Hong Kong before he reached twenty, and was quickly drawn into movie stunt work, a natural avocation for someone with his athletic ability and love of thrills. He quickly discovered, however, as did Chan several years before him, that being a stunt man in Hong Kong conveyed neither wealth nor status. It was not until 1993 that Hong Kong even had a stunt man's union. For jumping seven stories and landing on cardboard boxes – for some reason, air mattresses are seldom used in Hong Kong stunt work – Tong was paid less than $80. If he did the jump with his body in flames, he got $160. There was so much competition for work that when Tong mistimed a body flip and cracked his ribs, he kept quiet about it, fearful that someone would take his place. He felt compelled to take even insane risks, such as driving a car and setting off a bomb in the back seat. "In the Hong Kong movie business, if you refuse to do a job, they won't ask you to work again," he told me.

Tong's risk of injury was exacerbated by sleep deprivation: he recalls one two-month stretch in which he worked literally around the clock. "I sleep in my car at red light, at lunch time, whenever I'm not in the shot," he says. On one movie set, Tong had himself supported with wire in the middle of a swimming pool, so that he could doze standing up as crew members adjusted the lights. He managed to hide his profession from his parents until he broke his shoulder, an injury that put him out of work for three months without insurance. "Why do you have to be a stunt man?" he says his mother admonished him. "Today you jump ten floor, tomorrow fifteen, the next day they might require twenty, and sooner or later, you get killed." That got him thinking. Tong had a significant advantage over the vast majority of stunt men – a high-school education – and, at twenty-three, he set out to learn the mechanics of film-making, from pre-production to distribution, with the ultimate goal of becoming a director.

He did not retire from stunt work right away, however; he had certain specialties that kept him in demand. Because of his slender body, Tong was frequently called upon to double for actresses. ("I'm even willing to wear a bra," he recalls.) Stunt women are rare in Hong Kong; in the union, at last count, there were only 4, compared with 270 men. Actresses who do their own stunts and fight scenes are equally rare, although in the late 1980s one did emerge, a woman named Michelle Yeoh, whom Tong befriended and helped train. In a few years, she would rank as the top movie actress in Hong Kong, a female Jackie Chan.

Yeoh (pronounced "yo") is now in her mid-thirties, and comes from the small mining town of Ipoh in West Malaysia, where she grew up speaking English and Malay before learning Chinese. (When she adopted the name Michelle Khan for a number of her movies, she says her father remarked, "I didn't know you were Mongolian.") She has long, straight hair and high cheekbones and, for an Asian woman, a deep voice. As a teen, she enrolled in the Royal Academy of Dance in northwest England, with ambitions to become a ballerina, but in her first year she was incapacitated by a back injury. She transferred to another college in England, where she studied drama, and acted in plays by Shakespeare and Oscar Wilde. Upon returning home, she won the Miss Malaysia beauty pageant. A year later, she appeared in a television commercial with Jackie Chan, and came to the attention of a new film production company called D&B.

The D stood for Dickson Poon, a Hong Kong entrepreneur in his mid-twenties who had made a fortune in wristwatches and jewelry. Ease of entry is a notable characteristic of the Hong Kong film business; within a short time, Poon was one of Hong Kong's foremost movie executives.[1] In 1984, for a lark, Yeoh signed an acting contract with D&B and, within a year, she was cast in the lead role of a Hong Kong police sergeant in a movie called *Yes, Madam!* To prepare for the role, Yeoh trained intensively. "I literally lived at the gym with the stunt boys," Yeoh says. "They had a good time teaching me. I wasn't afraid to take falls."

Before long, Yeoh learned to punch and kick with tremendous speed. In the meantime, she spent hours in front of the mirror, working, she says, on "the facial expression, the conviction that I was fighting. You could be throwing a hard punch, but if your face doesn't say 'I'm gonna kill this guy,' the audience is not impressed." She had come a long way from ballet. Within the first five minutes of *Yes, Madam!* Yeoh clamps a book shut on a flasher's exposed parts and blows away four would-be robbers with an automatic and a shotgun. By the time she made her next feature, *Royal Warriors*, she was expected to do almost nothing but kick male butt. "My lines were like, 'Oh, well, we have to fight again,'" she told me. "We filmed the final scene in a little shack, beating the shit out of each other for seven days and nights. I ruptured an artery in my leg and dislocated my shoulder."

By 1987, Yeoh was engaged to Dickson Poon, and meanwhile she starred in another D&B slugfest, *Magnificent Warriors*. The action director for the film was Stanley Tong. Though Tong took an instant liking to her, he kept a professional distance, mindful that she was the boss's fiancée. One day, he was attaching some wire to her pants, in preparation for a stunt, when, he recalls, "She turned around with a strict face, and yelled, 'Stop pinching my bum!'" The stunt coordinator came running over, and Tong sputtered protestations of innocence, at which point, Tong says, "Michelle burst out laughing. She tells me, 'You look so serious; I have to think of something to break the ice.' My whole face was red for five minutes. That's how we become a good friend." Following *Magnificent Warriors*, Yeoh stood at the top of her profession, but after one more film Poon married her and persuaded her to retire.

1 It also helped that the company's co-founder was Sammo Hung, Jackie Chan's fellow student from childhood, who is called Bo (his Chinese name is Hung Kam-bo). Hence, D&B.

Three years later they were divorced, and Poon withdrew from film production.

During Yeoh's retirement, Tong continued his transition from stunt man to film-maker. He was one of two action directors for *Angel II* (1988) and assistant director for *Angel III* (1989), two sequels to a popular girls-with-guns movie. After that, he formed his own company, Golden Gate, and struck out on his own as the director of *Stone Age Warriors*, the 1990 movie about headhunters for which he tied himself with wire and plunged over a hundred-foot waterfall. (Tong to this day will not direct a dangerous stunt without pre-testing it himself.) Meanwhile, he kept in touch with Yeoh. "After Michelle get divorced, she's very depressed," Tong says. "So I tell her, 'Why don't we do a movie together?'"

A short while later, Tong got a call from Golden Harvest. Leonard Ho, the No. 2 man at the company, had been impressed with *Stone Age Warriors*, and to Tong's amazement, he asked whether Tong would be interested in directing Jackie Chan in *Supercop*, the third installment of the *Police Story* series. Since 1985, Chan had directed all but one of his own films, and Golden Harvest feared he might get stale. The company also hoped that an outside director would accelerate Chan's production schedule; on average, he took a year to make a film. Tong had to think about it. "I was worried," he says. "Jackie is the superstar. Maybe halfway in, I get fired, because movie is so personal – I like blue, he like red." After a week's deliberation, Tong spoke to Ho again, and said he'd accept only if Golden Harvest assured him of absolute control. Ho gave his word. Emboldened, Tong made a dramatic break with tradition, casting a woman – Michelle Yeoh – as Jackie Chan's action co-star.

Chan was a bit dubious. "Jackie has this thing – women should not fight," Yeoh says. "He likes them pretty and decorative. Luckily for me, Stanley thinks like I do." *Supercop* was Yeoh's comeback picture, and she made the most of it by performing a number of dangerous stunts, such as rolling off the top of a van and onto the hood of a fast-moving sports car. In the movie's climax, she hops on a motorbike, chases after a speeding train carrying the bad guys, rides off a steep hill, lands on the train, and ditches the bike on impact. (In order to do the stunt, Yeoh first needed to learn to ride a motorbike.) "When I see the movie now, I sit there and think I must have been mad," she says. Chan, who had sat glumly by the side of the train during the filming of the motorbike stunt, after vainly trying to talk Yeoh out of doing it, could not allow himself to be bested. In the same scene, he leaps off a building, grabs the rope ladder of an airborne helicopter, dangles a thousand feet over the city of Kuala Lumpur, crashes through a billboard, and jumps onto the train.

Jackie Chan's next collaboration with Stanley Tong was *Rumble in the Bronx*, which, to date, remains Chan's biggest international hit. Tong subsequently directed Chan in *First Strike*, a James Bond-style adventure film. Michelle Yeoh, in the meantime, was cast opposite Pierce Brosnan in *Tomorrow Never Dies*, the eighteenth install-ment of the James Bond series. Her last Hong Kong movie to date, *Ah Kam: The Story of a Stunt Woman*, a 1996 drama by the art-film director Ann Hui, came close to being her last movie ever. For one scene, Yeoh jumped off a highway bridge and plunged between cardboard boxes that were supposed to have softened her landing. She was hospitalized for a month. "The doctor told me if she wasn't so flexible, she either would have been killed or maimed for life," Hui says. "Michelle is really remarkable. Do you know what she said to me in the emergency room? She said, 'I'm sorry I ruined your shot.'"

True Crime: Triads in the Hong Kong Movie Industry

Despite the risks that some Hong Kong actors are willing to face on camera, the life of a movie star can be even more dangerous off the set. In Hong Kong, organized crime figures, who are known as triads, have exerted tremendous control over the industry. Only recently has triad infiltration of the movie business begun to diminish, but that is because the business has hit a down cycle, and there is less money to be made; triad societies are as opportunistic as they once were nationalistic. They originated in seventeenth-century China as secret societies dedicated to overthrowing the Manchus, who had conquered China in 1644 and established the

Qing Dynasty. The triads' mission was accomplished in 1911, when the Qing Dynasty was at long last toppled by the Republican Party, led by Dr. Sun Yat-sen, himself a triad. By then, however, the triad movement had degenerated into a criminal underground, with its world headquarters in Hong Kong. Today, Hong Kong has more than fifty triad societies, although only twelve to fifteen are active. They specialize in fields such as drug trafficking, money laundering, counterfeiting, and extortion.

In the early morning hours of May 4, 1992, the actress Anita Mui found herself in serious trouble with a triad. Mui, who is full-lipped and sultry, is sometimes called the Madonna of Hong Kong, because besides being an actress she is also a platinum-selling Cantonese-pop singer who likes to get down and dirty in her concerts and videos. She and some friends were giving a birthday party for her assistant in a private room at Take One, a karaoke club in Kowloon, where many movie industry people have their offices. It was prime time for Mui – she is a night owl, and notoriously difficult to roust for a daytime shoot – but she should probably have known better than to show up at a karaoke bar, since they are popular hangouts for triads. As it happened, a man named Wong Long-wai, who was both a triad and a movie producer – not an unusual combination in Hong Kong – was in another part of the club that morning, with his wife and at least one business associate.

Wong Long-wai was no one to trifle with. The triad society to which he belonged, the 14K, was a powerful one, and he was the head of a particularly violent ethnic faction called the Hunan Gang. Tony Deakin, a chief inspector in the Hong Kong Police Force, says the Hunan Gang became infamous in the 1980s for the way in which they robbed homes. "They would go in, tie everyone up, rape the women, eat the food, and spend ten to fifteen hours inside the premises before leaving," he told me.

Sometime that morning, Wong learned that Mui was at the club, and he evidently asked her to have a drink with him and sing a song. A social encounter between a film star and a triad is certain to have bad consequences. The next day, the triad invariably calls the star's manager with the news that the star has promised to appear in the triad's new film. Actors have reputedly been kidnapped and actresses raped for refusing to work for triads. Mui declined Wong's invitation, but, according to testimony from one of Wong's employees, she declined rudely – and in English. "Don't speak to me in English; I don't understand," Wong said, to which Mui responded, in English, "So what?" Wong slapped her.

The incident should have ended there, but other Hong Kong triad societies besides the 14K had an interest in the movie business, and not all of them were inclined to overlook an assault on a movie star. The following evening, Wong Long-wai was leaving a restaurant in the Wan Chai district of Hong Kong when he was confronted by three men, one of whom claimed to be Andely Chan, also known as the Tiger of Wan Chai. The Tiger was a race-car driver in his early thirties who had many friends in the movie industry including, it was said, Anita Mui. He was also a triad. According to testimony in a subsequent trial, one of the Tiger's men chopped Wong Long-wai in the arm with a knife, and the Tiger struck Wong in the face with a mobile phone. Wong was hospitalized for the knife wound. Two days later, someone slipped into Wong's hospital ward and shot him fatally in the head. Anita Mui immediately fled Hong Kong.

Many people were quick to criticize Mui, including Jackie Chan, with whom Mui had once been linked romantically; he said he had repeatedly warned her to stay away from nightclubs.[1] Chan is virtually the only movie star in Hong Kong who is immune to triad pressure, partly because he has the backing of a major, legitimate company, Golden Harvest, and partly because his movies are expensive and take a long time to make, whereas most triads want a fast buck. Willie Chan, Jackie's manager, has had grievous problems with triads, however. Managers in the Hong Kong movie industry perform a role akin to Hollywood agents, except that they rarely have multiple clients; there are no Mike Ovitzes in Hong Kong. Willie Chan was once the sole exception. In 1986, the top actress Maggie Cheung – who plays Jackie's long-suffering girlfriend in the *Police Story* series – asked Willie to represent her,

---

1 Since the incident at Take One, Anita Mui has acted in two Jackie Chan movies – *Drunken Master II* and *Rumble in the Bronx* – and each contains a scene in which a man strikes her in the face. The scene in *Rumble* was cut for the film's American release.

and when he agreed many other actors followed suit. "At my peak, I managed about forty-four artists," Willie told me. "But then the pressure from the triads became too great. They just said, 'I don't care what you do – I want this girl or this guy.' So a few years ago I decided to give up most of my artists." (He has just recently begun to rebuild his management stable.) Chan's agitation had become visible, and he refused to say more. Tony Deakin of the police says, "We were informed that a gun was pointed at Willie's head for release of the actor Andy Lau. Willie denies the incident, but I think the possibility of it being true is quite genuine."

Fortunately for Willie, he had never managed Anita Mui. In the months that followed Wong's murder, Mui lay low in the United States, Europe, and Japan. A grisly rumor circulated that the 14K wanted her leg in retribution, though there was no evidence that she had conspired in Wong's knifing or shooting, nor was she ever charged in connection with either offense. The Tiger, meanwhile, had been arrested in Macao as a suspect in the murder, and then released for lack of evidence, but he was scheduled to stand trial for the knifing.

On November 20, 1993, the Tiger finished second in the Macao Grand Prix, and was almost immediately disqualified when his race car was found to have illegal modifications. As he stepped out of a hotel in Macao around three o'clock the following morning, he was shot dead by three men wearing motorcycle helmets. After that, the matter seemed to be settled. No convictions resulted from either the Tiger's murder or Wong's, or from the knife attack on Wong. Anita Mui, who had returned to Hong Kong, kept quiet about the entire affair, except for complaining in a Singapore newspaper, "Which man would want to marry a woman who has so much trouble?"

Jet Li, the most popular martial-arts actor in Asia since Jackie Chan stopped making kung-fu movies, was another star who had a celebrated run-in with the triads. Li is a short, stocky man in his mid-thirties with the aspect of a boy and the grace of Gene Kelly. In his most admired films, such as *Fong Sai Yuk*, which features the former child star Josephine Siao as his kung-fu-fighting mother, he demonstrates a flair for comedy.

Li is the only major Hong Kong film star who grew up in Communist China. He was nineteen when he starred in his first movie, *Shaolin Temple*, a Hong Kong production filmed on location in China. The movie was a hit, and made him famous, though he was grossly underpaid – he received only a state subsidy. In 1988, he moved to California and got an American green card; in 1990, he settled in Hong Kong and signed with Golden Harvest. *Once upon a Time in China*, the smash hit of 1991, brought him superstardom – and left him with the bitter feeling that he was still grossly underpaid. Unable to resolve his money dispute with Golden Harvest, Li parted company with his manager and hired a new one, a man named Jim Choi.

Jim Choi had just begun producing films, but his first feature was a big-budget historical drama, *Shanghai 1920*, starring John Lone, who is perhaps best known to Western audiences for his role in Bernardo Bertolucci's *The Last Emperor*. Choi was mainland Chinese, in his mid-thirties, tall, slim, pale, and exceptionally well-mannered. The well-mannered part threw people off, because it was an open secret that Jim Choi was a triad who had made his fortune in Amsterdam in the heroin business.

It was all the more incongruous that Choi, needing a movie distributor, went into partnership with Shu Kei, a film critic and director of art films, including the well-regarded drama *Hu-Du-Men* (1996). "When I first got the call from him, I was kind of alarmed," Shu Kei told me. "But to be honest, he was one of the best partners I've ever worked with. Maybe he really wanted to abandon his past – I don't know. He was very serious about film-making, and he respected people. One time he had a slip of the tongue, and spoke an F-word in front of me. And he blushed."

Occasionally, there were reminders of Choi's hidden side. John Lone is notorious for making unreasonable demands, and one day, during the filming of *Shanghai 1920*, Choi insisted on giving Lone something he did not ask for – a bodyguard. Soon after that, Lone was getting a haircut when two assailants came at him with knives, only to be chased off by the bodyguard. "I assume it was a setup," Leong Po-chih, the director of *Shanghai 1920*, told me, laughing. "But after that, John was no trouble at all."

Jim Choi was just the kind of man to help Jet Li sort out his problems. By 1992, Li had far better relations with the People's Republic of China than he did with Golden Harvest, and when Li threatened to sue the film company, Choi backed him. Early that year, Golden Harvest voluntarily released Li from his contract, and Li turned his sights to his next project – a Jim Choi production. Choi was going to remake the 1967 swordfighting classic *Dragon Inn*, and he had cast Michelle Yeoh, who had just recently made her big comeback in *Supercop*, as Jet Li's co-star.

On April 16, 1992, Jim Choi stepped out of the elevator of his production company in Kowloon, and was mowed down by two men with guns who were dressed as security guards. Li and Yeoh were about to fly to Beijing for the start of filming when the news arrived that Choi was dead; the movie project was scrubbed.[1] Choi's murder was never solved, but the police entertained two theories, one of which was that he was killed in connection with his heroin business. The other theory was more ominous for the Hong Kong film industry. In the weeks before the shooting, Choi was heard arguing on the phone with another Hong Kong triad who wanted to use Jet Li in a movie; the police investigated reports that this triad had hired two hit men from south China to kill Choi for refusing to lend Li out. Jim Choi's death came just one month before the murder of Wong Long-wai, making 1992 a particularly bloody year for the Hong Kong movie business. The film industry had liked Choi, and had been willing to overlook his past, until the manner of his death brought it home. "His funeral was one of the least attended I have ever been to," Shu Kei says.

I caught up with Jet Li on the set of *My Father Is a Hero*, a film in which he plays an undercover cop from Beijing and Anita Mui plays a policewoman from Hong Kong. Directly across the street from Jackie Chan's office, the carpentry crew of the movie had built a two-story café out of wood and sugar glass, the type that breaks easily. One side of the café had been shattered by a car. In the center was an enormous waterfall, in which the water cascaded down a sheet of plastic mounted at a forty-five degree angle.

---

1 An alternate remake of *Dragon Inn*, starring Tony Leung Ka-fai and Brigitte Lin, was released that year.

Jet Li was wearing a black wool cap, a camouflage shirt, and green khakis. In person, Li seems as boyish and guileless as he does in his films. I was just about to ask him why he had hired Jim Choi when he excused himself to shoot his gun at the bad guys – Caucasians – while sliding down the waterfall. When he sat back down, he listened to my question, nodded politely, and said, in Mandarin, "I liked Jim Choi because he came from China, and his mentality was different from Hong Kong people. His approach was, 'If you have any problem, let me solve it; if not, we'll just be friends.'" Li said he knew nothing about Choi's past, or why anyone might want to kill him. A few minutes later, Anita Mui appeared on the set – an hour late, even though the director had sent a make-up person to her home to wake her up.

My Father Is a Hero was a production of a private company called Win's Group, which makes and distributes movies, and owns theaters. It was perhaps no coincidence that two movie stars with recent triad problems were in a Win's film. Win's is a refuge for actors when they get into trouble. The company was founded by two brothers named Heung Wah-keung and Heung Wah-sing, who are also known as Charles and Jimmy. While Jimmy has lately retreated from the movie business to pursue other interests, Charles has enhanced his influence in films by making bold investments in mainland China, and by becoming the majority shareholder in China Star Entertainment, a public company that distributes films and manufactures laser disks and videos. Next to Raymond Chow of Golden Harvest, Charles Heung is indisputably the most powerful figure in the Hong Kong movie industry today. Golden Harvest has Jackie Chan, but Win's has access to – and, in some cases, exclusive contracts with – a pantheon of other top stars. In March 1997, Golden Harvest and Heung's China Star formed a joint venture to supply movies to an ambitious new cable-television service.

Charles Heung is the son of the late Heung Chin who, in 1919, founded the Sun Yee On, by far the largest triad society in Hong Kong. Heung Chin reputedly collaborated with the Japanese during World War II; he was exiled to Taiwan in the 1950s, and died there. In early 1988, his first-born son, Heung Wah-yim – Charles's eldest brother – was convicted by a Hong Kong jury of being the Dragon Head, or boss, of the Sun Yee On, but the conviction was tossed out in late 1989 by Hong Kong's then Chief Justice, with the assent of two other judges, on an uncharacteristically liberal legal theory. Charles has repeatedly disavowed being a member of the Sun Yee On, but he has been identified as such by the United States Senate Permanent Subcommittee on Investigations. In January 1995, the Commission for Canada denied Charles a Canadian passport on the grounds that he was alleged to have a seat on the Sun Yee On's "ruling council" – and warned him that he might even be unwelcome as a tourist.

In Hong Kong film circles, however, Charles Heung is rather well liked, particularly after having parted company with his brother Jimmy, who isn't. In 1991, Gordon Chan directed the blockbuster comedy *Fight Back to School* for Win's, which was then jointly run by Charles and Jimmy, and he says he was paid pitifully; but he faults Jimmy, whom he describes as "very dangerous in the way he treats people." The director now has a distribution deal with Charles, and speaks of him, with apparent sincerity, as an honorable businessman – which is fortunate, since Charles has become virtually too big to avoid. (Tsui Hark, another top director, has also cast his lot with Heung.) In general, movie people make a distinction between "bad" triads and "good" triads, and when they complain about the involvement of gangsters in the film industry, they are usually referring to the ones who rape and kidnap and use other coercive means to get actors and actresses to sign contracts. Charles Heung is not considered the type to do anything like that. Then again, he doesn't have to – one suspects that many stars sign up with him because when they do, the bad triads tend to leave them alone.

Stephen Chiau, the star of *Fight Back to School*, for instance, was featured in several of Win's hit comedies, after having had difficulties with bad triads. (Unfortunately, as a consequence of working for the Heungs, he, too, has been denied a Canadian passport.) Chiau, who is often described as the Jim Carrey of Hong Kong, is an acknowledged master of what the Cantonese call *mo lai to*, or "makes-no-sense" comedy. Within Hong Kong itself, he rivals Jackie Chan as the biggest box-office attraction, but he is less popular elsewhere in Asia, because a lot of his humor is derived from wordplay, and is lost if one does not speak Cantonese. Andy Lau, who is both the biggest pop singer in Southeast Asia and a popular romantic leading man, is currently in business with Charles Heung. Before he struck up this arrangement, he had terrible problems with bad triads. In November 1993, his assistant, a twenty-six-year-old woman, wound up in the hospital after her apartment was fire-bombed. "There is lots of movie that is made by the gangster, and it was hard for me to reject that kind of project, so I just take it with a smiling face," he says.

Lau complains that the police never seemed terribly interested in triad activity in the film community. The police I spoke to did not agree – they said the problem was that movie people never wanted to testify. It was clear, however, that in the days leading up to Hong Kong's reversion to China, morale was low at the police department's Organized Crime and Triad Bureau. The Sun Yee On is thought to have infiltrated the Chinese Communist Party; indeed, Tao Siju, China's chief of police, has expressed support for "patriotic" triads, and, incidentally, he owns a night club in Beijing with Charles Heung. "The will to combat organized crime is lacking in Hong Kong now," Stephen Vickers, the former head of criminal intelligence for the Hong Kong police, told me. Even worse, police corruption by triads, a serious problem in Hong Kong in the 1970s, is evidently on the rise again. Chief inspector Tony Deakin says, "The Sun Yee On has all sorts of contacts within the police force. No one wants to admit it."

Deakin is a Eurasian – one quarter Scottish, three quarters Chinese – with an unmistakable case of reunification jitters. He is intimately familiar with both Charles and Jimmy Heung and seems to view the brothers as all-powerful. "No one in Hong Kong will talk to us about the Heungs unless they are willing to emigrate to Nigeria afterwards," he says. More ominously, he adds, "The Heungs can call a police station and find out what a witness has just reported." I found other members of the police force brusque on the subject of the Heungs. One senior police official granted me exactly fifteen minutes to ask questions, most of which he refused to answer, and, when I stood to leave, said, in clipped English, "Please understand – the Heungs are a sensitive topic around here. If I disclose information to you about the Heungs, I will be committing suicide.

I do not mean that the Heungs will kill me. I mean that my career will be finished."

One afternoon, I visited Charles Heung in his office in Tsimshatsui, at the southern end of Kowloon. Charles is a poised, handsome man in his late forties, with close-cropped hair, and a face that suggests vulnerability. He started out as an actor in kung-fu movies in Taiwan, and has acted occasionally in Win's films, such as *Arrest the Restless*, in which he played an incorruptible cop. Tiffany, his elegant second wife, who is Taiwanese, was formerly a model.[1] Heung was wearing an Italian suit and smoking Yves Saint Laurent cigarettes. He attributed the success of Win's to the competitive spirit for which the company was named. "We think in film business, every film is a battle, and you have to fight to win," he said. "The most famous star in Hong Kong have contract with us." He smiled.

It is pointless to ask someone in Hong Kong if he belongs to a triad society, because membership alone is a crime, but I raised the subject indelicately enough for Heung to catch on. He spoke at length in Cantonese to one of his employees, and she then told me, "Since you are curious to know the background of Mr. Heung, his family, to be honest, they do have a Mafia background, because his father was one of the heads. But the father died when Mr. Heung was very small, and he had very little knowledge of what was going on. Over the years, Mr. Heung has had to work even harder to overcome the negative effects of the family name." Heung admits that some people may fear him, but says his business philosophy is to get top actors and actresses and directors to make movies for him because they like him. "I tell you one thing, perhaps you understand a little bit," he says. "Maybe the actor shoot one film because they afraid of you. OK. But one or two or three more, you have to give what they want."

There is less of a stigma attached to declaring oneself a triad in Taiwan, perhaps because of the anti-Communist leanings of secret societies in the days of Republican China. (In 1927, a gangster-turned-politician named Chiang Kai-shek arranged for his

---

1 Charles Heung's first wife was Betty Ting Pei, the actress in whose home Bruce Lee died.

Shanghai-based triad society, the Green Gang, to slaughter hundreds of Communist Party members.) Taiwanese triads have long been active in the film industries of Taiwan and Hong Kong, and, to a surprising degree, they have a penchant for producing art films; perhaps this is because triads are preoccupied with honor and respect – what the Chinese call "face" – and it gains one face to win an award at a film festival. Yang Deng-kuei, the alleged boss of Taiwan's Northwest Gang, has been called the godfather of the Taiwanese movie industry. In early 1985, one of Yang's productions, a war film entitled *Soldiers at Ease*, was abruptly shut down by the Taiwanese government when it was reportedly discovered that the prop weapons being used on the set were real. Yang was arrested and charged with racketeering and arms smuggling, and spent the next four years incarcerated at Green Island, the Taiwanese equivalent of Alcatraz. Yang, who is diminutive and tough, has boasted that he gained face in prison by breaking his wrist, embedding a message of inmates' grievances in the splintered bone, and conveying that message to the outside world, via the prison infirmary. When he was released in 1989, he returned to the film business by producing Hou Hsiao-hsien's *A City of Sadness*, which won the Golden Lion Award at the Venice Film Festival.

Wu Ton, a short man with a missing front tooth, is another Taiwanese triad with film production credits – both in Taiwan and Hong Kong – and a prison record. His conviction, for murder, was no ordinary gangland killing. In 1984, a Taiwanese-born journalist named Henry Liu, who lived in San Francisco as a naturalized American, published an unflattering biography of Taiwan's president, Chiang Ching-kuo, son of the late Chiang Kai-shek. For that offense, Liu was targeted for death; the murder conspiracy went at least as high as the chief of Taiwan's military intelligence, and probably higher. Taiwan's largest triad society, the Bamboo Union, was recruited to the task, and Wu Ton, who was then known as the triad's "general executioner," was one of three Bamboo members who traveled to San Francisco to assassinate Liu. Though the three men carried off the murder, the San Francisco police were able to identify them, in part because the assassins had traveled to Liu's home on rented bicycles, which Wu Ton had signed for using his real name. Mortified by the scandal, the

Taiwanese government prosecuted the Bamboo hit team, the military intelligence chief, and two other intelligence officers for the murder. Wu Ton served six years of a life sentence. He began producing movies after his release; one of his credits is the 1993 action film *Butterfly and Sword*, which stars Michelle Yeoh.

Wu Ton even had discussions with the Hong Kong art-film director Stanley Kwan about producing the director's work. Kwan has not had a commercial success since his widely acclaimed *Rouge*, in 1987, a romantic ghost story starring Anita Mui. To help make ends meet, Kwan has had to direct television commercials for ice-cream and hamburgers, and, most recently, brassières. He says he did not connect Wu Ton with the Henry Liu murder until he saw old news clips of his producer-to-be in handcuffs. "I said, 'Oh, *that* is Wu Ton,'" Kwan told me. "But he treats me very well. He said,'I don't want you to make money for me – I want you to win an award for me.' I said, 'Boss, I will try very hard. But if I cannot get any award for you, then you kill me?'" Kwan no longer fears for his safety, however; Wu Ton has come to be viewed as a good triad.

In the past few years, one Hong Kong producer has emerged in the eyes of the movie industry as particularly bad. His name is Chan Chi-ming. The *South China Morning Post* has suggested that Chan is connected to a mainland Chinese brotherhood called the Big Circle, though he has never been convicted as such. "We believe he's been behind a lot of violence in getting actors for films," Tony Deakin says, adding, "We have absolutely no proof." Chan Chi-ming allegedly sent a script to the film star Chow Yun-fat, and when Chow didn't respond someone threw a cat's head into his courtyard. Chan is a former professional boxer in his thirties, married, with three children. He is superstitious, and is said to have gone into the movie business on the advice of a fortune-teller. A portrait of Chairman Mao hangs in his office. He produced his first movie, *Hong Kong Godfather*, in 1991. It starred Andy Lau.

Chan Chi-ming wanted Leslie Cheung, the star of *Farewell My Concubine*, to appear in his next project, but Cheung's movie company, Mandarin Films, refused to lend him out. The actor was busy completing Mandarin's release for the 1992 Lunar New Year, a comedy entitled *All's Well, Ends Well*. The first week of the Lunar New Year is the time of peak movie attendance in the

Chinese-speaking world, equivalent to our summer and Christmas seasons combined. On January 9, 1992, a month before the scheduled release of *All's Well, Ends Well*, five masked men armed with pistols and knives burst into Mandarin's film laboratory in Kowloon and demanded the negatives. One of the thieves was tried and convicted; in a confession – later recanted – he said he had committed the robbery for Chan Chi-ming, but Chan was never charged. *All's Well, Ends Well* opened as planned. "They stole the wrong negatives," Leslie Cheung told me.

The Mandarin Films robbery was more than the movie industry could tolerate. Five days later, during the morning rush hour, more than three hundred actors, directors, cameramen, screenwriters, and production crew members marched on Police Headquarters in the business district of Hong Kong. Jackie Chan was at the head of the parade, wearing a yellow armband. Among those marching beside him were Andy Lau, the comedy star Stephen Chiau, the top actress Carol Cheng, and the busty soft-porn star Amy Yip, whose movies include *Robotrix* and *Sex and Zen*.[1] The protesters carried a large banner that read "Show Business Against Violence," and handed the police a petition urging that the movie community be protected from extortion. The march came to be known as a demonstration against triads, though in fact it was a demonstration against bad triads. As a result of the march, the police established a new division called the SIT – Special Investigation Team – to deal with triad abuses in the film industry; in 1994, the SIT was dissolved without having made a significant case.

Five months after the parade, however, Chan Chi-ming's career in motion pictures was interrupted when, during a business trip to Shenzhen, a city in south China, he was arrested and jailed. He was initially accused of arms smuggling, which carried the death penalty, but the charges were reduced to unlawful sexual intercourse with one of Shenzhen's numerous prostitutes. (It is widely believed that the Heungs lured Chan to Shenzhen and used

---

1 Yip, who reportedly insured her thirty-six-inch breasts against "injury or shrinkage," complained that triads had forced her to be photographed entirely nude in a movie – a circumstance which, despite the highly erotic nature of her films, she had long avoided. "When people have seen you completely naked they are not curious about you any more," she told a newspaper.

their influence to arrange his arrest. When I asked Charles Heung if this was true, he laughed and said, "Of course not true. I am not so big power!") After a year of incarceration, Chan Chi-ming returned to Hong Kong and, to the amazement of the movie industry, relocated his company, Wang Fat Film Production, directly across the street from the office of Charles Heung. Chan promptly produced his second film, *Once a Black Sheep*, which starred Carol Cheng.

Chan Chi-ming agreed to speak with me about his career. I arrived at his office at the appointed time, but found only his sister Betty, and a hapless young movie director named Chris – he wouldn't tell me his last name – whom Chan had enlisted as a translator. The office held an enormous altar with a green pagoda roof, and incense burned in a polished brass receptacle. Spread across a table were stills from Chan Chi-ming's soon-to-be-released new movie, which originally had been called *Shattered Promises*, but now was called *Bomb Lover*. Chris waited with me for one hour, then two. At five o'clock, Chan at last arrived. He has a dark complexion and large, sensual lips, and was dressed, improbably, in a herringbone jacket, a floral tie, and tortoise-shell glasses. I quickly discovered that Chan defies interviewing. Mostly, he giggled, or made cryptic pronouncements, such as "The movie business is like a flying dragon." ("Don't ask me," Chris said. "I'm just the translator.") I was reminded of something Tony Deakin had told me – that Chan claims his Chinese jailers injected him with substances that rendered him "basically a retard." Chan suggested that I pray at his altar, and asked what religion I belonged to; when I told him, he said, ominously, "Will the God of the Jews protect you?" I asked how he had managed to get a big star like Andy Lau to act in his first movie. "It was fate," Chan said. What were his ambitions in the movie business? "I want to be like Sir Run Run Shaw," he said. "I admire him. Because he is very tight with money. Like the Jews." I felt it was time to leave.

Go West: John Woo, Tsui Hark, Ringo Lam, Chow Yun-fat, and the Lure of Hollywood

Oddly enough, for all the problems the industry has had with triads, its movies make them seem heroic. Perhaps the blame lies with John Woo, who, before his move to Hollywood, was the acknowledged master of the Hong Kong gangster film. The triads in John Woo movies are modern gun-toting versions of honorable Chinese swordsmen, and he has them slaughter one another with operatic grandeur. Woo is fascinated with the themes of loyalty and brotherhood: in his acclaimed film *The Killer* (1989) – probably the best-known Cantonese-language movie in the world – a professional hit man and the cop who is stalking him discover they share the same code of honor.

Woo came to the gunplay picture surprisingly late in his career: it took him eighteen features, more than half of them comedies, to find his metier. The day I met Woo, in Los Angeles, he was dressed in black, down to a pair of zippered boots. He is a short, modest man who greets visitors with a bow, and it takes a little while to discover the quiet maniac under the surface – the man who, in the word of the character actor Simon Yam, is "crazy about blood and bomb." For me, that discovery came when Woo described how he nearly blew up his favorite leading man, Chow Yun-fat, of whom he is enormously fond, to get the proper effect in the climactic scene of *Hard-Boiled* (1992), the last movie Woo directed in Hong Kong. In that scene, Chow Yun-fat runs down the narrow corridor of a hospital that is about to explode, and Woo was unhappy because the stunt co-ordinator and special-effects man would not set off the blast until Chow was almost out of the frame. "They are afraid to kill the actor," Woo told me. "But then the shot have no meaning – it doesn't feel any danger. So I give the cue to blow up the whole thing by myself. Some of the explosion was pretty close to his body, and Chow Yun-fat was really run for his life." He laughed.[1]

---

1 Woo also blew up a house behind a fleeing Chow Yun-fat during the filming of *A Better Tomorrow II* (1987) and, in the finished movie, one can see Chow's look of consternation as his hair catches fire.

Woo was born in Canton in 1946, but four years later, to escape Communism, he and his family moved to the slums of Hong Kong, where they lived in a succession of tin shacks. He says he witnessed a lot of street violence growing up. He also spent a good part of his childhood at the movies, and developed a strong preference for European and American films over the local product. His father, who had been a scholar and teacher in China, contracted tuberculosis in Hong Kong and spent ten years in the hospital; he died when Woo was sixteen. Woo's schooling was sponsored by an American family through the Christian Church. He says his early ambition was to become a priest – "I wanted to help people" – but the seminary rejected him as too "artistic."

At twenty-two, after a few years of tinkering with a borrowed 16mm camera, Woo got a job at the Cathay Production Company as a script supervisor, then moved over to its larger competitor, Shaw Brothers, as an apprentice to the martial-arts director Chang Cheh. He was twenty-seven when he directed his first movie, a chop-socky called *The Young Dragons*, which was financed independently by a friend who had just made a windfall. Golden Harvest released the film after heavy re-editing. "Too violent," Woo says. Woo made several more kung-fu films – including *Hand of Death*, featuring a still-struggling Jackie Chan – but his first big hit was *Money Crazy*, a screwball comedy he wrote and directed for Golden Harvest in 1977. Woo was suddenly a hot property, but he was dissatisfied. He didn't want to make comedies; he wanted to make *Bonnie and Clyde* and *The Wild Bunch*. The executives at Golden Harvest were shocked – after all, his comedies were successful.

Six years later, Woo was hired by Cinema City, a new independent film studio founded by Karl Maka, Dean Shek, and Raymond Wong, three actor-director-producers. Cinema City had a formula: slick, wholesome family pictures, mostly comedies. Woo had been typecast as a funnyman, but he was running out of ideas; before long, he had a reputation as box-office poison. The studio transferred him to its business office in Taiwan to work in distribution, though he also found time to direct two flop comedies in a row, one of them a lame remake of Neil Simon's *The Sunshine Boys*, called *The Time You Need a Friend*. He took to drink. Peter

Chow, a movie industry veteran who runs a self-named film distribution company in New York, recalls that Woo's nickname during his stint in Taiwan was "the best director" because, in Cantonese, the word for "best" sounds like the word for "drunken derelict." It was the time Woo needed a friend; fortunately, one came to his rescue.

The friend was Tsui Hark, one of the biggest names in the Hong Kong movie business. Until recently, Tsui had so many successes, both as a director and producer, in so many different genres, that the industry consistently looked to him to determine what the next fad would be. He effectively launched the special-effects fantasy film in Hong Kong as the director of *Zu: Warriors from the Magic Mountain* (1983); revitalized the spook genre as the producer of *A Chinese Ghost Story* (1987); and re-invented the martial-arts epic as the director and producer of *Once upon a Time in China* (1991). He is considered the master of the comic-strip style of Hong Kong film-making, but also an outstanding woman's director; *Peking Opera Blues*, his 1986 film about three women caught in the political intrigue of 1913 China, is one of the most respected works of the Hong Kong cinema.

Tsui Hark (pronounced "Choy Hok") has a goatee beard, a weak chin, and angry eyes – the face of a movie villain, a role he has played on occasion. He was born in China in 1951, spent his childhood in Vietnam, his teen years in Hong Kong, and his early twenties in Texas, studying cinematography at the University of Austin. After a stint as a documentary film-maker in New York, he returned to Hong Kong at the end of 1976 and joined the television network TVB. It was a golden era in Hong Kong television, and Tsui found himself among a group of experimental TV directors who would soon break into movies as part of the Hong Kong "new wave." Tsui made the break in 1979. He made angry films. His third feature, in 1980, *Dangerous Encounter of the First Kind,*[1] is nihilistic in the extreme – its heroine amuses herself by driving pins through the brains of mice.

Some people doubted that Tsui would get to make another movie

1 Also known as *Don't Play with Fire.*

after that, but Karl Maka and Dean Shek, of Cinema City, staked him to his fourth picture. Why they ever believed that Tsui was suited to their brand of wacky comedy is anyone's guess, but Tsui obligingly directed a wacky comedy called *All the Wrong Clues . . . For the Right Solution*, a spoof of the George Raft-style gangster film, with Karl Maka as Al Capone. It won Tsui a Golden Horse Award for Best Director of 1981. (The Golden Horse is Taiwan's Oscar, for which any Chinese-language film is eligible – provided, of course, it does not come from mainland China.) The following year, Cinema City scored its first huge hit, *Aces Go Places,* concerning the adventures of a jewel thief; and in 1984, Tsui directed *Aces Go Places III*, a James Bond send-up which, in addition to a Chinese cast, featured the original actors who played Jaws and Oddjob in the Bond movies, and Peter Graves of the television series *Mission: Impossible*. It was a blockbuster.

No one would describe Tsui Hark as new wave any longer, but he was certainly a success. In April 1984, Tsui and his wife, Nansun Shi, founded their own company, Film Workshop. Around this time, John Woo hit the skids. "John and my husband would go drinking, and tell stories, and pour their hearts out," Shi recalls. Woo spoke of his frustrated ambition to break out of comedy and make gangster films. In 1985, at Tsui's invitation, Woo returned to Hong Kong and began writing the script of *A Better Tomorrow*, the story of Kit, a police cadet; his older brother, Ho, who (Kit learns to his horror) is a triad, and Ho's partner, Mark. Woo would direct the film, and Tsui, for the first time in his career, would produce.

It was not an ideal partnership. Tsui admits that as a producer "I get too involved in the project, and there is not enough room for some directors to breathe. John Woo is very much independent." Woo clearly won out in *A Better Tomorrow*, which bears his male-bonding thumbprint. (Indeed, Tsui had wanted to recast the film as the story of three women, in the manner of his *Peking Opera Blues*, of the same year.) For the pivotal role of Mark, Woo says he was looking for a Chinese version of the suave French actor Alain Delon, and it appears he could not have chosen better. Chow Yun-fat is six feet tall and matinee-idol handsome, with big hands that look comfortable holding a Beretta. No one associated with *A Better*

Tomorrow could have predicted its phenomenal success, though audience reaction at the sneak preview, in August 1986, was a good indicator. "The people went crazy," Woo recalls. (By tradition, Hong Kong movies are tried out at a midnight show on the Saturday before the official première.) *A Better Tomorrow* became the top-grossing film in Hong Kong history up to that time, spawned scores of imitations, and set off a fashion craze for the designer sunglasses and trench coat worn in the movie by Chow Yun-fat – no small feat, since Hong Kong is too humid for trench coats.

Tsui and Woo reprised their roles as producer and director the following year to make *A Better Tomorrow II*. They fought over the script and the edit, and the film suffered. Woo has largely disowned it, apart from the relentless final shoot-out, which he describes as "a mad painting." (The movie is also notable for providing one of the closest calls that ever befell Stanley Tong, who was a stunt double for Leslie Cheung. Woo asked Tong to leap off a pier and onto a speeding motorboat, but Tong bounced off the motor, narrowly missing its blades, before figuring out how to time the jump successfully.)

Next, Woo proposed a prequel, to be set in the war-torn Vietnam of the 1960s. Tsui seized on the idea and directed *A Better Tomorrow III* himself, a feminist departure from Woo in which Chow Yun-fat is taught how to shoot a gun by femme fatale Anita Mui. The movie, also known as *Love and Death in Saigon*, was shot on location, the first Hong Kong picture since the war to be filmed in Vietnam. Tsui had not returned to Saigon since his childhood, and found that nothing worked properly. "The tanks they gave us don't move, and when you start the helicopter, the propeller flies off," he recalls. Worse, the pyrotechnics expert provided by the government to create the film's explosions blew himself up and was killed.

Woo and Tsui teamed up as director and producer for the last time in 1989. The result was *The Killer*. The film was financed by an entertainment conglomerate called Golden Princess, which had Chow Yun-fat, who plays the title role, under contract. *The Killer* made John Woo and Chow Yun-fat internationally famous, and effectively ended Woo's friendship with Tsui Hark. All remaining civility between the two men broke down in 1991, when Tri-Star bought the story rights to *The Killer* for a possible American remake, with Richard Gere in mind for the hit man, and Denzel Washington as the cop. (The picture is still in development.) Tsui insisted on sharing in the buyout, even though Woo had sole credit as the screenwriter. "Sorry!" Tsui said, shaking his head angrily, when I brought up the subject. "The story line of *The Killer* was written by me."

Sitting in his office on a studio lot in Los Angeles, Woo was reluctant to talk about his rift with Tsui. "We just have different ideas," he said. "I still think he's a great talent." Terence Chang, who had accompanied Woo to Hollywood as his business partner and producer, listened, and squirmed with impatience. Chang had been the general manager at Tsui's production company, Film Workshop, but after *The Killer*, he and Woo left to form their own company, Milestone Pictures, with Lynda Kuk.

"Let me put this on the record," Chang said, interrupting. "After *A Better Tomorrow II*, Tsui said John screwed up the movie, and asked me to fire him. I refused. So Tsui rejected every idea proposed by John, including *The Killer*, until John was broke. Can you imagine? Here's a top director, and he's borrowing money from Chow Yun-fat. John was so stupid; he got offers to leave Film Workshop for a lot of money. 'No, I'm loyal to Tsui, because he gave me my second chance . . . .'"

"Yeah," Woo said. "If somebody say something bad about him, I was so angry, I almost want to beat up the guy."

"Finally, Chow Yun-fat went to the boss of Golden Princess and insisted on doing *The Killer*. Tsui wanted to disown the film. He said it was shit."[1]

In 1990, after parting company with Tsui, Woo finally got to direct his own account of wartime Saigon, called *Bullet in the Head*. (He wisely filmed it in Thailand.) *Bullet in the Head* does not feature Chow Yun-fat, and bears no relation to the *Better Tomorrow* series, except that it, too, concerns the bonds of brotherhood, which, this time around, are severely tested in a climate of war and greed. Though remarkably unpleasant for a

---

1 This version of events is confirmed by Jasmine Chow, the wife and business adviser of Chow Yun-fat; see page 81.

John Woo movie – it includes a torture sequence in a Vietcong interrogation camp that appears to have been inspired by *The Deer Hunter* – he considers it his best work to date. Many critics agree with him.[1]

John Woo's difficulties with Tsui Hark did not begin to prepare him for the culture shock of working for Universal Pictures in Hollywood. When he made his last four movies for Golden Princess, he told me, "Even the boss from the studio is not allowed to see any footage. Every day, I can shoot based on my instinct, and I can put the new stuff in any minute. I only need to deliver the final print." Within reason, this is the norm in Hong Kong. Even those directors who work for triads – a fate that Woo avoided – never complain of creative interference. As the director Wong Kar-wai puts it, "It's better to deal with a godfather than an accountant."

Hard Target, Woo's first American movie, starring Jean-Claude Van Damme, involved a lot of accountants. "I just didn't get used to the system here," Woo said, shaking his head. "Too many meeting, too many politic. So many people get their input in the script. The people have so much worry and fear, and sometimes they are afraid to make any decisions. So you have to deal with them, and waste time and energy on those kind of things . . . ."

Woo enjoyed making *Hard Target*, however; he found the camera crew and the stunt group entirely up to Hong Kong standards, and had the highest praise for the cast members – particularly Lance Henriksen, who played the movie's central villain, and who, for one scene, agreed to be set on fire. The star was a different story. "Jean-Claude Van Damme is like a little boy," Terence Chang said. "While the film was being edited, he was in another building, cutting his own version, and trying to get Universal to use it. His cut was ludicrous. He took out scenes with the other actors, and substituted himself, in slow motion. He said, 'People pay to see me, not Lance Henriksen.'" Van Damme was ultimately overruled, but not without a fight. "So ridiculous," Woo said. In Hong Kong, the movie stars are unpampered and

---

[1] *Bullet in the Head* is the top-ranked movie in the critics' poll conducted for Chapter 4 of this book.

businesslike – Anita Mui is considered a temperamental actress because she is occasionally late – and movie publicists don't even exist.

After completing *Hard Target*, which was modestly successful, Woo signed an exclusive two-year deal with Twentieth Century Fox. He spent eight months trying to develop an adventure movie to take place in the Brazilian rain forest, but gave up after casting and script problems proved insoluble. Fox then hired him to direct *Broken Arrow*, an action film about stolen nuclear warheads, starring John Travolta and Christian Slater. The budget was $60 million – twelve times the cost of Woo's most expensive Hong Kong movie. Though Woo and Travolta got along famously, Chang says that because of studio politics, "John was miserable most of the time during that picture." Against Woo's wishes, the studio replaced his entire stunt team and forced out his director of photography, causing the camera crew to quit in protest. Fox originally had planned to release *Broken Arrow* for Christmas, 1995, but held it until the following February, an indication that the studio lacked confidence in the movie. It was one of the top-grossing films of 1996. "You know what's the barometer of that movie being successful?" Chang says. "People are starting to be nice to me."

All the same, Woo knows his days of unfettered artistic freedom are behind him. "In Hong Kong, I feel I work like a painter," he told me. "In Hollywood, I also work like a painter, but somehow my hand is tied up by rope, and I need to struggle very hard because somebody pull me back." He sighed. "But I still think I can do something here."

Directing a Jean-Claude Van Damme movie appears to be an initiation rite for Hong Kong film-makers who want to work in Hollywood. Tsui Hark recently directed *Double Team*, with Van Damme and basketball star Dennis Rodman, for Columbia Pictures. Van Damme's previous movie, *Maximum Risk*, was directed by Ringo Lam.[1]

To many Hong Kong film fans, Ringo Lam is the darker, more

1 For Lam's assessment of *Maximum Risk*, see page 102.

cynical alternative to John Woo. His movies are no less violent, but they do not dwell on Woo's themes of honor and chivalry. "I don't believe in the hero," he says. "There's only antiheroes." In *Full Contact* (1992), the normally suave Chow Yun-fat gets a buzz cut, a motorcycle jacket, and a switchblade; his nemesis is a smiling homosexual sociopath. Lam, who was born in Hong Kong, joined TVB in 1973 as a trainee, and worked at the television network for five years, alongside Tsui Hark and Ann Hui. He moved to Toronto in 1978, and studied film-making at Canada's York University, before returning to Hong Kong as a full-time director. His biggest critical and commercial success was *City on Fire* (1987), in which Chow Yun-fat plays an undercover cop who gets mixed up in a botched jewel heist.[1] Since 1989, Lam's movies have been more popular in the United States than at home. Lam believes he is still being punished for a thoughtless remark he made following the Tiananmen Square Massacre of June 4 of that year: after the news media carried the story of the massacre unremittingly for days, Lam suggested they might take a break and show the Dragon Boat Festival.

Chow Yun-fat has also decided to go Hollywood. After signing with the William Morris Agency, spending a year in Los Angeles, and working hard to improve his English, Chow accepted the lead role in *Replacement Killers*, an action film that casts him, not surprisingly, as a hired gun. He drops by John Woo's house every Sunday for a cookout, and expects to work with the director again.

Though Chow is arguably one of the most charismatic screen actors in the world, Hollywood may not be ready for a star as genuinely nice as he is. He grew up on Lamma Island, a rural section of Hong Kong that he compares to the sticks of Tennessee, and he is a man of few pretensions. Despite having set off a fashion craze for designer sunglasses and sleek trench coats, he says he felt more comfortable playing a country bumpkin in Mabel Cheung's 1987 film *An Autumn's Tale*. Chow has an irresistible ear-to-ear grin and a little boy's hyperventilating laugh. I interviewed him over lunch at a Chinese restaurant in Hong Kong, and when I

1 The movie was the obvious inspiration for *Reservoir Dogs.*

declined to eat, because I was too busy taking notes, he fed me dumplings with his chopsticks.

Chow stumbled into acting at eighteen after answering an ad for a training program at TVB; by 1976 he was one of the stars of *Hotel,* a primetime soap opera. "I played a very romantic lover, very charming," he told me. After a few years, he attempted to make the transition to movies. He proved his mettle as a serious actor, first as a boat person in Ann Hui's *The Story of Woo Viet* (1981) and then as a wartime drifter in Leong Po-chih's *Hong Kong 1941* (1984), for which he won the Golden Horse award for Best Actor. But he still could not shake his image with moviegoers as a TV soap-opera hunk in the wrong medium.

John Woo and *A Better Tomorrow* changed that forever. Chow was immediately elevated to the top rank of Hong Kong film stars; by the early 1990s, his only peers were Jackie Chan, the martial artist Jet Li, and the comedian Stephen Chiau. Production houses inundated him with scripts, contracts, and money. The triads sought him out as well, a task made more difficult because he avoided all night life – a typical outing for Chow was a trip to the market to buy fish and vegetables for his mother. Though the cat's head that was tossed anonymously into his courtyard made him nervous, his move to Hollywood was motivated by boredom, not fear. A decade after *A Better Tomorrow,* he was still typed as a gunslinger and antihero. "Always the production house want to see Mr. Chow carrying the gun," he said. "Nobody want to take a risk. They copy, copy, copy, copy. It is not interesting anymore." (Presumably, it will be a bit more interesting in English.)

At the time of our lunch, Chow was slated to appear in two more Hong Kong movies – "Then I'm a free man," he said. One of them was already in the can. It was called *God of Gamblers' Return,* the sequel to one of Chow's biggest hits. He plays a gambler so gifted that he can tell how the dice will fall by the rattle of the cup; Charles Heung, the powerful producer whose father founded the Sun Yee On, plays his friend and armed guard. Chow invited me to the première of *God of Gamblers' Return* and said he would introduce me to Jimmy Heung.

"But you don't have to worry when you meet with Jimmy,

because there will be a lot of bodyguards beside you," Chow said.
"And they all got the trench coat and the sunglasses."

The Two Mr. Wongs

I did not notice bodyguards at the première of *God of Gamblers'*
Return, but my eyes were on the director, Wong Jing. To be more
accurate, my eyes were on Wong Jing's mouth. Two weeks earlier,
at about three in the afternoon, as Wong Jing was about to enter his
office in Kowloon, three men jumped him from behind and bashed
his teeth in. Wong Jing is a squirrelly man with large glasses who
has a reputation for being talkative, though when the police
questioned him about the assault – after his dental surgery – he was
mum. "We firmly believe he got beaten up for something he said,
because his attackers concentrated on his mouth," Tony Deakin
told me. "Maybe he was talking about certain people behind their
backs." I asked Charles Heung for his reaction to the assault. "We
will leave it to the police to solve," he said. Then he laughed.[1]
    Wong Jing is one of the most successful directors and producers
in Hong Kong. His father, Wong Tin-lam, was also a film director,
but of highbrow dramas, whereas Wong Jing is often called the
Cantonese Roger Corman. Even in a cinema known for its
exploitation films, he stands out. *Naked Killer* (1992) a movie he
wrote and produced, features a team of emasculating lesbian
assassins in hot pants. In *High Risk* (1995), which he wrote and
directed, a helicopter crashes into a skyscraper, and its whirring
blades slice innocent bystanders in half. In *Chinese Torture*
Chamber (1994), which he wrote and produced, a woman is
accused of murdering her husband with a powerful aphrodisiac
that caused his penis to explode – a scene that is played out to the
tune of "Unchained Melody." Wong's output is alarming – before
turning forty, he had directed more than fifty films, all from his own
scripts, and produced many more – though not all his efforts have
had his full concentration. "Wong Jing is a funny guy," Chow Yun-

---

1 Wong Jing has since ended his longtime partnership with Win's and signed a
production deal with Golden Harvest.

fat said recently. "He put the camera right there and say 'Action!,' then look for some good horse in the horse racing" – he mimicked flipping the pages of a racing form – "then he look up and say, 'Cut!'"

A few days after the première of *God of Gamblers' Return*, Wong Jing invited me to his office, which overlooks Victoria Harbor; before sitting down to talk, he lit three incense sticks and genuflected to Buddha in silent prayer. He was wearing jeans and a red sweater with a Dakar racing insignia. He brushed off his assault as insignificant, saying, "If the guys really hate me, they would injure me more." Wong, who is married, with two daughters, describes himself as "a little bit workaholic"; on a typical day, he rises at six to write, stops by his office at ten to handle administrative chores, and spends the afternoon on the set. He has a degree in Chinese literature, and started out as a scriptwriter for TVB before directing his first movie, at twenty-five, for Shaw Brothers. Wong admires Hollywood films – his favorites are *The Cincinnati Kid*, *It's a Mad, Mad, Mad, Mad World*, and *Die Hard* – and if you were to combine those three pictures, and add a modicum of bad taste, you might come up with something resembling *God of Gamblers' Return*. In the opening scene of that movie, a mad Taiwanese card shark and his henchmen kill Chow Yun-fat's pregnant wife and place the fetus she was carrying in a jar; then Chow Yun-fat and Charles Heung shoot down twenty-two of the henchmen. After that, the movie becomes a screwball comedy, with a couple of explosions and high-speed chases thrown in. It was one of the big hits of 1995.

Wong knows his success has made him unpopular in the film community, and he is unrepentant. "Why should I apologize?" he said. "In my opinion, a movie ticket is a vote." I did not realize quite how unpopular he was, however, until I spoke to Ann Hui. "No, I don't like him," she told me. "Do you know what he said about my film *Song of the Exile*? He said, 'Who wants to watch the autobiography of a fat woman?' For maybe ten years, he's been an object lesson in how to make successful bad movies." When I made a reference to Wong's beating, Hui giggled. "I can't say I'm sorry," she said.

*

If the industry resents Wong Jing for being so successfully schlocky, it equally resents Wong Kar-wai, a director who is noncommercial to the point of defiance. Wong Kar-wai is a native of Shanghai, a large man with a broad face, who, like Wong Jing, got his start as a scriptwriter for TVB. He subsequently became a staff writer at Cinema City, which sacked him after he spent a year on salary without producing a script. He ended up scratching for work in Mongkok, a rough section of Hong Kong infested with triads, and drew on the experience as the writer and director of his first movie, *As Tears Go By* (1988), a deglamorized gangster film in the vein of Martin Scorsese's *Mean Streets*. It was a hit both commercially and critically, but it did not represent the kind of movie that Wong really wanted to make – it was far too straightforward. He was reading Manuel Puig, and taking inspiration from the Argentinian novelist's way of telling a story with the pieces all jumbled.

Wong kept his artistic agenda to himself, however. After the success of *As Tears Go By*, Wong's producer, Alan Tang, was happy to finance the director's next movie, asking only to be told the title of the film (*Days of Being Wild*) and who was in the cast (six major stars). Leslie Cheung, in the lead role, plays a violent young man in 1960s Hong Kong who breaks the hearts of a pair of girlfriends before taking off for Manila to search for his mother; beyond that, it's difficult to describe the plot. On the strength of the movie's hot director and all-star cast, Alan Tang was able to pre-sell *Days of Being Wild* to distributors all over Asia before Wong had shot his first frame.

When those distributors saw the final cut, in early 1991, Wong says, "they all fainted." *Days of Being Wild* was an unconventional film for any movie market; coming from a supposedly commercial director, in Hong Kong of all places, it was an act of apostasy. Critics adored the film – it regularly turns up on lists of the best-ever Hong Kong movies – but it died at the box office. Wong says Alan Tang had been so certain of a hit that he had promised his wife diamond jewelry, "but after the première, he told her, 'Forget it.'" Still, Wong adds, "he never said an unhappy word to me" – though he declined to produce Wong's next movie.

Wong did not have to look hard for a new backer, however. Actors longed to work with him, and his ability to attract stars was still unmatched. Besides that, producers were convinced that *Days of Being Wild* was a fluke – something Wong needed to get out of his system before returning to the commercialism of *As Tears Go By*. Wong announced that his next movie would be an adaptation of *The Eagle Shooting Heroes*, a classic novel of the martial arts, and that its cast would include five of the six stars of *Days of Being Wild*, plus the Taiwanese-born Brigitte Lin. She had recently become a sensation all over Asia for her role in *Swordsman II*, a martial-arts film produced by Tsui Hark. Wong had also secured the services of Sammo Hung, Jackie Chan's old schoolmate, as his action choreographer. Scholar Films, a production company owned by Tsai Sung-lin, a wealthy Taiwanese businessman, bankrolled the new movie, which was called *Ashes of Time*. It seemed foolproof.

It wasn't. *Ashes of Time* must rank with the most self-indulgent pictures ever made. Wong took his all-star cast to the Yuli desert of China, shot hundreds of thousands of feet of film, and changed the script at liberty from day to day. After two years, the movie had run several million dollars over budget, and was still unfinished. Shu Kei, the director and critic, was called in to help raise money to complete the film; he was alarmed when he saw the rushes. "I felt there was a story somehow going on, but I could not quite make out what it was," he says. *Ashes of Time* was finally released in late 1994. It is visually sublime – the Australian-born Christopher Doyle won a Golden Horse for his cinematography – but on one viewing, at least, the story line is indiscernible. It failed commercially.

While working on *Ashes of Time*, Wong Kar-wai tossed off another movie – self-produced – in a mere two months, and many consider it a superior effort. *Chungking Express* is made up of two separate stories, each about a lovelorn cop in present-day Hong Kong; it has been compared stylistically to the films of Jean-Luc Godard. Though the movie's Korean distributor, who invested in it because it featured Brigitte Lin, was crushed when he saw it – she plays a gun moll in a blonde wig, and is barely recognizable – *Chungking Express* did good business throughout Asia. Wong's self-indulgence was back in evidence for his most recent film, *Happy Together*, about a gay male couple in Buenos Aires. He began filming in mid-1996; by the following March, he was in the editing room, and, according to Chris Doyle, had not yet worked out the story line. Two months later, *Happy Together* was shown in competition at Cannes, and won Best Director – the first top prize awarded to a Hong Kong film at Cannes since King Hu's 1971 *A Touch of Zen*. Perhaps because his pictures seem to be growing more accessible, the Hong Kong movie industry has warmed a little to Wong Kar-wai, though art-film directors remain a mistrusted breed in the city. Wong, for his part, denies that he makes art films. "I think I'm a not very successful commercial film director," he says.

Reunification Blues

When I began watching Cantonese-language movies, I was convinced that censorship must be nonexistent in Hong Kong. I was mistaken. In 1987, the Hong Kong legislative council passed the Film Censorship Bill, empowering a government bureau to censor movies that, among other things, are deemed likely to corrupt morals or encourage crime. One of the first movies to suffer was Ringo Lam's *School on Fire* in 1988 – not so much for its extreme violence, but because it depicted students corrupted by triads. The bureau considered banning the film entirely, until, Lam recalls, he and his producer "almost kneel down and beg." It was finally released in Hong Kong with thirty-six cuts, and even more in Taiwan, where, Lam says, "they chopped out all the scenes in school, and just left the 'on fire.'"

Nowadays, the movie would probably be released intact. In the past several years, the censorship bureau has spent far less time worrying about morals than about one of the other criteria for restriction – pictures that might damage good relations with other territories. For "other territories," read mainland China. Hong Kong's nervousness about the change of sovereignty is expressed nowhere more clearly than in its cinema, which is devoid of politics. Indeed, given the industry's self-censorship when it comes to China, the ratings bureau is probably unnecessary. About the most daring political reference I've seen in a Hong Kong film came at the end of *Supercop*, when Jackie Chan's Hong Kong police officer joked to Michelle Yeoh's Chinese inspector that it didn't matter which government got the bad guys' loot, since 1997 was just around the corner. Even the Tiananmen Square Massacre, which touched off a powerful emotional reaction in Hong Kong, is considered too touchy a subject for a movie. The director Ann Hui tried to raise money for years to make a film about Hong Kong's reaction to the massacre, and, she says, "I was treated like someone with leprosy." She adds, "Right now in Hong Kong, there's a lot of anxiety in the air."

For good reason, considering Beijing's undisguised contempt for artistic freedom. The mainland director Zhang Yimou, for instance, was forced to cancel an appearance at the 1995 New York Film Festival because the Chinese government was unhappy with the content of a documentary, by another director, to be screened at the festival. The following year, Communist officials unsuccessfully tried to pressure the Disney Company into dropping Martin Scorsese's *Kundun*, a feature film concerning the Dalai Lama. Under the terms of the Sino-British Joint Declaration, Hong Kong will be permitted to preserve its laws and its free-enterprise system for fifty years after its accession to China provided, of course, that China keeps its word. "Who knows? The Chinese government, their policy can change every day," the director Stanley Kwan says. Kwan's *Red Rose, White Rose* was filmed in Shanghai, and the experience left him shaken. He discovered that the mainland government's policy is to confiscate all negatives and, after a review by censors with an eye to political and sexual content, allow the director to take home no more than ten thousand feet of film – about two hours' worth – for post production. "So that means if you have a new idea after you get the final censor cut, no way can you do it," he says. One of the love scenes in Kwan's movie did not meet China's stringent anti-pornography standards, and had to be smuggled out. As a penalty for the smuggling, Kwan was barred from filming on the mainland for two years.

Hui had a similarly bad experience filming a scene in Shenzhen for *Ah Kam: The Story of a Stunt Woman*, her recent film starring Michelle Yeoh. The Chinese censors insisted that she excise a scene in which female employees at a karaoke bar attempt to lure customers on a rainy night. "It's not even a seduction scene," Hui told me, shaking her head. At least, she said, the censorship bureau in Hong Kong is composed of several university graduates, and if one disagrees with their rulings, there is a board of appeal, of which Hui is a member. "But in China I just get a sheet of paper telling me what to cut. It comes from one bureaucrat whose taste is questionable, and fluctuating all the time."

Hui also worries that, under Chinese sovereignty, Hong Kong film-makers will be forced to cater to the tastes of mainland Chinese – peasants, she says, who go for "mindless kung-fu flicks" – a situation that she describes as "economic censorship." The Hong Kong film industry, has, in fact, long faced economic censorship from an entirely different quarter, the Republic of Taiwan, where ticket sales traditionally covered as much as 20 per cent of a Hong Kong movie's budget. Only a decade ago Taiwan blackballed Hong Kong film-makers or actors who so much as shot on location in China. (Tony Leung Ka-fai, the star of Jean-Jacques Annaud's *The Lover*, was unable to get acting work for two years – "Not even one movie," he says – after appearing in a film shot in the mainland in 1983.) Taiwan's future economic role in the Hong Kong movie industry remains an open question.

Until recently, the mainland has provided little income if any to the Hong Kong movie business, and what's worse is that the Communist government has condoned, and officials have even profited from, the piracy of Hong Kong films. (Indeed, copyright protection of any sort is notoriously lacking in China.) There is no guarantee that China will become a significant source of revenue for Hong Kong film-makers after 1997, though the potential rewards of tapping into a hitherto closed market of a billion two hundred million people could be tremendous. "The China market is our future," Charles Heung told me confidently. In August 1993, Heung opened a multimillion-dollar, 200,000-square-foot movie studio in Shenzhen, and announced a deal with a Chinese company to build theaters and video-rental outlets across China. Two months later, Golden Harvest made a similar announcement. Win's Group and Golden Harvest now have distribution rights in China for all non-pirated Hong Kong videos and laser disks. "There will be a lot of teething problems," Raymond Chow said, sounding rather less confident than Heung. "But it is a very important step in the right direction."

One added benefit of Golden Harvest's joint-venture deal is that Jackie Chan's most recent films are now officially sanctioned in China. Nevertheless, he seems to have his eye fixed, for the moment at least, on the United States. In 1996, he flew to Australia to shoot an English-language film called *Mr. Nice Guy*, which was directed by his old Peking Opera classmate Sammo Hung; Chan plays a television chef who has to fight for his life after inadvertently acquiring a videotape of a Mob hit. During the filming of one stunt, he fell two stories, twisted his neck, and ended up, for the zillionth time, in the hospital. When I asked Chan if he had made preparations for the reversion of Hong Kong to China, I was not surprised by his answer. In essence, he said, why should he worry about politics, when every day on the set could be his last day alive?

2 Film-makers

Selected Interviews and Filmographies

Fredric Dannen

I have never envied the celebrity journalist. During my two and a half years at *Vanity Fair* in the early 1990s, I heard many stories from colleagues about the circles of publicity Hell a journalist needed to pass through in order to get an interview with a Hollywood movie star. Nothing like that – thank goodness – exists in Hong Kong. I found movie people there to be so accessible, and generous with time, that I was left with far more material than I could fit comfortably into the preceding chapter. The interviews that follow are intended, therefore, as a supplement. Some of the subjects, such as Tsui Hark, had, I felt, more to say for themselves than the chapter could accommodate; others, such as Peter Chan, were absent from it altogether. As a further supplement, I have included filmographies, either selected or complete as indicated.

Jackie Chan (actor, director, producer) and Willie Chan (manager)
Peter Chan (director, producer)
Sylvia Chang (actress, director, producer, writer)
Leslie Cheung (actor)
Chow Yun-fat (actor) and Jasmine Chow (spouse, business adviser)
Christopher Doyle (cinematographer)
Ann Hui (director)
Sammo Hung (actor, director, producer)
Stanley Kwan (director)
Ringo Lam (director)
Andy Lau (actor)
Clara Law (director) and Eddie Fong (director, writer)
Tony Leung Ka-fai (actor)
Jet Li (actor)

Anita Mui (actress)
Josephine Siao (actress)
Stanley Tong (director)
Eric Tsang (actor, director)
Tsui Hark (director, producer, actor)
Anthony Wong (actor)
Wong Jing (director, producer, writer, actor)
Wong Kar-wai (director, writer)
John Woo (director, producer, writer) and Terence Chang
    (producer, manager)
Simon Yam (actor)
Michelle Yeoh (actress)
Yim Ho (director, writer)
Ronny Yu (director, producer)

JACKIE CHAN, Actor, Director, Producer
Sing Lung
Born Hong Kong, 1954

Jackie Chan (right) with   Jackie Chan with Maggie
Sammo Hung in *Project A*   Cheung in *Twin Dragons*

WILLIE CHAN, Manager
Chan Chi-keung
Born Malaysia, 1941

Jackie Chan and Willie Chan, though not related, are the oldest-
running artist and manager team in the Hong Kong cinema. An
account of how their partnership began can be found on page 18.

Jackie Chan in *Police Story*

Willie Chan with Quentin Tarantino

QUESTION: *How do you come up with a Jackie Chan movie?*
JACKIE CHAN: When the audience see my movie, they are more interested in action than story, so a lot of time, my story very simple. First thing, how many fight scene? Of course, there is a big fight scene at the end, a middle one, a light fight scene, a little big scene – maybe five fighting in the whole movie. Then I plan it. One fighting on the boat, maybe one fighting in the office, one fighting in the restaurant, one fighting in the swimming pool. OK. Then, how many comedy I put inside? OK. (Claps his hands.) Then we start the story.

You can spend more time on just one of those action sequences than on all the non-action scenes combined.

Yes. We do the acting scene one and a half day, but when we do action scene, like the scene [at the end of] *Drunken Master II*, we take four months. In American film, you do that, they sue you.

Don't your doctors tell you to knock off the dangerous stunts?

Every doctor tell me stop, but I can't, really. I know the audience likes what I do, and even I get hurt, the audience said, don't stop doing this kind of dangerous things, we love your movie. If some movie I'm not doing good enough, they say, aah, this time not so good. Yeah. I don't know what can I do. I want to stay number one. Some action actor change, and they lose audience. I believe Stallone lost his audience for some period; now he's coming back. So I'm scared to change. As long as I'm doing very crazy things, the audience keep coming.

Didn't your near-fatal accident while filming Armour of God *change your outlook at all?*

It doesn't change my movie life, but it change my thinking. After I almost die in Yugoslavia, I'm in the hospital, and I think, people die very easy, and you don't know when. Aah. Many things I didn't do in my life, I'm very regret. Then I'm thinking, if I want to do something, I do it right now.

How good a fighter are you, really?

Many people better than me. I think everybody say Jackie Chan martial arts very good, because I'm famous. Even my bodyguard [Ken Lo], seven time heavyweight champion, he can kill you by one kick. But when I fight with him, he was like this (shakes). Because I am famous. Same thing Bruce Lee. He's very good martial artist, but not like now people say. At the time he get famous, people tell me, Bruce Lee, his punch around one hundred, two hundred pounds. Now he is the legend, his punch can break the wall down.

Are you too famous in Asia?

In Hong Kong, it's OK, because everyone treat me like a friend. But I cannot go out in Korea, Taiwan. You know, one Japanese girl die already, jumped to the subway. I must have a responsibility. After the girl suicide, I go to Japan, tell all the fans, don't dream one day you are Jackie Chan's wife. I'm not a god, I need my life. I'm the normal people.

You seem to be tremendously popular in Japan.

This makes me very happy (points to poster on office wall). This is from a big newspaper in Japan, the hundred most famous people in the movies. America has fifty-one, Japan has two, and Hong Kong only one. Not Bruce Lee. Me.

What is Jackie Chan afraid of?

WILLIE CHAN: He's funny. He's a very brave guy, but he's very afraid of the injection needle. If he goes to the doctor for an injection, he will still pull me along, and grab my hand, and actually yell. Anything else he's not scared of.

Have you ever tried to talk him out of doing a stunt?

There's no way to. We've been together so long, I daresay he trusts me completely. He would get my opinion for any business venture he would enter, whether he buys a house, what I think of a new girlfriend. But on movies, he won't talk to me. He's so sure of what he wants to do, and nothing will stop him from doing the stunts. I don't think even his father can do it.

Does he have many girlfriends?

He has a *lot* of girlfriends – some more special, some less special. He's not ready to be tied down yet, let's put it that way. He's a very energetic guy. You can't get him to sit down, except on a long flight. He knows there isn't anything he can do on a plane, so he sleeps thirteen hours. Here he doesn't sleep much at all.

Filmography
Jackie Chan

1962 Big and Little Wong Tin-bar (child actor)
1963 Love Eternal (child actor)
1964 The Story of Qiu Xiang-lin (child actor)
1972 Police Woman (martial-arts director, actor)
1972 Fist of Fury (stunt double)
1973 Not Scared to Die (actor)
1973 The Heroine (martial-arts director, actor)
1973 The Little Tiger of Canton (actor)
1974 Stranger in Hong Kong (actor)
1974 Golden Lotus (actor)
1975 All in the Family (actor)
1975 Hand of Death (actor)
1976 New Fist of Fury (actor)
1976 Shaolin Wooden Men (actor)
1976 The Killer Meteors (actor)
1976 To Kill with Intrigue (actor)
1977 Iron-Fisted Monk (martial-arts director)
1977 Snake and Crane Arts of Shaolin (actor)
1977 Magnificent Bodyguards (actor)
1977 Snake in the Eagle's Shadow (actor)
1978 Half a Loaf of Kung Fu (actor)
1978 Spiritual Kung Fu (actor)
1978 Dragon Fist (actor)
1978 Drunken Master (actor)
1979 The Fearless Hyena (actor, director)
1979 Fantasy Mission Force (actor)
1980 The Young Master (actor, director)
1980 The Big Brawl (actor)
1980 The Fearless Hyena II (actor, director)
1981 Cannonball Run (actor)
1982 Dragon Lord (actor, director)
1983 Winners and Sinners (actor)
1983 Cannonball Run II (actor)
1983 Project A (actor, director)
1984 Wheels on Meals (actor)

1985 My Lucky Stars (actor)
1985 The Protector (actor)
1985 Twinkle, Twinkle Lucky Stars (actor)
1985 Heart of the Dragon (actor)
1985 Police Story (actor, director)
1986 Armour of God (actor, co-director)
1987 Project A II (actor, director)
1987 Rouge (producer)
1988 Dragons Forever (actor)
1988 Police Story II (actor, director)
1988 The Inspector Wears Skirts (producer)
1989 Miracles (actor, director)
1991 Operation Condor (actor, director, producer)
1991 Island of Fire (actor)
1991 Center Stage (producer)
1992 Twin Dragons (actor)
1992 Supercop (actor)
1993 City Hunter (actor)
1993 Crime Story (actor)
1994 Drunken Master II (actor, co-director)
1995 Rumble in the Bronx (actor)
1995 Thunderbolt (actor)
1996 First Strike (actor)
1997 Mr. Nice Guy (actor)

PETER CHAN, Director, Producer
Chan Ho-san
Born Hong Kong, 1962

Peter Chan directs and produces films for the United Filmmakers Organization, or UFO, one of the most successful new movie companies in Hong Kong. Chan co-founded UFO in 1991, in reaction to the major studios, which were enthusiastically making formula swordplay and action pictures for a market that was rapidly becoming saturated; UFO's success came from avoiding genre films in favor of something new for Hong Kong – urban dramas in the American mold.

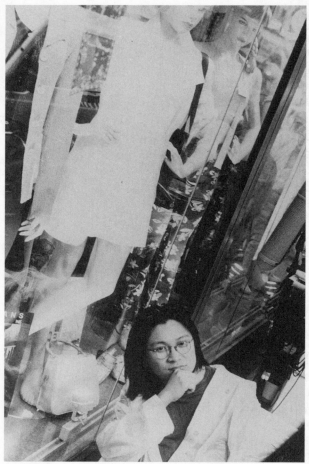

Peter Chan

Chan, for his part, received a United States education, first at an American high school in Thailand, where his family lived during his childhood, and later as a film major at the University of California in Los Angeles. He dropped out of UCLA at twenty-one to work as an interpreter on the set of John Woo's last movie for Golden Harvest, *Heroes Shed No Tears*, which was filmed in Thailand in 1982 (it went unreleased for five years), and then was hired as production manager and assistant director for three Jackie Chan films, including *Armour of God*.

In 1987, Peter Chan got a job in distribution and sales for Alan
& Eric, a production company named for Alan Tam, the singer and
actor, and Eric Tsang, the actor and director. Chan, who wears his
hair long and dresses casually, was forced to look corporate, but his
year at the short-lived company – it folded after the stock-market
crash – taught him business rudiments that later proved useful.
After a brief stint at Impact, another production company, Chan
created UFO with Tsang, and the directors Jacob Cheung and Lee
Chi-ngai (who is called Chi Lee). Today, UFO has two additional
partners.

QUESTION: *A lot of critics refer to UFO movies as "yuppie" films.*
PETER CHAN: I hate that term. Hong Kong people don't even know
what a yuppie is. In Chi Lee's film *This Thing Called Love*, the
couple drive a Honda Civic. That makes them yuppies? If you like
to say there is a UFO formula, I think our films are about ourselves.
Most of our films are about the loss of innocence, friendship,
disillusionment, the difficulty of living with people. City folks'
problems.
But would you agree your films bear a strong American influence?
I think that influence was inevitable. We grew up watching
American films. The last film I produced for Impact, *Yesteryou,
Yesterme, Yersterday*, was loosely based on the concept of [the
American television series] *The Wonder Years*, which I liked
immensely. I thought we should have something like this in Hong
Kong.
And when that film did not get released, you formed UFO.
That's right. We were pissed off at the studios. Our first UFO film
was *Days of Being Dumb*, in 1992, a light look at two kids who
wanted to be triads. It was not a big hit, but it did all right. After
that, we hit the down slump of the Hong Kong film industry, and to
save the company, we had to make a film for a Taiwanese
distributor in two months. We had no script. So, for the first time,
I directed with my UFO partner Chi Lee, knowing that as a co-
director, I would not feel so "auteur," and we could finish the movie
fast. He directed half the scenes, and I directed half. We wrapped in
six weeks, spent two weeks on post-production, and shipped it out
to Taiwan. The film was *Tom, Dick and Hairy*. I was excited about

that film; it was finally the kind of movie I had always wanted to make. It was released in Taiwan with a ton of promotion – and it died flat. We were all very disillusioned. I remember getting on a flight to New York, and we were talking about closing down UFO, and doing something else. UFO was about to be history. But then, a month later, *Tom, Dick and Hairy* was released in Hong Kong, and it was an overnight success.

So that was the movie that really put UFO on the map.

It changed all our lives. Then, two months after that, we released *Yesteryou*, and it became another hit. So we had two hits in two months. Then we put out *He Ain't Heavy, He's My Father*. We were disappointed, because we thought we had a good idea, but the execution was all wrong. And it was a bigger hit than *Tom, Dick and Hairy*.

That takes us to 1994.

At that point, Leslie Cheung comes in. He had a contract to work with us when we started UFO two years earlier, but he did not honor that contract until we became big. He called and said, "Let's do that movie." So we had to come up with a star vehicle for Leslie. But it was difficult to design a role for him, because he's bourgeois and pretty, and most of my films are about down-and-out small potatoes. We came up with the idea for *He's a Woman, She's a Man*, in which he plays a star record producer. And that film became the biggest box-office hit for UFO.

It didn't hurt Anita Yuen's career, either.

She's not contracted to us, yet she's been in almost every one of our films. Her début film was a supporting part in *Days of Being Dumb*, and she had a great supporting role in *Tom, Dick and Hairy*.

When you created UFO, was Cinema City your model? After all, Eric Tsang, one of your partners, had been part of the inner circle at Cinema City.

I think we are very different from Cinema City, as much as Eric wants to disagree. He always wants to recreate the Cinema City utopia of fifteen years ago. In those days, [Cinema City co-founder] Karl Maka would say, "Let's do this," and seven people rushed into the same project. There was no auteur. I keep telling Eric, we cannot do that in this day and age. My generation is more individualistic. I also think Cinema City was different because it was owned by [the entertainment conglomerate] Golden Princess. The money came from them. So Cinema City was not really independent. Though I must say, Golden Princess was a good boss – probably the best ever. They didn't think they were creative people, they just did distribution, and let you decide what you wanted to make. As opposed to Golden Harvest, a company that thinks they know everything there is to know about movie-making, when actually they're sitting in an office wearing suits and ties.

Doesn't UFO have a production contract with Golden Harvest?

Yes, they got UFO. Recently, they've been buying all the talent. You know, they got Wong Jing's company, too. Golden Harvest is trying to become a monopoly, and now Win's Group is the only other force to reckon with. And I hope Win's will get bigger, because if Golden Harvest is the only film-maker company in Hong Kong, the world will be hell.

You certainly are *individualistic.*

Most of the film-makers in UFO are very stubborn. That's what brought us up and made us produce hits in the early 90s – we knew what we wanted to do, and we would not follow the trend. But in the long run, that individualism will probably also bring about our downfall.

What do you mean?

In a film industry with a turnover as fast as Hong Kong, we may not be able to compete in the long run. [Wong Jing's] *Young and Dangerous* came out in January 1996, and was a big hit; by July, the third sequel was out already. We could not do that. After *Tom, Dick and Hairy* made money at the box office in April 1992, we didn't come up with our next film until Christmas. And that was fast for us. It took me two years to do *Age of Miracles*. So we could never beat the system.

You seem to be more collaborative as a company when it comes to screenplays, though.

I've never had one screenwriter finish a whole film for me. I'll come up with a story idea, and then I'll call in my regular brainstorm group of screenwriters and story consultants. But that's the way Hong Kong works. If I were working in Hollywood, I'd have a stack of spec scripts on my desk. We have no spec scripts here. The writing culture is nonexistent in Hong Kong. We have a minimum of novelists. It is a reading-intensive city, but we read newspapers and gossip magazines. I think Hong Kong people are not patient enough to read a book.

Is there anything else about Hollywood you'd like to see in Hong Kong?

No one in Hong Kong has long-term planning. We are not trained to make decisions five weeks before shooting. It's a very guerrilla kind of film-making – that's why it's cheap. It's cheap because the system is cheap. We don't have unions, and we work in a very chaotic, no-schedule sort of way. We decide things on the spot.

I've heard you complain that acting talent is too expensive, however.

Yes. Because of the bidding war we had a few years ago when we were going strong, actors' prices have gone up triple. Leslie Cheung is getting 5, 6 million.[1] Maggie Cheung is getting 1 million for the movie I'm shooting now. Eighty per cent of the talent is getting double what they're worth. Will they reduce? No. A lot of actors would rather not work than lower their price.

Aren't there some stars who can justify their cost because they can open a movie?

Stephen Chiau, Jet Li, and Andy Lau can open a film. Leslie needs a good role. But no actress in Hong Kong can open a film, except Michelle [Yeoh], because she's an action star.

And, of course, Jackie Chan. You were his production manager on Armour of God – *is it true that movie was out of control?*

It was like *Apocalypse Now.* I think Golden Harvest spent two times the budget they should have. They flew in tons of people to Yugoslavia – thirteen or fourteen directors. Stanley Kwan was assistant director, William Chang was the art director, and Eric Tsang was the director for some of the best scenes. He should have received a directing credit with Jackie; it wasn't fair. We had the crème de la crème of the Hong Kong film business. And when Jackie got hurt, we all stopped for about a month, but we were not allowed to go back to Hong Kong. For a while, there was less activity in Hong Kong, because everyone was in Yugoslavia.

1 Hong Kong dollars. To convert to United States dollars, multiply by 0.128.

How did you film the stunt at the end, where Chan appears to leap off a cliff onto a hot-air balloon?
We did the cliff in Hong Kong and the balloon in France. He jumped onto the balloon from a helicopter, and the balloon just folded on him. He was suffocating. Then he had to maneuver himself down from the balloon and into the basket. We were quite worried there.

Do you like Hong Kong movies?
No. I can't say I like Hong Kong movies, even though I'm making them. One or two films a year I enjoy immensely. But I don't think any Hong Kong film-maker is a big fan of Hong Kong movies. We don't have a clue why you American people like them so much.

Filmography

1984 Wheels on Meals (assistant production manager)
1985 The Protector (assistant director)
1986 Armour of God (production manager)
1986 Sworn Brothers (associate producer)
1987 Heroes Shed No Tears (production assistant)
1989 News Attack (producer)
1989 Whampoa Blues (producer)
1990 Curry and Pepper (producer)
1991 Alan and Eric: Between Hello and Goodbye (director, producer)
1992 Days of Being Dumb (producer)
1993 Tom, Dick and Hairy (co-director)
1993 Yesteryou, Yesterme, Yesterday (producer)
1994 He Ain't Heavy, He's My Father (co-director, co-producer)
1994 Twenty Something (producer)
1994 Over the Rainbow, Under the Skirt (producer)
1994 He's a Woman, She's a Man (director, producer)
1995 Happy Hour (producer)
1995 Heaven Can't Wait (screen story)
1996 Age of Miracles (director, producer)
1996 Who's the Woman, Who's the Man (director, producer)
1996 Comrades, Almost a Love Story (director, producer)

SYLVIA CHANG, Actress, Director, Producer, Writer
Chang Ai-chia
Born Taiwan, 1953

Sylvia Chang in *Eat Drink Man Woman*

Western audiences may know Sylvia Chang best for her small but memorable portrayal of an aging father's young fiancée in Ang Lee's *Eat Drink Man Woman*, in 1994, but by then she had acted in almost fifty other films, often in starring roles. Chang has also distinguished herself as a director, producer, and screenwriter, as well as a recording star with seven platinum albums to her credit. She is an actress of range, who has performed in art-house drama (*That Day on the Beach*) and screwball comedy (*Aces Go Places*); her film-making talents probably found their widest expression in *Passion*, a 1986 film about adultery and betrayal, for which she was director, writer, and star. Recently, Chang became the managing director of a Taiwanese cable-television network aimed at the youth market.

Chang was born in Taiwan, but spent her early teen years in New York. On her return home, she became a singer and presenter on television, and was soon offered an acting contract by Raymond Chow of Golden Harvest. She picks up the story from there:

QUESTION: *You were only eighteen when Golden Harvest signed you up.*

SYLVIA CHANG: Yes. In those days, they made you live in a dormitory in back of the studio. They told me, you'll be pleased with the dorm – Bruce Lee used to stay there. But it was very spooky, like a ghost house. They gave me a flat with another person, who I think was supposed to spy on me. They had a lot of restrictions – you cannot have a boyfriend, you cannot see reporters.

Your first picture was . . . .?

A kung-fu movie called *Flying Tigers*. It was banned in Taiwan. The reason is very funny. Some member of Chiang Kai-shek's son's family went to look for a Chinese film and saw the title – Oh, *Flying Tigers*, it must be about the air force. So they showed it, and found out it was all kung-fu fighting, and drug-dealing in the memorial hall for Sun Yat-sen. They got so mad, they banned the film, and passed a regulation that a script had to be approved before [a Taiwanese citizen] can make it.

Was that a typical film for you at Golden Harvest?

Yes. I was the reaction person in martial arts films, a very weak person. The ironic thing was, I learned martial arts as a kid. Years later, when I made *Aces Go Places*, I got to use my skills. But none of the people at Golden Harvest knew I had them. Thank God; otherwise I'd have been fighting, and bruised all over.

How long were you signed for?

Five years. But after a year, I told Mr. Chow that I didn't feel this was what acting was about, and it was not really suitable for me, and he released me from my contract. It was nice of Mr. Chow; he usually freezes you in the refrigerator. He gave me a comment which I always remember, and was a lot of help to me. He said, "I don't know why you look much prettier in person, but you're not very photogenic." So he was not very satisfied with me on the screen.

How was that helpful?

I agreed with him. But then I said, "That doesn't mean I cannot act." I look at a lot of Western movie stars, they don't have to look so great if they're serious about acting. Then, luckily, I started to win awards. Now people categorize me as a character actress.

I understand Raymond Chow gave you your first break as a director.

Yes. Mr. Chow always knew I wanted to direct, and a few years after he released me from my acting contract, he asked me to take over as director for *Once upon a Time*. That's a melodrama. It was sad; the original director was hit by a car, and he died.

Have you ever felt sex discrimination in Hong Kong as a woman director?

I've been very lucky. People say the Chinese are very male chauvinist, and a woman has no status, but I've always been well treated here. But I recently directed a film in New York called *Siao Yu*, and I was not treated well at all. The [American] producer just wanted to push me to get everything in the can. If I looked for another angle to do a shot, they'd say, "Oh, there she goes again." The crew was very rude. Very rude. All these years, I never had these problems in Hong Kong.

Dickson Poon, the retailing mogul who used to be married to Michelle Yeoh, produced your film Passion. *That seemed an unusual film for him.*

Dickson didn't know much about drama, and he was very much against it. But he knew that I had Cora Miao and George Lam [two top actors] in the cast, so he felt it was safe. When it was nominated for a lot of awards, he went to the ceremony, and when I had to go on stage, he offered to hold my bag. Before that, he was never even friendly. Some people just like to be in lights.

Tell me about your role in Aces Go Places.

That was my very first try at comedy and action, and it was really fun. I had never done this kind of action acting, and some scenes took at least forty takes.

Tsui Hark later directed you in Aces Go Places III, *and in* Shanghai Blues.

Oh, man, Tsui Hark – he's crazy. Once you go into a studio with him, you never know when you're going to come out. He has so much energy. We had not really a fight, but after *Shanghai Blues* came out, I went to see it. I was not very happy with it. Everybody loved that film, but I thought it should be better, because we devoted so much time to it.

Selected Filmography

1978 Once upon a Time (director)
1979 Legend of the Mountain (actress)
1979 The Secret (actress)
1982 Aces Go Places (actress)
1982 Crazy Romance (actress)
1982 He Lives by Night (actress)
1983 Aces Go Places II (actress)

1984 Aces Go Places III: Our Man from Bond Street (actress)
1984 The Funniest Movie (actress)
1984 Funny Face (actress)
1984 Shanghai Blues (actress)
1986 Aces Go Places IV (actress)
1986 The Flower Floating on the Sea (actress)
1986 Passion (director, writer, actress)
1987 The Game They Call Sex (co-director, actress)
1987 Seven Years Itch (actress)
1988 Chicken and Duck Talk (actress)
1988 Soursweet (actress)
1989 Eight Taels of Gold (actress)
1989 All About Ah Long (actress)
1990 Full Moon in New York (actress)
1990 The Fun, the Luck, and the Tycoon (actress)
1990 Queen of Temple Street (actress)
1991 A Rascal's Tale (actress)
1991 Sisters of the World Unite (co-director, co-writer, actress)
1992 Mary from Beijing (director)
1992 That Day on the Beach (actress)
1992 Three Summers (producer, writer)
1992 Twin Dragons (cameo)
1993 C'est la Vie, Mon Cherie (cameo)
1994 Eat Drink Man Woman (actress)
1994 In Between (director, writer, actress)
1995 I Want to Go on Living (actress)
1995 Siao Yu (director, writer)
1996 Tonight Nobody Goes Home (director, co-writer)

LESLIE CHEUNG, Actor
Cheung Kwok-wing
Born Hong Kong, 1956

Leslie Cheung was educated in England, and began his career as a pop singer in 1977, under contract to the Hong Kong television network RTV. He went on to record a number of hit albums for PolyGram before retiring from singing in 1989 to concentrate on acting. (He recently embarked on a brief comeback concert tour.)

Leslie Cheung in *A Chinese Ghost Story*   Leslie Cheung

Cheung's breakthrough in movies had come three years earlier when he was cast as Kit, the angry young police cadet, in John Woo's *A Better Tomorrow*; in 1993, he achieved worldwide fame on the art-house circuit as the effeminate opera singer in the mainland Chinese movie *Farewell My Concubine*, directed by Chen Kaige. In 1996, he starred in Kaige's *Temptress Moon*.

I met Cheung one evening, well past midnight, in the back room of a supermarket in the remote Chai Wan district of Hong Kong, where he was filming a scene for Tsui Hark's Lunar New Year comedy *The Chinese Feast*. He had the lead role, as a young triad who becomes a chef. His hair was streaked with red dye, and he wore a sweater tied around his neck; as he spoke, he gestured dramatically with his cigarette. Cheung has a reputation for being bitchy – when John Lone beat him out for the role of a Japanese transvestite in the movie *M. Butterfly*, he reportedly said of his rival, "He looked pretty, but he cannot be compared to me" – and, in my conversation with him, he wasted no time on diplomacy.

QUESTION: *Did you set out to be a performer?*
LESLIE CHEUNG: Not at all, actually. I studied textiles. Which has

Leslie Cheung on the set of *Ashes of Time*

helped me, because once you can sing and act, you have to know how to dress yourself.

Your first movie, in 1980, was called Erotic Dream of the Red Chamber. *That doesn't sound like a propitious beginning.*

I thought it would be a big opportunity for me to go into the movie business, because the company making the film had a famous actress under contract. It turned out to be a disaster, a low-budget blue movie, very indecent. And the dialog was terrible. After that, I made some more low-budget movies, of better quality. But my main event was still the singing career, which turned out to be pretty big during 1984. My greatest hit at that time was "Monica," which sold a million copies.

Yet five years later, you gave up singing.

One day I woke up and decided, well, this is the time for me to do some good movies. So I had a big concert tour – like, thirty-three consecutive concerts in Hong Kong; I still hold the record – and then I quit. It's very unreasonable for me to work at both singing and acting. As an actor, you can go much further – traveling back and forth in time, playing different characters. It's like having more lives during your lifetime.

You seem to have a knack for choosing good roles; at least a half dozen of your films are standard repertory at Hong Kong film festivals in the United States.

My own preferences are *A Better Tomorrow, Rouge, Days of Being Wild*, and, especially, *Farewell My Concubine*. I was disappointed *Farewell* did not get the Oscar for Best Foreign Picture. [It lost to *Belle Epoque* of Spain.] There must be some politics involved.

You told me earlier that Golden Harvest would not allow Jackie Chan to star opposite you in Farewell *because of the film's homosexual overtones.*

Yes. It was stupid of them, because that was a great film. Jackie was a little disappointed, too, because he couldn't make that movie with me. We are very good friends. Somehow it seems he's always acting in those kung-fu movies, and it's very hard for him to do a breakthrough. I'm telling him, this is the right chance.

Do you think he could have handled the role as well as Zhang Feng-yi did?

(After a pause) It would be different. Very different. I can't say he is going to be the best, because of the language barrier. I'm not so sure about his Mandarin.

Did you sing in Farewell?

No, that's the only thing I didn't do. I'm a perfect tenor, but I'm not a soprano.

But normally, you don't use a voice double.

I won't allow myself to do that, unlike some people. Especially for the past three or four years. I want to have my quality controlled. That's why I will do a maximum of three movies in a year, and only one movie at a time. Anita Yuen, my co-star in this movie [*A Chinese Feast*], she's doing two or three at a time; she's the hottest female in town now. When I work with somebody, I have to trust them first. I am in this movie because Tsui Hark is my friend, and he's very professional. His movie is going to be, maybe not great, but at least above average.

Are you going to try to concentrate on art films?

I'll do all types. The only thing I can't do is kung-fu, though with some stand-ins I might. But, of course, the great directors want me to do great dramas.

Do those directors include Zhang Yimou of China?

I don't think so. Because his movie is telling mostly about the lower-class people in China, like farmers, and people from very deserted areas. It doesn't fit into my image, I'm sorry to say. In Chen Kaige's *Temptress Moon*, I get to play a Teddy boy in Shanghai, in the 1920s. A decadent part. It's more like me.

Are there any Hong Kong directors you haven't worked with that you'd like to?

Ann Hui. Her luck wasn't with her the past few years, but she's a great director.

I noticed that on your list of personal favorites, you mentioned Wong Kar-wai's Days of Being Wild, *but not his subsequent* Ashes of Time.

I spent too much time on that. Wong Kar-wai is a very nice guy, but he changes his mind a lot, and it's very hard for the actor or actress to follow him. And he had problems with the script this time; I think it has been laying there for too long. We started shooting in 1992, and he wasn't finished until the end of '93. And then all my dialog was transferred to the voice-over, which is quite unfair to me. It seems like I don't have any acting to do. So I think the movie has some very great images, but the script is a disaster.

Would you make another movie with him?

It depends. I have to read the script first. He is a very promising director, but somehow I find it very difficult to work with him, especially he's killing a lot of time for me, and I am not making a lot of money. [In August, 1996, Cheung flew to Argentina to play a male hustler in Wong Kar-wai's *Happy Together*, a gay love story inspired by the writings of Manuel Puig.]

Did you find John Woo difficult?

Not at all. John is more professional. He seldom changes the script, and he has a heart for all the characters in the movie – you understand what I'm saying? I talked with him when I was in Los Angeles for the Oscars, and there might be a chance of working with him again.

But otherwise, you don't seem especially eager to make Hollywood films.

I passed up a lot of opportunities, because I don't think it's the right thing for us to go and work in Hollywood, since we work very comfortably in Hong Kong. We are the stars, right? I'd rather be one of the best in Asia then just a stand-in in Hollywood. But I do like Los Angeles. The last time I was there, I asked all the drivers and chauffeurs why they were in L.A. And they all gave me the same reply: because we want to be an actor. I was thrilled. When you go back to your hotel tonight, ask the taxi driver why he lives in Hong Kong. He won't tell you to be an actor.

Chow Yun-fat is giving Hollywood a try.

Let's cross our fingers. He's very good. But he has to watch his diet, he's getting fatter. A lot fatter. (Puffs his cigarette.) I'm sorry to say it, but I think his prime time has slipped away.

Selected Filmography

1980 Erotic Dream of the Red Chamber
1982 Crazy Romance
1982 Last Song in Paris
1982 Nomad
1984 Double Decker
1984 Fate
1984 Intellectual Trio
1985 For Your Heart Only
1986 A Better Tomorrow
1987 A Better Tomorrow II
1987 A Chinese Ghost Story
1987 Rouge
1988 Fatal Love
1989 Aces Go Places V: The Terracotta Hit
1990 A Chinese Ghost Story II
1991 The Banquet (cameo)
1991 Days of Being Wild
1991 Once a Thief
1992 All's Well, Ends Well
1992 Arrest the Restless
1993 All's Well, Ends Well Too
1993 The Bride with White Hair
1993 The Bride with White Hair II
1993 The Eagle Shooting Heroes
1993 Farewell My Concubine

1994 Ashes of Time
1994 He's a Woman, She's a Man
1994 It's a Wonderful Life
1994 Long and Winding Road
1995 The Chinese Feast
1995 Phantom Lover
1996 Temptress Moon
1996 Shanghai Grand
1996 Tri-Star
1996 Who's the Woman, Who's the Man
1997 Happy Together

CHOW YUN-FAT, Actor
Born Hong Kong, 1955

JASMINE CHOW, Spouse, Business Adviser
Born Singapore, 1959

Chow Yun-fat is one of the best-known movie stars in Asia – and soon, he hopes, in the United States. In February 1997, production began on his first Hollywood movie, *Replacement Killers*. Though

Chow Yun-fat in *Hard-Boiled*

Chow Yun-fat in *A Better Tomorrow*

Chow's English was charmingly maladroit at the time the following interview took place, his English skills have improved dramatically since his move to Los Angeles; Jasmine, his pretty, no-nonsense wife, who moved there with him, jokes that he seems to have "swallowed a thesaurus." For details about Chow's family background and career history, please consult pages 46–8.

QUESTION: *Did you anticipate the success of* A Better Tomorrow?
CHOW YUN-FAT: No. Never. I always hope the boss can make money, but what I enjoy is the moment when I'm acting. And up to finish the film, everybody not very optimistic about this film. Even the boss of Golden Princess. But then, going to see the première, you can feel the atmosphere in the cinema. The audience is very excited, shouting, clapping hands. This never happen in a Hong Kong movie. I love it.
JASMINE CHOW: And the box office every night was good. The money coming in was so great.
Your life changed after that.
CHOW YUN-FAT: It changed a lot. I make more movie, and I make more money. (Jasmine laughs.) And I also make more injury.
John Woo has almost killed you a couple of times.

JASMINE CHOW: He has stitches around his eyes from *The Killer*, the effects of the gunshots outside the church.

CHOW YUN-FAT: In *A Better Tomorrow II*, the grenade goes off in the house, and the heat and fire push me off the camera, and some of my hair burned already.

JASMINE CHOW: John is crazy with explosive.

You also wrenched your back carrying Dean Shek in one of the Brooklyn scenes of A Better Tomorrow II.

CHOW YUN-FAT: That shot, I'm carrying him in the warehouse, quite close to the waterfront, and in the warehouse is a lot of water. So that accident happened because so slippery. I lost my balance, and my back twist, and I cannot move any more.

JASMINE CHOW: On the flight all the way from New York City to San Francisco, he has to sleep on the floor and crawl to the toilet. John Woo has injured him a lot. I want to kill John Woo.

Do you plan to work with Woo in Hollywood?

CHOW YUN-FAT: Love it.

What caused the rift between Woo and Tsui Hark?

CHOW YUN-FAT (After a pause): Such a long story.

JASMINE CHOW: It happened when *The Killer* was successful. Tsui Hark didn't support this project at all, but when this movie got fame everywhere, Tsui Hark knew he needs to get this recognition back. Fighting for that. Tsui wants John to declare he's the rightful owner of the film. Quite a tedious argument on this. In the end John gave up. John doesn't like argument. I know John was very sad, he lost a good friend. John is a very melancholy person.

Tsui Hark directed you in A Better Tomorrow III. *How was that experience?*

CHOW YUN-FAT: Tsui Hark is a very good director, very creative, very sensitive. For my own way, I think I cannot communicate with Tsui Hark. I cannot feel it. We are going two different directions. Maybe sometime we can make another movie, but not at this moment. After *A Better Tomorrow III*, he tried to invite me another kind of story. I turned him down.

Tell me about Ringo Lam.

CHOW YUN-FAT: Ringo Lam, he's another kind of director, he like the things very real, raw. He would never let the actor feel very soft or comfort in the location.

JASMINE CHOW: He's like a mad dog on the set. I couldn't believe it, this guy has no sympathy at all. You don't feel pain, he's not happy.

CHOW YUN-FAT: He like the actor, actress, the crew members, to share the sadness of the director (laughs).

Filmography
1976 The Reincarnation
1976 Learned Bride Thrice Fools Bridegroom
1976 Massage Girls
1976 The Hunter, the Butterfly, and the Crocodile
1977 Hot Blood
1978 The Private Lives
1978 Miss "O"
1980 See-Bar
1980 Joy to the World
1980 Police Sir
1981 Executioner
1981 The Story of Woo Viet
1982 The Postman Strikes Back
1982 The Head Hunter
1983 The Bund (television movie)
1983 The Bund, Part II (television movie)
1983 Blood Money
1983 The Last Affair
1984 Love in a Fallen City
1984 The Occupant
1984 Hong Kong 1941
1985 Women
1985 Why Me?
1986 Rose
1986 Witch from Nepal
1986 Dream Lovers
1986 The Missed Date
1986 100 Ways to Murder Your Wife
1986 The Lunatics
1986 A Better Tomorrow
1986 Love unto Waste

1986 The Seventh Curse
1986 A Hearty Response
1986 My Will, I Will
1987 City on Fire
1987 Tragic Hero
1987 Scared Stiff
1987 Brotherhood (cameo)
1987 Rich and Famous
1987 The Romancing Star
1987 An Autumn's Tale
1987 Flaming Brothers
1987 Spiritual Love
1987 Prison on Fire
1987 A Better Tomorrow II
1988 The Eighth Happiness
1988 Tiger on Beat
1988 Fractured Follies
1988 Diary of a Big Man
1988 The Greatest Lover
1988 Cherry Blossoms
1988 Good-bye, Hero
1988 City War
1989 All About Ah Long
1989 Wild Search
1989 The Killer
1989 Triads: The Inside Story
1989 A Better Tomorrow III: Love and Death in Saigon
1989 God of Gamblers
1990 The Fun, the Luck, and the Tycoon
1991 Once a Thief
1991 Prison on Fire II
1992 Now You See Love . . . Now You Don't
1992 Hard-Boiled
1992 Full Contact
1994 Treasure Hunt
1994 God of Gamblers' Return
1995 Peace Hotel
1997 Replacement Killers

CHRISTOPHER DOYLE, Cinematographer
Born Sydney, 1952

Christopher Doyle

Ashes of Time: Brigitte Lin

Christopher Doyle has been called the finest director of photography currently working in the Chinese cinema, a curious circumstance for someone who is neither Asian nor a photographer by training. At eighteen, he dropped out of a literature program at the University of Sydney to join the merchant marines, worked on an Israeli kibbutz, and then ended up in Bangkok, where he posed as a Western doctor to help a con man sell quack medicine. After studying Chinese in Hong Kong in the late 1970s, he moved to Taiwan, where, as a founding member of a theater workshop, he learned to handle a still camera. In 1980, he shot episodes of Taiwan's acclaimed nonfiction television series *Travelling Images*, and came to the attention of the movie director Edward Yang, who hired him as cinematographer for *That Day on the Beach*. Yang stood by Doyle even after the studio cameramen went on strike in protest of the Australian's hiring; the film won the award for Best Cinematography at the Asia-Pacific Film Festival.

Since then, Doyle has worked with other leading Chinese directors, including Chen Kaige, Patrick Tam, Stanley Kwan, and Shu Kei; but he is most closely associated with Wong Kar-wai, who has relied on the Australian exclusively since directing his second feature, *Days of Being Wild*. Doyle's cinematography for Wong's *Ashes of Time*, which was shot in the Yuli desert of China, earned him a Golden Horse in 1994. He has since shot Wong's *Happy Together* in Buenos Aires, and published several books of still photographs.

QUESTION: *How important was* Days of Being Wild *to your career?*
CHRISTOPHER DOYLE: Even before we started, it was being hailed as the film of the year. I had two assistants collapse from nervous exhaustion beforehand, and it was a stressful thing for a lot of the crew members. Maggie Cheung hated me at the time, because we were often doing retakes for technical reasons. I thought, this film is either going to make me or break me, but if Wong Kar-wai is giving me this trust, I should try to rise to it. Since then, I don't worry about my reputation.
I understand you shot quite a lot of the never-completed Days of Being Wild II, *in which Tony Leung Chiu-wai was to star as a gambler.*

A great deal of film, yes. Andy Lau was to be an underworld criminal, and we shot a whole sequence with him in the Walled City of Hong Kong, a no-man's land where all the drugs come from. It was a depressing place to be. So many rats, so hot, dangerous, and claustrophobic. We shot there for three weeks.

And never used one frame.

Listen, if I was to cry about the amount of footage on the cutting-room floor. . . . One day, my creative team and I gave a seminar on *Ashes of Time* to the Hong Kong Society of Cinematographers. We spoke for four hours. It was so depressing – they didn't care about the esthetics of the whole thing, they just wanted to know what filters I used. And when we were finished, they said, "We're considering drafting up a contract that stipulates how much of the footage that is shot must appear in the finished film." I said, "Fuck this. I'm never going to talk to the people again."

How much unused footage was there on Ashes of Time?

I don't want to know. It's very high.

Give me an example of something you didn't use.

There's a question of whether Brigitte Lin's brother actually exists. So we shot a scene – it could be a dream sequence – where she carries the body of her dead brother through the desert. The woman I was with at the time was a still photographer on the set, and she looked very much like Brigitte. She dressed up as the brother, and Brigitte tried to carry her, but the sand was too soft, and she sunk down to her calves. So we changed it around and made Brigitte the dead brother. We spent a whole day on that, but it was physically impossible.

Sammo Hung is listed as the action director for Ashes of Time. *What exactly was his role?*

Because of the dynamics of the whole thing, we had to have an action director. But how can one be an assistant director to Wong Kar-wai? It's a contradiction in terms. How can another director work out what Wong Kar-wai wants, when it evolves from day to day? So we just tried to make each fight sequence stylistically different, and fall in with the general style of the film. I was usually traveling back and forth, lighting one set, and then rushing to another side of the sand dunes to keep everything under control.

The script of a Wong Kar-wai film is just a point of departure.

I don't even bother with it any more. I assume the film is going to be about time and space and identity and isolation. And probably it's going to be in the spaces he says it'll be in – probably. Even the time period can be left till a week before shooting. When we got to Buenos Aires [to film *Happy Together*] he was still deciding whether the film would take place in the 1990s or the 1960s. One day, after we'd been there for six months, he suddenly said to me, "Buenos Aires is like a grid. The streets are all parallel." I said, "Yeah?" He said, "Therefore, this film must be a grid. Leslie Cheung and Tony Leung [the male leads] are the horizontals, and we need to find the verticals." So he brought in two more actors. They sat around for months waiting for him to figure out where they go. He has me running around, he has someone calm and collected in William Chang [the art director], he has crazy people throwing out ideas, and he's got some of the best actors in the world. From that, he picks and chooses, and the film forms day by day.

Filmography

1981 That Day on the Beach
1986 Noir et Blanc
1987 Soul
1987 Burning Snow
1989 My Heart Is that Eternal Rose (co-cinematographer)
1991 Days of Being Wild
1992 Peach Blossom Land
1992 Beijing Bastards (co-producer)
1993 The Red Lotus Society
1994 Ashes of Time
1994 Chungking Express
1994 Red Rose, White Rose
1995 Fallen Angels
1995 The Peony Pavilion
1995 Out of the Blue
1996 Temptress Moon
1996 Four Faces of Eve
1996 Comrades, Almost a Love Story (actor)
1997 Happy Together

ANN HUI, Director
Hui On-wah
Born Manchuria, 1948

Ann Hui

The Spooky Bunch

Like the protagonist of her semi-autobiographical movie *Song of the Exile*, Ann Hui is the daughter of a Japanese mother and a Chinese father, with a university education in London – in her own case, two years of film school. Upon graduating, in the mid-1970s, she returned to Hong Kong, where she had spent part of her childhood, and worked as an assistant to the late director King Hu. She subsequently became a director of dramatic series and documentaries at television station TVB, alongside other emerging film-makers of the Hong Kong new wave, including her then boss, Patrick Tam. In 1979, she made her début feature, *The Secret*, a well-regarded thriller that appears to have been inspired somewhat by Roman Polanski (whose *Chinatown* is one of Hui's favorite films). After a hit comedy, *The Spooky Bunch*, Hui changed direction sharply, and won international acclaim with a pair of gut-wrenching dramas concerning the lives of Vietnamese refugees – the latter film, *Boat People*, was given its première at Cannes.

Unlike other new-wave directors who had been her contemporaries at TVB – notably, Tsui Hark – Hui has resisted the lure of commercialism. She turned down numerous offers to make more mainstream Hong Kong movies, including a chance, in 1992, to

Boat People

direct *Fong Sai Yuk*, a martial-arts film starring Jet Li. (She did, however, provide assistance to the film's director, Corey Yuen; for instance, the memorable villain in the movie, Zhou Wen-zhou, who has gone on to become a martial-arts star in his own right, was Hui's discovery.)

When I first met Hui, toward the end of 1994, many people considered her to be past her prime. After directing two television dramas, *The Prodigal's Return* and *A Boy and His Hero*, Hui had returned to feature film-making with *Summer Snow*, a drama about a middle-aged woman forced to care for a father-in-law with Alzheimer's Disease. She was modest about the film's prospects, though I soon discovered that she is always modest, if not brutally frank about her own perceived shortcomings. (She can be equally brutal in her assessment of other film-makers; see, for instance, her comments about the director Wong Jing, on page 49.) Hui invited me to a screening of *Summer Snow*, and when the lights came on, the consensus among the audience was that her comeback was assured. Indeed, not only did *Summer Snow* sweep both the Golden Horse and Hong Kong Film Awards, but in January, 1997, on the strength of the movie, Hui and lead actress Josephine Siao became two of the last-ever Hong Kong citizens to be honored by Queen Elizabeth with the title of MBE – Member of the Most Excellent Order of the British Empire.

Hui was disappointed in her follow-up movie, *Ah Kam: The Story of a Stunt Woman*, and, for budgetary reasons, unable to make the improvements she sought. (Moreover, the star of the film, Michelle Yeoh, was badly injured on the set.) Fearful of post-reunification censorship by the Chinese government, Hui is considering working outside of Hong Kong. Should that fail, she says, "I'll try to keep my mouth shut and survive here."

Filmography

1979 The Secret
1980 The Spooky Bunch
1981 The Story of Woo Viet
1982 Boat People
1984 Love in a Fallen City

1987 Romance of Book and Sword
1987 Princess Fragrance
1988 Starry Is the Night
1990 Song of the Exile
1991 My American Grandson
1991 Zodiac Killers
1993 Fong Sai Yuk (associate producer)
1994 The Day the Sun Turned Cold (co-producer)
1995 Summer Snow (also: producer)
1996 Ah Kam: The Story of a Stuntwoman
1996 Who's the Woman, Who's the Man (cameo)

SAMMO HUNG, Actor, Director, Producer
Hung Kam-bo
Born Hong Kong, 1950

Sammo Hung (right)

When film-maker Ann Hui needed someone to play the master stunt director in her recent film *Ah Kam: The Story of a Stunt Woman*, she cast Sammo Hung, a multitalented Hong Kong movie personality who, among other things, *is* a master stunt director. His contributions to the modern Hong Kong cinema have been considerable – notably, as the director of cult classics such as *Eastern Condors* and *Encounters of the Spooky Kind,* and as an action and martial-arts star. On screen, Hung tends to play comic roles, the natural consequence of being a living contradiction – a fat man of extraordinary agility. In *Winners and Sinners,* he leaps over a flaming buffet table, crashes through a window, and lands on a stone patio; in *The Owl vs. Bumbo,* he takes to the dance floor and does a creditable soft-shoe routine.

One of four children born to Shanghainese parents, Hung was sent to the same draconian Peking Opera school attended by Jackie Chan. He was the eldest boy at the academy, and Chan grew up respectfully calling Hung his *dai go dai,* or Biggest Brother. (Though Hung, like Chan, was subject to beatings from the schoolmaster, he played his old teacher sympathetically in *Painted Faces,* a 1988 biopic that netted him a Golden Horse for Best Actor.) In the early 1970s Hung applied the skills he learned at the school as an extra and stunt man; in the opening of Bruce Lee's *Enter the Dragon* (1973), for instance, Hung gets the stuffing knocked out of him by Lee. When Hung met Lee for the first time on the set, he was eager to put the martial-arts legend to the test. "I see him coming," Hung told me, "so I ask him, 'You really fight?' He say yes. 'So can we try?' He say yes. We just started fighting, and he make one move – he kicks real fast, and just stop here." Hung pointed to a spot about a millimeter from his forehead, and smiled. "So, yes, he's a real fighter."

In recent years, Hung has continued to act in and direct movies, but he only occasionally agrees to work as an action director. He made one such exception for the art-house director Wong Kar-wai, for the existential swordplay epic *Ashes of Time,* which was filmed in the Yuli desert of China. "I like working with Wong Kar-wai; he's a very good director, you know?" Hung says, adding, however, that the finished film was not to his taste. "I told Wong Kar-wai, 'Very boring.'"

Though between 1983 and 1988, Hung directed Jackie Chan in five films, the two men stopped working together after that, and there was talk of friction between them. Hung denied this when I first met him, at his office in a run-down building in Kowloon. (He has since moved.) Hung, who was wearing a gold bracelet and had a ponytail tied in a knot, picked up an old, framed school photograph to show me, taken when he was a chubby boy in his early teens, and Jackie Chan was a starved-looking adolescent with a crewcut. Not long after our meeting, Hung served as action director for Chan's auto-racing movie *Thunderbolt*, and more recently he flew to Australia to direct *Mr. Nice Guy*, Chan's first English-language film in more than ten years. Hung shows no sign of slowing down; apart from the old photo, he keeps a large poster in his office that apparently expresses his credo: "Get up early, sleep well, have 70 per cent of your stomach filled, run a lot, laugh a lot, don't get mad, never get old."

Selected Filmography

1975 Hand of Death (actor, action director)
1975 The Man from Hong Kong (actor, action director)
1977 Broken Oath (actor, action director)
1977 Iron Fisted Monk (actor, director)
1977 Shaolin Plot (actor, action director)
1978 Enter the Fat Dragon (actor, director)
1978 Warriors Two (actor, director)
1979 Game of Death (actor, action director)
1979 Knockabout (actor, director)
1980 By Hook or by Crook (actor, action director)
1980 Encounters of the Spooky Kind (actor, director)
1980 The Victim (actor, director)
1981 Prodigal Son (actor, director)
1982 Carry on Pickpocket (actor, director)
1983 Project A (actor)
1983 The Dead and the Deadly (actor, action director, producer, co-writer)
1983 Winners and Sinners (actor, director)
1983 Zu: Warriors from the Magic Mountain (actor)
1984 The Owl vs. Bumbo (actor, director)
1984 Wheels on Meals (actor, director)
1985 Heart of the Dragon (actor, director)

1985 It's a Drink, It's a Bomb (producer)
1985 My Lucky Stars (actor, director)
1985 Twinkle, Twinkle Lucky Stars (actor, director)
1985 Yes, Madam! (producer)
1986 Eastern Condors (actor, director)
1986 Millionaire's Express (actor, director)
1986 Spooky Spooky (actor, director)
1986 Where's Officer Tuba (actor, producer)
1987 Righting Wrongs II: Blonde Fury (producer)
1988 Dragons Forever (actor, director)
1988 Lai Shi, China's Last Eunuch (actor, producer)
1988 Painted Faces (actor)
1988 Paper Marriage (actor)
1989 Eight Taels of Gold (actor)
1989 Encounters of the Spooky Kind II (actor, action director)
1989 Fortune Code (actor)
1989 Pedicab Driver (actor, director, producer)
1990 Island of Fire (actor)
1990 Pantyhose Hero (actor, director, producer)
1990 Shanghai, Shanghai (actor, producer)
1990 She Shoots Straight (actor, producer)
1990 Skinny Tiger and Fatty Dragon (actor)
1991 Daddy, Father and Papa (actor)
1991 Ghost Punting (actor)
1991 Lover's Tear (actor, producer)
1991 My Flying Wife (actor)
1991 Operation Scorpio (producer)
1991 Slickers vs. Killers (actor, director, producer)
1991 The Banquet (actor)
1991 Touch and Go (actor)
1992 Moon Warriors (director)
1992 Painted Skin (actor)
1993 Blade of Fury (actor, director)
1993 The Eagle Shooting Heroes (action director)
1993 The Kung Fu Cult Master (actor, action director)
1994 Ashes of Time (action director)
1995 Don't Give a Damn (actor, director, producer)
1995 Thunderbolt (action director)

1996 Ah Kam: The Story of a Stuntwoman (actor)
1996 How to Meet the Lucky Stars (actor)
1996 Somebody up There Likes Me (actor)
1997 Once upon a Time in China and America (director)
1997 Double Team (action director)
1997 Mr. Nice Guy (director)

STANLEY KWAN, Director
Kwan Kam-pang
Born Hong Kong, 1957

Stanley Kwan (standing) and   *Center Stage:* Maggie Cheung
Winston Chao on the set of *Red*
Rose, White Rose

Novices seeking an introduction to the Hong Kong cinema are
often urged by aficionados to see Stanley Kwan's 1987 ghost story
Rouge, though in many respects it is an atypical Hong Kong movie.
While the ghost story is a staple of the industry, *Rouge* was made
almost entirely without special effects; it relies on Kwan's

Rouge: Anita Mui and Leslie Cheung

atmospheric direction, and the acting, to convey a sense of the spirit world. Further, it is that rare hybrid – a movie that succeeded both as a commercial venture and as an art-house film. Kwan has not had a bona fide hit since *Rouge*, and, according to film critic Tony Rayns, who assisted him on his recent documentary, *Yang ± Yin: Gender in Chinese Cinema*, he doesn't care all that much. In recent years, however, Kwan has had to scrape for financing, and one of his potential backers was a Taiwanese triad.

In shunning commercialism, Kwan takes after his mentor, Ann Hui, with whom he worked at TVB in the mid-1970s. He had joined the television station, after graduating from Baptist College in Hong Kong with a communications degree, in hopes of becoming an actor – a career that never got off the ground. Instead, he learned film-making as an assistant director on three of Hui's early films, and on Patrick Tam's *Nomad*, before directing his first feature, *Women*, in 1985. The following year, Kwan found himself in Yugoslavia, as the assistant to Eric Tsang, who had been hired by Golden Harvest to direct Jackie Chan's Indiana Jones knockoff, *Armour of God*. Though Kwan left the production midway, he was on hand to witness Chan's near-fatal fall from a tree, for which the actor required brain surgery. "It was just terrible," Kwan recalls. "Jackie says, 'Oh, it was nothing,' but suddenly, we saw blood coming from his ear."

Kwan stuck with Golden Harvest to make *Rouge*, with Jackie Chan as producer, and Chan's manager, Willie Chan, as "co-ordinator." When the director showed the rough cut to the studio bosses, including co-founder Leonard Ho, he recalls, "They're all scared. They could not imagine that the ghost was treated this way. They couldn't see any somersault, or special effect." Kwan says Ho wanted him to reshoot the film, "but Jackie and Willie – especially Willie – stay on my side," and the movie was released unchanged in Taiwan, where it was an immediate hit. It went on to win Best Picture and Best Director at the Hong Kong Film Awards. Caroline Thompson, who wrote the screenplay for *Edward Scissorhands*, recently optioned the story for an American remake, which she plans to direct.

Four years later, Jackie Chan produced Kwan's *Center Stage* (also known as *Actress*), a biopic about silent-movie actress Ruan Ling-yu – the Chinese Garbo – who committed suicide at twenty-five. It was a critical success, but, Kwan notes, "It definitely lose money for Golden Harvest." Kwan, for his part, says, "I'm really not satisfied with the film now; I think the concept can work much better," and he has similar feelings about his more recent *Red Rose, White Rose*. He adds, "I really appreciate the comment of Krzysztof Kieslowski" – the Polish director of the "Three Colors" trilogy – "who said that after you finish the film, you cannot get another chance, and you've got to face the mistakes that you made. So he thought that was really suffer for the director."

Filmography

1979 The System (assistant director)
1980 The Beasts (assistant director)
1980 The Spooky Bunch (assistant director)
1981 The Story of Woo Viet (assistant director)
1982 Boat People (assistant director)
1982 Nomad (assistant director)
1982 The Postman Strikes Back (assistant director)

1983 The Last Affair (assistant director)
1985 Women
1986 Love unto Waste
1987 Armour of God (assistant director)
1987 Rouge
1989 Hearts No Flowers (producer)
1990 Full Moon in New York
1990 Ming Ghost (producer)
1991 Center Stage
1992 Too Happy for Words
1994 Red Rose, White Rose
1996 Yang ± Yin: Gender in Chinese Cinema

RINGO LAM, Director
Lam Ling-tung
Born Hong Kong, 1955

Ringo Lam

Full Contact: Chow Yun-fat

Ringo Lam has referred to himself as a "dark-faced god," because of his penchant for temper tantrums on the set, and some people in the industry seem put off by him. "He's not particularly friendly," says John Woo's producer, Terence Chang. I'm pleased to report that my own encounters with Lam have been pleasant and stimulating. At our first meeting, he was accompanied by his shy Chinese-Canadian wife Mabel, and we covered some of the basics of his film career. (For additional detail, please refer to pages 45–6.)

QUESTION: *How did you get the name Ringo?*
RINGO LAM: Years ago, I went to a party and met a girl who asked me if I had an English name. I said I don't have any. So she said, I like the Beatles – what about I name you Ringo? I said fine. I like the Beatles, too.
When you joined television station TVB in 1973 as a trainee, you started out as an actor?
For seven months, nine months. But I didn't like my face being shown on screen. After that, I worked as a production assistant, until 1978. Since there is not much job satisfaction working for a

TV station, I quit and went to Toronto to study film [at York University].

Did you complete your studies?

No. I got citizenship in Canada, but I never finished my film study. I went back to Hong Kong in 1981 to work as a director. It's really a rough time. I didn't get a chance to start my first film until the end of '82.

That was the ghost story/comedy Esprit d'Amour?

Yes. That film is initiated by another director, Leong Po-chih. He completed one third of the movie, and then there is an argument between him and Karl Maka, the boss of Cinema City – I don't know what it's about – and Maka asked if I could finish the film. I have no choice, I needed food. So I just do the best I can, and the movie turned out to be quite successful.

Maka eventually asked you to direct him in the fourth installment of Cinema City's biggest hit comedy series, Aces Go Places.

I accepted for two reasons. One, *Aces Go Places* enjoyed a huge budget by Hong Kong standards, and I was always curious how to spend so much money. The second reason, I wanted to work with Karl Maka and find out who this guy is. On screen, he's a comedian. But off screen, he's so serious – the master of Cinema City.

Apart from that, you didn't want to make the film?

No, because I prefer drama. But at Cinema City, you have to do comedy, OK?

After that, however, Maka let you switch to drama.

I guess he liked me. He said, "Ringo, I know you don't like comedy very much. Now I give you a budget, and you do one project on your own, according to what you like." So, at that time, I read in the newspaper about a jewelry shop in Tsimshatsui that was robbed by a gang of robbers, and their plan was already known to the police. I went to court to see who are these robbers. So tough. And I find out they didn't dress well, and everybody look like a loser. I do more research on this case, and it turn out to be the story for *City on Fire.*

Your first drama was a hit.

Yeah. And I won the Best Director in the Hong Kong Film Awards. And Chow Yun-fat won the Best Actor.

City on Fire *also became the inspiration for the American film* Reservoir Dogs.

That seems to me very natural. Everybody learn from others; my film learns from America directors. And because of the success of this *Reservoir Dog* [sic], that helped my publicity in the States. If there was no *Reservoir Dog*, I think today nobody even think about *City on Fire*.

Did you like Reservoir Dogs?

A couple of scenes, not the whole movie. I like the scene where the guy is dancing, playing with the knife, and cut the victim (laughs).

Chow Yun-fat starred in your next movie, Prison on Fire.

After *City on Fire*, I didn't know what's to be my next project. Then my brother, Nam Yin, he had a lot of friends in the gangster world, he knew a lot of characters in that circle. So he fed me with details. I found a scriptwriter, and we finished the first draft of *Prison on Fire* in seven days. It turned out to be my most successful movie.

I was surprised to learn that Full Contact *was not a success in Hong Kong. In America, it's probably your most popular collaboration with Chow Yun-fat.*

Of my five films with him, that one got the worst box office in Hong Kong. I think the audience like Chow Yun-fat dressed well in a suit and tie. In *Full Contact*, he's such a macho guy, in a leather jacket.

Chow Yun-fat thought he looked out of shape in the movie.

I told him to keep fit. It's both our fault. I should have gone to his house and done the exercise together with him.

Burning Paradise, *your one and only costume film, is also far more popular in the States than it is in Hong Kong.*

That one is expensive. It cost more than 23 million Hong Kong dollars. A big loss for Golden Harvest.

For some reason, your movies haven't fared as well in Hong Kong in the 1990s as they did in the 1980s.

(After a pause) I think the film critics here dislike me. Maybe because I say something about June 4th [the day of the Tiananmen Square Massacre, in 1989].

What did you say?

After all the bloodshed in Beijing, everybody is crying, and showing so much emotion in the media. Almost every fifteen minutes the television repeat the same news. Everybody is so sad. OK. I feel sad, too. But the thing last too long. After two, three weeks, I said, "Can we break for awhile? Let's have the Dragon Boat Festival." Oh. All of a sudden, everybody came after me. I said, "I'm sorry," and I went to Singapore and stayed there for a month. There were threats sent to my company. After that, all my movies didn't get a good response.

[During a more recent visit to Hong Kong, I took Lam to dinner, and afterward we dropped by a hotel lounge to discuss the making of his first Hollywood movie, Columbia Pictures' *Maximum Risk*, starring Jean-Claude Van Damme. Lam, as usual, was wearing military-style fatigues – his fashion statement. He ordered a cognac and a cigar, and told me what had transpired.]

In the summer of 1995, I finish *The Adventurers*, and then I pay a visit to Toronto to see my parents. All of a sudden, the phone ring, and a producer from L.A. want me to make a picture with Jean-Claude Van Damme. It's been my dream, hoping that one day I can work on a Hollywood project, and learn the Hollywood system.

You were aware, were you not, that John Woo had a rather unpleasant experience making Van Damme's Hard Target *for Universal?*

I heard a lot of rumor how John Woo have trouble with Van Damme. But I just figure, everybody have ego, and if I can suppress mine, that will help a lot.

So, did you have a problem with Van Damme?

No, we are still friend. My problem is with the studio. I think maybe the studio doesn't know how much they changed my movie.

What happened?

(After a pause) See, the way I make *School on Fire, Prison on Fire*, my characters are very contradictory. Always gray, not black and white. That happens over and over again in my movie. So I apply the same thing on Natasha [Henstridge, the female lead in *Maximum Risk*]. I just do it naturally. And she become the most dangerous character to Jean-Claude. She can betray him, trap him, put him in danger.

Columbia let you do that?

Yes. They respect me, and support my vision all the way through production. And even in post-production.

So what went wrong?

(Sighing) Then they invite an audience and have a screening test. The audience fill out some forms, and maybe their comment is not very clearly expressed, and the studio executive have to guess what they mean. And that is dangerous. There's a column to rate the actor and actress, and the audience don't like Natasha. They don't say her performance is not satisfactory – maybe they don't like her because her character is not lovable. You have to guess. So then the studio want me to change her character. Boy and girl meet each other, and walk hand in hand, and have fun and adventure. Because Jean-Claude movie should be very simple, right? A simple story, kicking ass. So I reshoot three days, and it change the whole story. That's what make me crazy. If they cut the action scene, that's OK. But they pull out the root.

Do you still recognize it as your film?

I think just one or two shots, that's Ringo Lam. But the movie doesn't belong to me any more. Still, I shouldn't complain too much. I'm already lucky enough to have people finance my first Hollywood movie. (Sadly puffs his cigar.) A lucky guy, Ringo Lam. Mr. Lucky.

Filmography

1983 Esprit d'Amour
1984 The Other Side of Gentleman
1985 Cupid One
1986 Aces Go Places IV
1987 City on Fire
1987 Prison on Fire
1988 School on Fire
1989 Wild Search (also: producer)
1990 A Moment of Romance (co-producer)
1990 Undeclared War (also: producer)
1991 Prison on Fire II
1991 Touch and Go
1992 Twin Dragons (co-director)
1992 Full Contact (also: producer)
1994 Burning Paradise

1995 The Adventurers
1996 Maximum Risk

ANDY LAU, actor
Lau Tak-wah
Born Hong Kong, 1961

Andy Lau in *Drunken Master II*

One of the hardest-working people in an industry known for its grueling schedules, Andy Lau has moved in the opposite direction from Leslie Cheung. While Cheung gave up a successful singing career to pursue film acting full-time, Lau has lately cut down on his own once-prodigious film output to devote more time to recording and touring as a singer. Today, Lau is quite possibly the most popular male vocalist in Asia, a feat he accomplished on sheer willpower. His rugged looks – "lean, mean, with that trademark aquiline nose" (*South China Morning Post*) – made him a natural leading man for the movies, but his voice was considered too harsh for Cantopop. All that changed in 1990, with the release of his fifth album, *Can It Be Possible*, which went multi-platinum. Three years later, Lau became the first Asian singer to sign an endorsement contract with Pepsi-Cola.

Since the early 1980s, Lau has appeared in numerous Hong Kong film classics, including one of his first movies, Ann Hui's *Boat People*, in which he played a young Vietnamese at an internment camp. Wong Kar-wai cast him as a triad in his own début film, *As Tears Go By*, and as a soulful cop in *Days of Being Wild*. (Lau was said to have been somewhat displeased with the latter role, because he was made to wear a police cap that obscured his face.)

Lau is one of six siblings from Taipo, a poor rural village in Hong Kong's New Territories. Like Chow Yun-fat before him, he joined TVB as an actor-trainee in 1981, and achieved almost immediate popularity on television. But in 1985, he had a contract dispute with the station. "I just wanted to get away," Lau says. "I want to make two movies a year, and they want me to keep on doing the TV series for the rest of my life. So they put me in one daily program, and I just sit there for one and a half years and wait for the contract to finish. In the end, they told me, 'You're really a tough guy.'"

After breaking free, Lau averaged closer to ten movies a year, well into the 1990s. "It's very strange in Hong Kong," he says. "The popular actor is not so many, and if you get popular, every film company tries to find you." Among the companies that sought him out were those run by triads. For a few years, he was happy to take on the workload. "Chow Yun-fat told me, 'Try to do all the movie, and don't let the other people have a chance,'" he says, laughing. But by the early 1990s, it had got to be too much. "By that time, I'm a worker, not an actor," he says. "I just try to make sure the way I walk, or talk, or smoke, is different in one movie from the other."

The overexposure did not hurt Lau's movie career, and he remains one of the biggest box-office draws in Asia. His performance as a motorcycle racer in Derek Yee's *Full Throttle*, for instance, helped make that film one of the smash hits of 1995. I asked Lau why, when so many film stars are also recording stars, the movie musical is almost nonexistent in the modern Hong Kong cinema. He says the reason is budgetary, but that, if the opportunity arose, he'd been happy to make a Hollywood-style musical in Cantonese, adding, with a smile, "We can call it *East Side Story*."

Selected Filmography

1982 Boat People
1982 Once upon a Rainbow
1984 Everlasting Love
1985 Twinkle, Twinkle Lucky Stars
1985 The Unwritten Law
1986 Sworn Brothers
1987 In the Blood
1987 Magic Crystal
1987 Rich and Famous
1987 Tragic Hero
1988 As Tears Go By
1988 Lai Shi, China's Last Eunuch
1988 The Truth
1989 Casino Raiders
1989 City Kids 1989
1989 The First Time Is the Last Time
1989 Fortune Code
1989 God of Gamblers
1989 Long Arm of the Law III
1989 News Attack
1990 Dragon in Jail
1990 God of Gamblers II
1990 A Home Too Far
1990 Island of Fire
1990 Kawashima Yoshiko
1990 The Last Blood
1990 A Moment of Romance
1990 Return Engagement
1990 Stars and Roses
1991 The Banquet (cameo)
1991 Casino Raiders II
1991 Dances with the Dragon
1991 Days of Being Wild

1991 Don't Fool Me
1991 Hong Kong Godfather
1991 Kung Fu vs. Acrobatic
1991 Lee Rock
1991 Saviour of the Soul
1991 The Tigers
1991 Tricky Brains
1991 Zodiac Killers
1992 Casino Tycoon
1992 Casino Tycoon II
1992 Come Fly the Dragon
1992 Game Kids
1992 Gun-N-Rose
1992 Handsome Siblings
1992 Moon Warriors
1992 Saviour of the Soul II
1992 What a Hero
1993 Days of Tomorrow
1993 Future Cops
1993 The Perfect Exchange
1994 Drunken Master II
1994 Drunken Master III
1994 A Taste of Killing and Romance
1994 The Three Swordsmen
1994 Tian Di (also: producer)
1995 The Adventurers
1995 Full Throttle
1996 A Moment of Romance III
1996 Shanghai Grand
1996 Thanks for Your Love
1996 What a Wonderful World
1997 Armageddon

CLARA LAW, Director
Law Cheuk-yiu
Born Macao, 1957

Clara Law

EDDIE FONG, Director, Writer
Fong Ling-ching
Born Hong Kong, 1954

Clara Law and Eddie Fong are one of the most respected wife-and-husband teams in world cinema, and their movie collaborations – notably *Autumn Moon*, directed by Law from a script by Fong – seem to have international appeal. (The film won the Golden Leopard at Locarno in 1992.) They are also a prime example of Hong Kong reunification jitters, having settled a few years ago in Australia. When I met with them, in Sydney, they were in the process of editing *Floating Life*, their first Australian movie.

QUESTION: *How did you happen to settle in Australia?*
CLARA LAW: We did it gradually. My parents and siblings have

lived here for years, and Eddie and I spent a month here in 1992, on our honeymoon.

Your honeymoon? Weren't you married in 1989?

Yes. The day after our wedding, I flew to New York to make *Farewell China.*

I see. So you spent a month in Australia in 1992 . . . .

And then we came back in 1993 to do post-production for *Temptation of a Monk.* In 1994, we decided to move here. We sort of gradually found that our audience is not just Hong Kong – it's a select group, but it's worldwide. And to be honest and very frank, I would not like to be under the régime of the Communist government.

You're worried about censorship?

Oh, yes, everybody will have to worry about that. *Temptation of a Monk* was banned in China.

Hong Kong is not the most hospitable place for an art-film director, would you agree?

It didn't make life easy for us. It's been like walking a tightrope, trying to make films that are meaningful and not just entertainment.

Eddie Fong

Eddie and I found ourselves very lonely working there.

Did you ever aspire to commercialism?

After I made *Reincarnation of Golden Lotus*, which was a box-office hit, I was tempted. My thought at that time was, do one commercial film and one art film. But when I made *Autumn Moon*, I felt such freedom and relief and happiness, I began to see that I could not make a film purely for commercial reasons.

Do you work on all of Clara's films?

EDDIE FONG: Yes. Even if I'm not involved in the writing, I work as associate producer for her. Because most of the time, the producer will trust me to handle the budget.

How did you two meet?

CLARA LAW: Through his writing. I had finished my studies in England, and at that time, Eddie'd just finished his second feature. I thought his scripts were very good. So I approached him and asked if he'd be interested in writing my first feature [*The Other Half and the Other Half*]. Without pay.

You went for that?

EDDIE FONG: Sure. At that time, I was quite fed up with the film industry in Hong Kong. Until I met Clara, I didn't know if I wanted to work in film at all any more.

Why?

My second film was a disaster. It's called *Cherry Blossoms* – not the title I wanted. It was the last Shaw Brothers film, and I was still shooting it, in Japan, when Shaw Brothers stopped all production. Then Shaw Brothers sold it to Golden Harvest, and Golden Harvest asked me to shoot some more nude scenes, because they didn't think the film was commercial enough. I refused to do that. After that, they didn't allow me to touch the film any more. I was so frustrated.

And then you met Clara . . . .

And I started working with her. I figured, it's better to have two people struggling together, rather than one. After I worked with her on two films, I thought, maybe I should direct another one myself. So when Clara directed *Farewell China* in New York, I started to direct *Kawashima Yoshiko*.

How was that experience?

Not good. Since I've got two big stars in the movie [Andy Lau and

Anita Mui], Golden Harvest wants the film to be shown during the summer holidays. And summer movies are really short, because the theaters like to have many screenings per day. So I got pressure that the film has to be within ninety minutes. I don't think I can do that. Finally, I got one version of one hundred and eight minutes, for the Venice Film Festival, and then I cut it down to ninety-three minutes for the Hong Kong version.

Which was still too long?

No, because the projectionist in Hong Kong runs it at twenty-eight frames per second [instead of the normal speed of twenty-four], so the film can finish earlier for another screening. It's the craziest thing.

The last film you directed in Hong Kong, Private Eye Blues, *seemed close to mainstream entertainment. Yet some people think they detect a hidden political message.*

They're right. It's about betrayal, like what happened in 1989 with the student movement [at Tiananmen Square]. But in the Hong Kong cinema, you have to disguise everything.

CLARA LAW: Because the golden rule is, don't talk about politics. Otherwise it will be a flop. They proved it with *Farewell China*. I guess the majority of the Hong Kong audience, they want to have fun, and if you force them some truth, they find it hard to take.

Are there any Hong Kong directors whom you admire?

The director I most admire is Hou Hsiao-hsien [of Taiwan]. You need a lot of guts to do the things he does. Hong Kong directors do not have that guts.

Tell me about your latest film, Floating Life.

It's the story of a family from Hong Kong that immigrated to Australia, and they're broken apart because of the different culture, until they find their balance and come back together.

I understand the Australian government helped foot the bill.

Yes, it's the first Cantonese-speaking film to be funded by the Australian government. It has a mainly Australian-Chinese cast, and maybe half the cast never had any acting experience. That's OK, because they make a very credible family. I always thought this film should not have stars.

Is it possible that Hong Kong film-making will actually improve under mainland Chinese sovereignty?

Maybe – if you believe any suffering will help creativity.

Filmography
Clara Law

1988 The Other Half and the Other Half
1989 The Reincarnation of Golden Lotus
1990 Farewell China
1992 Autumn Moon (also: co-producer)
1992 Fruit Punch
1993 Temptation of a Monk
1993 Erotique (co-director)
1996 Floating Life (also: co-writer)

Filmography
Eddie Fong

1980 The Beasts (co-writer)
1982 Coolie Killer (writer)
1982 Nomad (co-writer)
1984 An Amorous Woman of the Tang Dynasty (director, writer)
1987 Cherry Blossoms (director, writer)
1988 The Other Half and the Other Half (writer)
1988 Lai Shi, China's Last Eunuch (writer)
1989 A Fishy Story (co-writer)
1989 The Reincarnation of Golden Lotus (writer)
1990 Farewell China (producer, writer)
1990 Kawashima Yoshiko (director)
1992 Autumn Moon (co-producer, writer)
1992 Fruit Punch (co-producer, writer)
1993 Temptation of a Monk (co-writer)
1993 Erotique (co-producer, co-writer)
1994 Private Eye Blues (director, writer)
1996 Floating Life (co-writer)

TONY LEUNG, Actor
Leung Ka-fai
Born Hong Kong, 1957

Tony Leung is one of the best-known Hong Kong actors in the West, thanks to his role as a Chinese man who has an affair with a young French woman in Jean-Jacques Annaud's sexually graphic

Tony Leung in *The Lover*

film *The Lover*, from the novel by Marguerite Duras. His fame in
the West might have come sooner: he says he was offered the title
role in Bernard Bertolucci's *The Last Emperor*, but turned it down
because of a copyright dispute between Bertolucci and the Hong
Kong director Lee Hong-cheun, who, in 1983, gave Leung his first
movie role, playing the same character. "Everybody think I'm very
stupid, and that I lose a great chance," Leung told me. "But I don't
want to unplease director Lee."

Leung says his childhood was rather like the one depicted in the
film *Cinema Paradiso*. His father was a Hong Kong projectionist,
at a theater that showed mostly Western movies, and Leung spent a
good portion of his youth seated in the back row. After graduating
from college, he enrolled in the training program for actors at TVB,
but dropped out after nine months because he needed to earn a
living. In the early 1980s, he and some friends launched an
entertainment magazine, through which Leung met director Lee,
who was about to shoot a movie entitled *The Burning of the
Imperial Palace* in mainland China – an almost unheard-of location
for a Hong Kong film at the time. To his amazement, Leung was
not only offered the lead, but went on to win Best Actor at the Hong

Kong Film Awards. It proved a mixed blessing: he became a star overnight, but no one would cast him in a movie for almost two years, because Taiwan, the largest export market for Hong Kong films, blacklisted him for acting in the mainland.

Leung got off-camera work at Cinema City, where he apprenticed to both Tsui Hark and John Woo, and says that, with Tsui's help, the Taiwanese boycott finally was lifted. Before long, he was one of the most in-demand actors in the Hong Kong cinema; in 1993, his peak year, he averaged a movie a month, all in lead roles. "Maybe it's a very bad habit, but I think Hong Kong people don't want to work slow," he says. "And, comparing to Hollywood stars, we don't earn so much."

Toward the end of 1994, however, his career was once again in jeopardy. He had displeased the actress Cheung Man, who had been given a production company by the powerful, and feared, movie producer Jimmy Heung, whose father founded the Sun Yee On triad society. The actress had cast Leung in her film *Dream Lover*, and, after shooting had wrapped, she demanded that he postpone his next movie assignment to reshoot some scenes. Leung declined, even after Cheung Man held a tearful press conference accusing him of reneging on his contract. He was reluctant to talk about the contretemps, although, he says, "What she tell the newspapers is not true, and this piss me off." Since that time, Leung's movie output has slowed down, and he has tentatively embarked on a second career, as a pop singer.

Selected Filmography

1983 Burning of the Imperial Palace
1986 Fire Dragon 1986
1986 Lady in Black
1986 Laser Man
1987 People's Hero
1987 Prison on Fire
1988 Gunmen
1989 A Better Tomorrow III: Love and Death in Saigon
1989 Sentenced to Hang
1990 Farewell China

1990 Her Fatal Ways
1990 Island of Fire
1990 Queen's Bench III
1990 She Shoots Straight
1991 Au Revoir, Mon Amour
1991 The Banquet
1991 Center Stage
1991 The Lover
1991 The Raid
1991 Red and Black
1991 This Thing Called Love
1992 92 Legendary La Rose Noire
1992 All Men Are Brothers
1992 Dragon Inn
1992 King of Chess (also: co-writer)
1992 Misty
1992 Once upon a Time a Hero in China
1993 The Black Panther Warriors
1993 Boys Are Easy
1993 The Eagle Shooting Heroes
1993 Flying Dagger
1993 Ghost Lantern
1993 He Ain't Heavy, He's My Father
1993 Lover of the Swindler
1993 The Perfect Exchange
1993 A Roof with a View
1993 Rose, Rose I Love You
1993 The Sting II
1993 Tom, Dick and Hairy
1994 Always Be the Winners
1994 Ashes of Time
1994 God of Gamblers' Return
1994 He and She
1994 I Will Wait for You
1994 It's a Wonderful Life
1994 Long and Winding Road
1994 Lover's Lover
1994 To Live and Die in Tsimshatsui

1995 The Christ of Nanjing
1995 Dream Lover
1995 Lover of the Last Empress
1995 A Touch of Evil
1996 Evening Liaison

JET LI, Actor
Li Lian-jie
Born China, 1963

Jet Li in *Fist of Legend*

Since the death of Bruce Lee in 1973, scores of imitators have made movies using pseudonyms such as Conan Lee, Rocky Lee, and the like. Despite the similarity of name, Jet Li has always been an original, and, since his breakaway hit of 1991, *Once upon a Time in China*, he has been the most popular martial-arts star in Asia. Although he says that Bruce Lee was his boyhood idol, when he subsequently remade Lee's *Fist of Fury*, as *Fist of Legend*, the result was less an homage to the late star than a radical reinterpretation of what had been a virulently anti-Japanese film.

Though Li stands only about five foot six, he is powerfully built; Michelle Yeoh, who costarred with him in *Tai Chi Master*, says she was constantly terrified that one of his blows would accidentally connect with her. Li is a private man who, in interviews, shuns almost any topic apart from *wu shu*, the high-kicking martial-arts style he has helped popularize ever since he was a boy growing up in Communist China. He began learning the fighting technique when he was eight, and took five gold medals in the national championships at the age of twelve. A year earlier, he made his first trip to the United States, to perform in a *wu shu* troupe for President Nixon at the White House. "I was just a small child," he recalled, speaking in Mandarin. "And since it was just the opening of diplomatic relations between China and the United States, I was afraid that any mistake I committed would cause national harm." The performance went flawlessly, and the United States left an indelible impression on Li. "I was very curious about the tall buildings and all that stuff," he says.

Li was not yet twenty when he was asked by a Hong Kong production company to star as a fighting priest in *Shaolin Temple*, a kung-fu movie shot on location at the authentic temple in Hunan Province. Though, as expected, the picture was banned in Taiwan, it caused a sensation in Hong Kong, Singapore, and other parts of Asia. Six years later, in 1988, Li, who had been paid only a state subsidy for his work in motion pictures, obtained a two-year exit permit from the Chinese government, and settled in San Francisco with a Chinese actress, whom he subsequently married and divorced. In between, they had two children. (It is subject he does not discuss.) Though Li was issued an American green card, he never learned to speak English.

After Li's exit permit expired, he moved to Hong Kong, rather than return to Beijing, and signed up with Golden Harvest. His movie stardom had waned, but after Tsui Hark and Golden Harvest featured him as the Cantonese hero Wong Fei-hung in *Once upon a Time in China*, he was bigger than ever. (For more detail about Li, and his subsequent rift with Golden Harvest, please consult pages 27–9.) Li told me that Wong Fei-hung was a natural role for him, a person much like himself – as he put it, "young and innocent, and daring to do things that are impulsive."

Selected Filmography

1982 Shaolin Temple
1984 Shaolin Temple II: Kids from Shaolin
1986 Born to Defend (also: director)
1986 Shaolin Temple III: Martial Arts of Shaolin
1988 Dragon Fight
1989 The Master
1991 Once upon a Time in China
1992 Once upon a Time in China II
1992 Once upon a Time in China III
1992 Swordsman II
1993 Fong Sai Yuk
1993 Fong Sai Yuk II
1993 Kung Fu Cult Master
1993 Tai Chi Master
1993 The Last Hero in China
1994 Bodyguard from Beijing (also: producer)
1994 Fist of Legend
1994 New Legend of Shaolin (also: producer)
1995 High Risk
1995 My Father Is a Hero
1996 Black Mask
1996 Dr. Wai in "The Scripture with No Words"
1997 Once upon a Time in China and America

ANITA MUI, Actress
Mui Yim-fong
Born Hong Kong, 1963

Anita Mui did not agree to be interviewed; quite possibly she was
wary of being asked about The Incident. In 1992, Mui got into an
angry confrontation with a triad in a karaoke bar, and by the
following year, through no apparent fault of her own, two people
were murdered as a consequence (see pages 25–7). Mui is, by all
reports, an unhappy woman. Her father died when she was a baby,
and, at the age of four, she began vocal training under the tutelage
of her mother, a veteran Chinese opera singer. By eight, to help
support her family, Mui was singing in nightclubs, and at nineteen,

Anita Mui

she won the top prize in a television-sponsored talent contest. She went on to become the most popular female vocalist in Hong Kong, though she was frequently accused of corrupting the city's youth with her raunchiness. (At one sold-out concert, she stripped down to her black lingerie and wriggled on the floor with four male dancers.)

Mui appeared in her first movie in 1982, and rapidly developed into a top film star, equally adept at drama and comedy. For her role in *Rouge*, as the ghost of a prostitute searching for her lover in modern-day Hong Kong, she won the Golden Horse Award for Best Actress. She has demonstrated a flair for action as well – as a gun moll opposite Chow Yun-fat in *A Better Tomorrow III*, and as a costumed superheroine in *The Heroic Trio* and its sequel, for instance. Mui has never married, though for a time she was linked romantically with Jackie Chan, who not only broke off their affair, but cast her as his stepmother in *Drunken Master II*; she retaliated by nearly stealing the picture.

Selected Filmography

1982 Last Song in Paris
1984 Fate
1985 Musical Dancer
1986 100 Ways to Murder Your Wife
1986 Inspector Chocolate
1987 Happy Bigamist
1987 Rouge
1987 Scared Stiff

1987 Trouble Couples
1988 The Greatest Lover
1989 A Better Tomorrow III: Love and Death in Saigon
1989 Fortune Code
1989 Miracles
1990 Kawashima Yoshiko
1990 Shanghai, Shanghai
1991 Au Revoir, Mon Amour
1991 Saviour of the Soul
1991 The Top Bet
1992 Justice, My Foot!
1992 Moon Warriors
1993 The Heroic Trio
1993 Executioners
1993 Fight Back to School III
1993 The Magic Crane
1994 Drunken Master II
1995 My Father Is a Hero
1995 Rumble in the Bronx
1996 Who's the Woman, Who's the Man

JOSEPHINE SIAO, Actress
Siao Fong-fong
Born Shanghai, 1947

Josephine Siao was once called the Shirley Temple of Hong Kong, a child star of the 1950s and 1960s, celebrated for her family pictures and musicals. Today, most American fans of the Hong Kong cinema know only her adult work – such as her uproarious performance as Jet Li's kung-fu-fighting mom in *Fong Sai Yuk*, and her bittersweet portrayal of a retiring opera star in the recent *Hu-Du-Men*. When we met, I had just attended a screening of Ann Hui's *Summer Snow*, which starred Siao, who had yet to see the movie herself. Despite my enthusiasm, Siao had grave misgivings about the film – she was unconvinced that Hui's subject matter, Alzheimer's Disease, would go over well with audiences. Her performance subsequently won her the Best Actress award at the Berlin Film Festival, and resulted in her receiving an MBE from Queen Elizabeth.

Josephine Siao in *Summer Snow*

Siao's English is impeccable – she has taught the language on television, and also published a best-selling book on Western etiquette – though before our meeting, she sent me a letter advising that an interview might be difficult. She lost all the hearing in her right ear at age two, and, she said, had become nearly deaf in her left ear since 1990. At her request, we met in the conference room of a hotel, because, she explained, "my gadgets do not work so well in noisy places." Siao did not seem to miss a word I said, and I thought perhaps she had exaggerated her condition, until Ann Hui later told me that Siao often has to lie down after a conversation, because the strain of using her hearing aid left her exhausted. I was all the more amazed at Siao's acting skill – her deafness is indiscernible in her movies – and all the more grateful for the interview.

QUESTION: *How did you become an actress?*
JOSEPHINE SIAO: I came over to Hong Kong from Shanghai with my mother when I was three. My father had passed away. A friend of my mother's said, "There's a job for your daughter, a one-shot deal. Would you like to take it?" My mother said OK, because we

needed the money for our meals. So she sent me into the film business, and I just didn't stop. I had my mother and myself to support, and a half-brother and half-sister in Shanghai. At that time, in the 50s, they were making a lot of family films, so they needed children running around.

Did you have professional management?

Just to arrange filming schedules, not to negotiate. That was done by ourselves. And the studios really took advantage. By the time I reached twelve, I had to work thirty hours nonstop, if necessary. Even when I was younger – nine, ten – I was always overworked. That was the way they shot films. At least people were kind to me. My mother had a tougher time. For a lot of films, we didn't get paid.

Did you work primarily for one studio?

No, I was a freelance artist. At the time, Shaw Brothers and Cathay turned out only Mandarin films, but we also had a Cantonese movie industry. I made movies in both Mandarin and Cantonese. The Mandarin films had bigger budgets, and they were thought to be better produced. But I think the overall quality of acting was superior in the Cantonese film industry.

Who do you have in mind?

I worked with all the top stars. There was one called Ng Tso-fan, and another was called Cheung Ying. When I started to play the lead, I worked with Wu Fung and Lui Kei. These were big names then. All Cantonese.

Do you recall any of your earlier pictures?

When I was eight, I made one with Shaw Brothers called *Mei Goo*. I won the Best Child Actress Award at the South East Asia Film Festival.

Your Mandarin films included musicals?

Yes, I was forced to sing, even though I had lost my hearing in my right ear. So I didn't like singing.

How did your work schedule affect your education?

I had a tough time. I had to stop school for many years, and work with private tutors. But I had a very good English teacher, from Cambridge. He was very nice to me.

Your résumé says that between 1952 and 1968, you acted in two hundred feature films.

I was lucky, because most child stars reach a predicament stage between eleven and fifteen – not yet an adult, but no longer a child – and they fade away. But I had training in Peking Opera, and they needed people who knew swordfighting. That's why I kept getting jobs, and never stopped.

Yet there came a point when you did stop.

I retired when I was twenty-one. I didn't like the film business, and I told my mother I wanted to head off. [Appropriately, her farewell picture at the time was called *The True Story of a Rebellious Girl*, in which Siao played a female James Dean.] So in 1968, I moved to the United States for four years to get a communications degree from Seton Hall University. I thought I wanted to get behind the camera, although somehow they keep getting me to act.

Isn't Seton Hall in New Jersey?

That's right. So I was picking up a New Joisy accent. I lived in South Orange, because we had relatives there. I stayed with them for a year, and then I moved out. I wanted to know what American life was about, and I figured, if I live with a Chinese family, I'll never learn. So I spent three wonderful years with a Jewish family. I ate gefilte fish, and I had a nice Jewish mother trying to marry me off to doctors and lawyers. I'm a converted Jew.

Did you graduate?

Yes, I got my BA degree. I was a bit overage for college, but I was very happy. I came back to Hong Kong, but I wanted to get my mother to move with me to the United States, so I could get my Master's, and then get a job. We sold our house, but then I found out from friends that my mother didn't want to leave Hong Kong. You saw *The Joy Luck Club*? Chinese mothers don't tell you what they really want. So I stayed here and made a few Mandarin films for the Taiwan market. [In 1976, Siao also starred in and co-directed *Jumping Ash*, a hit crime drama about drug trafficking, from a script by retired police detective Philip Chan.]

And then . . . . ?

I got married, and moved to Taiwan. He was an actor in Taipei. My mother said, "Why don't you just live together?" But I was so conservative in those days, and I said, "No, I have to be married." She was right, because the marriage lasted only three months. I came back to Hong Kong, and worked in television and film. I had my own production company.

One of the movies you produced, and starred in, was Ann Hui's comedy The Spooky Bunch, *which is considered a classic. You also became the only woman ever to play the lead role in a John Woo movie, the comedy* Plain Jane to the Rescue.

That was produced by my company. John Woo was in a very bad mood then, and I think that movie was one of his lows. Afterwards, he put it nicely to me. He said, "I'm sorry, but at that time, I wasn't myself."

You folded your company not long after that.

I decided it was too tough being a producer in Hong Kong. I don't think we have a fair system for independents – it's not like in the States. The distributors make their own films, and they monopolize the market. If you bring a film to them, no matter how good it is, they save all the best showing times for themselves – Christmas, Chinese New Year. I don't think that's healthy. So I quit production, got married, and moved to Australia.

Why Australia?

My husband worked for Rupert Murdoch. He got transferred there. I thought I would never make a movie again. But after two years, he was transferred back to Hong Kong.

And you were lured back into films.

They asked me to make a film with Stephen Chiau, and I quite like him. [The movie was called *Fist of Fury 1991 II*.] Lousy film. It sold very well.

Two years later, you made Fong Sai Yuk, *with Jet Li.*

I didn't want to do it – I turn down most offers. But I feel quite bad if I turn them all down.

You said you had Peking Opera training as a child. Did you do your own fighting in the movie?

I did the close-up scenes. I had to train in *wu shu* with two teachers from Beijing, because Jet Li is really good, and I didn't want to look stupid next to him. The best thing that happened to me with *Fong Sai Yuk* was that I had the chance to learn Chinese martial arts. I still practice every day. The Peking Opera school that my mother sent me to was good enough for films in those days – I learned how to stand, and hold a sword. But it wasn't a full course, like Jackie Chan had. He was indentured to his school; my mother paid for me to go. If you paid, they didn't beat you up – but they also didn't teach you that much.

Have you considered working in Hollywood?
Not unless I could work with people like Robert De Niro or Jack
Nicholson. I went to a couple of Hollywood parties in early 70s,
and found the people very competitive – everybody trying to
outsmart everybody. That's not a place for me. And my handicap is
tough for a director. Unless people know me for a long time, they
might find me a nuisance.

So what are your career plans?
I'm working on an MA degree in child psychology from Regis
University, in Denver, but I'm studying at home. I have two
daughters to take care of.

Do you want them to be actors?
I don't encourage it.

Selected Filmography

1956 Mei Goo
1958 Nobody's Child
1960 Nineteen Heroes of the Green City
1967 I Love A-Go-Go
1967 Diamond
1968 Winter Love
1968 Window
1968 A Purple Stormy Night
1969 The True Story of a Rebellious Girl
1974 Hiroshima 28
1974 Girlfriends
1974 Rhythm of the Sea
1976 Jumping Ash (also: co-director)
1980 The Spooky Bunch (also: producer)
1982 Plain Jane to the Rescue
1987 The Wrong Couples
1991 Fist of Fury 1991 II
1993 Always on My Mind
1993 Fong Sai Yuk
1993 Fong Sai Yuk II
1995 Summer Snow
1996 Hu-Du-Men
1997 Mahjong Dragon

STANLEY TONG, Director
Tong Kwai-lai
Born Hong Kong, 1960

Stanley Tong (pointing) on the set of *First Strike*

Stanley Tong is a Hong Kong success story, a former stunt man who went on to direct three of the biggest-grossing Asian movies of all time, all starring another former stunt man, Jackie Chan. Each of those films – *Rumble in the Bronx*, *Supercop*, and *First Strike* – has had a successful run in American movie houses. He is currently directing Leslie Nielsen in *Mr. Magoo* for Disney. Tong's greatest achievement, however, may simply be that he is still alive. To this day, Tong will not allow an actor to attempt a dangerous stunt without first testing it himself. Before asking Chan to jump off a building and grab the rope ladder of an airborne helicopter for a scene in *Supercop*, for instance, he gave Chan a demonstration. "I fall three times," he says, before nailing the jump on his fourth try. "Then I tell Jackie the trick of how to avoid the fall." (For more detail about Tong, please consult pages 20–24.)

Selected Filmography

1987 Magnificent Warriors (action director)
1988 Angel II (action director)
1989 Angel III (assistant director)
1990 Stone Age Warriors
1992 Supercop
1993 Project S
1995 Rumble in the Bronx
1996 First Strike

ERIC TSANG, Actor, Director
Tsang Chi-wai
Born Hong Kong, 1953

Eric Tsang

I met Eric Tsang at a fried-chicken restaurant under the elevated subway in the Williamsburgh section of Brooklyn, where he was between takes in the role of a triad with a heart of gold in Peter Chan's *Comrades, Almost a Love Story*. He had been to New York only once before, to play an odious lecher – one of his stock characters – in Chinese-American director Wayne Wang's *Eat a Bowl of Tea*. Tsang told me his English was rusty, and said the young woman seated next to him would translate, if need be. The woman turned out to be his co-star, Maggie Cheung, who politely declined to be interviewed herself, and whose translation services proved unnecessary.

Tsang is one of the most recognizable character actors in the Hong Kong cinema, a compactly built man with a squeaky voice, whose filmography is too extensive to reproduce here in full. He was a professional soccer player until, at age twenty, one of his fans, the director Lau Kar-leung, asked him to work as a stunt man. When Tsang protested that he did not know kung-fu, Lau assured him that if he could kick a soccer ball, he could kick around the bad guys in his movies. Before long, Tsang turned his hand to writing scripts; his credits include Lau's *The 36th Chamber of Shaolin*, and Sammo Hung's Bruce Lee parody, *Enter the Fat Dragon*.

In the late 1970s, Tsang became friendly with the actor and producer Karl Maka, who recruited Tsang for his new studio, Cinema City. Together, they developed the concept for the *Aces Go Places* comedy-adventure series, in which, Tsang says now, Maka and Sylvia Chang were supposed to be Richard Burton and Elizabeth Taylor, and Sam Hui was James Bond. Tsang directed the first two movies in the five-part series, and they caused a sensation. "The audience, they're crazy about it," he says of the first film. "At some theaters, too many people are asking for tickets, and broke the windows, and the police had to come out."

Tsang became a member of the so-called Gang of Seven at Cinema City, a governing board that judged the merits of every new film project. But, like fellow board member Tsui Hark, he was never made an equity partner in the studio, and, in 1984, he left to go into business for himself. In 1991, he became one of the founding partners of the United Filmmakers Organization, a consortium of young directors. Tsang works on the business side, generating the budgets for UFO films by pre-selling them to theater chains all over Asia. "The directors just want to make movies; they don't want to have to worry money," he told me. "I worry for them."

These days, Tsang, who married young and has four children, acts far more often than he directs. "I like directing, but you have to waste half a year to direct a film," he says. "You act film, you can make seven or eight in a year, and earn more money." Tsang's acting has won him numerous awards, including, in 1991, a Golden Horse for his starring role in *Alan and Eric: Between Hello and Goodbye*. He says he thought his acting had improved from working with Wayne Wang on *Eat a Bowl of Tea*, because the director had encouraged him to tone down his frenetic body language, and express himself more through the dialog. "After that," he says, "I work with other directors in Hong Kong, and they're asking me, 'Eric, how come you turn slow? Before you act quite fast.' I said, 'Aah! It was because maybe I get some influence from Wayne Wang.' "

Selected Filmography

1975 The Dragon Lives Again (actor)
1978 The 36th Chamber of Shaolin (writer)
1978 Enter the Fat Dragon (writer)
1979 The Challenger (director)
1981 All the Wrong Clues . . . For the Right Solution (actor)
1981 Chasing Girls (actor)
1982 Aces Go Places (director)
1982 Till Death Do We Scare (actor)
1983 Aces Go Places II (director)
1983 Play Catch (actor)
1984 Double Trouble (director)
1984 Funny Face (actor)
1984 My Little Sentimental Friend (actor)
1985 My Lucky Stars (actor)
1986 Shanghai Express (actor)
1987 Final Victory (actor)
1987 It's a Mad Mad Mad World (actor)
1987 Sacred Stiff (actor)
1987 Seven Year Itch (actor)
1987 Trouble Couples (actor, director)
1987 You're My Destiny (director)
1988 Golden Swallow (actor)
1988 Keep on Dancing (actor)
1988 The Other Half and the Other Half (actor)
1989 Eat a Bowl of Tea (actor)
1989 Fatal Vacation (actor, director)
1989 Fortune Code (actor)
1989 News Attack (actor)
1989 Pedicab Driver (cameo)
1989 Reincarnation of Golden Lotus (actor)

1990 Curry and Pepper (actor)
1990 The Last Blood (actor)
1991 Alan and Eric: Between Hello and Goodbye (actor)
1991 Gigolo and Whore (actor)
1991 The Banquet (actor)
1991 The Tigers (director)
1992 Come Fly the Dragon (director)
1992 Days of Being Dumb (actor)
1992 Handsome Siblings (director)
1992 Once upon a Time a Hero in China (actor)
1993 Bogus Cops (actor)
1993 Chez 'n Ham (actor)
1993 Lady Super Cop (actor)
1993 Master Wong vs. Master Wong (actor)
1993 Vampire Family (actor, director)
1993 Yesteryou, Yesterme, Yesterday (actor)
1994 Always Be the Winners (actor)
1994 He's a Woman, She's a Man (actor, producer)
1994 Moonlight Boy (actor)
1994 Oh! Yes Sir! (actor)
1994 Over the Rainbow, Under the Skirt (actor)
1996 How to Meet the Lucky Stars (actor, producer)
1996 The Age of Miracles (actor)
1996 Those Were the Days (actor, director, producer)
1996 Who's the Woman, Who's the Man (actor)
1996 Comrades, Almost a Love Story (actor)

TSUI HARK, Director, Producer, Actor
Born Canton, 1951

My scheduled twenty-minute interview with Tsui Hark ran more than five hours, at the end of which, he showed no sign of fatigue. I was not surprised: in film circles, Tsui is known for marathon work sessions that can last three days nonstop.

Tsui Hark was born in Canton, but raised in the Chinese section of Saigon. His father was a pharmacist with a large family – sixteen sons and daughters from three marriages. It was the father's hope that at least one of his sons would become a doctor, but an artistic

Tsui Hark (right) on the set of *Double Team*

streak ran through the family, and none obliged. Tsui says, for instance, that his eldest brother became an actor, "and I was quite influenced by the romantic lifestyle he had." Meanwhile, the father undermined his own ambitions for Tsui by visiting movie studios on trips to Hong Kong, and bringing back photographs that his son found fascinating. Tsui was ten when he made his first film. "Me and three schoolmates used to perform a magic show on stage at the end of every school year," he says. "One day, we went to a camera store next to my house, and they had an 8mm camera they couldn't sell, because the neighborhood is not very rich. The owner said, 'Are you interested in this kind of camera? I can rent it to you.' So we got the camera for three days, and shot ourselves making the magic show."

When Tsui was fourteen, he was sent to Hong Kong for his secondary education, and three years later, successfully applied to Southern Methodist University in Dallas, Texas. After a year at SMU, he transferred to the University of Austin. "I just want to get in the film business," Tsui told me, "and one way is to go study film,

Peking Opera Blues: Brigitte Lin, Cherie Cheung, Sally Yeh

Swordsman II

and then come back to Hong Kong and apply for a job. Texas is the first school that accept me." Did his father approve? "He believed I was studying pharmacy."

QUESTION: *What was your impression of Texas?*

TSUI HARK: I was very confused and frustrated. I couldn't get used to that kind of place, where the houses are very scattered. It's quite different from Hong Kong. After three years, I feel like, it's boring here – better to go back home and start from zero. But I wanted to go around America first. So in 1974, I went to New York. And I got stuck there.

You found New York to be more like Hong Kong?

Just like Hong Kong. Very business, very crowded, very stink, and people very nervous.

Where did you stay?

I rent an apartment with a friend on Delancey Street [on the Lower East Side of Manhattan]. That was terrible. One day they broke through the wall and got our money – all twenty buck. There's a big hole in the wall, and we didn't know how to fix it.

In New York, you worked with Christine Choy, the documentary film-maker?

Yes. She had a grant to make a film called *From Spikes to Spindles*, a history of the Asian-American.

How quickly after your return to Hong Kong did you land a job at TVB, the television network?

Within a month.

Because you had a film degree from the United States?

They never even looked at my résumé. What is important is the energy you have, and I was quite anxious to get a job. They asked me what I want to do. I said, "Anything – but the most thing I want is to be a drama director." They said, OK. And I start working as a series director.

Chow Yun-fat was under contract at TVB at that time, right?

We work together once. He play a side character in one of my series – tear-jerking kind of series called *The Family*. It's about 104 episodes: people die, get rich, get divorced. One hour every evening, primetime. We have five director for the whole series. Ringo Lam was one of them. His desk is right in front of mine.

So many important new directors came out of TVB . . . .

Yes – the new wave (laughs). I never understood why they call us that. I asked Ann Hui one time. Because the French new wave, everybody got this philosophy, to make film more realistic, more vérité. Our new wave never have this philosophy behind it.

You were at TVB for nine months . . . ?

Then I went to another station, CTV, for six months. I make a costume drama called *Golden Dagger Romance.* That one became a talking point among the television circle, because I shot it in quite a filmic way, with a portable camera. So then the movie people are interested in me.

Your first movie was Butterfly Murders.

Just an idea I have – sort of like a detective story, with a martial-arts background, and sci-fi kind of color. I didn't know anything too much about film-making. I just grab the narrative line and shoot the plot. Later I found out that making a movie is different from shooting a story.

How was Butterfly Murders *received?*

It's really a flop. People get very disappointed in the film. And it was supposed to be low budget, but I think I get a big head, and I spent maybe 3 million Hong Kong dollars. I was quite scared that I ruin some people's life, that I use too much money.

Nevertheless, you turned around and made another movie, about cannibalism – We're Going to Eat You.

That's a film with a lot of Roger Corman elements. It didn't turn out to be good, either. This glorious title of new-wave director! (Laughs.) I became very disappointed in myself. I was thinking about not making film any more – do something else, teach in school or something.

Instead, you directed Dangerous Encounter of the First Kind – *a nasty piece of work.*

At that time I was quite angry, and I tried to do something anarchistic. When you don't care what you put on the screen, a heavy burden is lifted from your shoulder, and you start to make film like a student. And that becomes effective in some way. That film did not do good business, because too violent, and it doesn't have a star. But I enjoyed the process of it.

[Tsui went on to join Cinema City, and directed two hit comedies for the studio; meanwhile, he made the landmark fantasy film *Zu: Warriors from the Magic Mountain*, for Golden Harvest. He soon created Film Workshop, and became John Woo's producer for four films, including the world-famous *The Killer*, before the two men had a falling-out. For more information on this phase of Tsui's career, please consult pages 40–43.]

Why are you and John Woo no longer friends?

I don't understand what happened. Suddenly we just stopped talking to each other. A lot of people around him just got hostile. I remember one time, John got an award for *The Killer*, and nobody informed me. That's my beginning of thinking there is something wrong between us. I was very shocked.

You took control of A Better Tomorrow III. *Was that your first time back to Vietnam?*

Yes. I want to go back there and see what happened. I met some friends and relatives who tell me very shocking stories of the war. But I found out that Thailand is a better place to film this sort of movie – better equipped.

Your state-supplied pyrotechnics expert got killed, I understand.

We want to know how big is the explosion, so he went home to mix all these different portion of chemicals, and smoked a cigarette outside, and stamp it out with a plastic slipper. The butt stick to the slipper, and his whole house went into the air. He died right away, and one of his assistant, 90 per cent of his skin was all burned out. We have to send him to a hospital in Bangkok, but first we have to go through a whole process to get a paper so he can get in the plane. He lived anyway.

Were you happy with the film?

(After a long pause) Happy with film? I think it was out of control, that film. It's too long.

Don't you like any of your movies? How about Peking Opera Blues? *That's been described as your masterpiece.*

That was interesting for me – using three actresses to play all the roles usually played by male actors in a traditional Hong Kong film. But I still feel disappointed, because it was shot in Hong Kong instead of Peking. The street and background is not right.

So what do you consider to be your best movie?

Before, I thought it was *Once upon a Time in China*. But I look at it again, and I found so many problem with the film that I changed my mind.

Do you like American films?

A lot. *Citizen Kane* is one of those. Howard Hawks is very interesting. I like John Ford, Francis Coppola. Frederick Wiseman's documentaries are interesting, too. And I got very amazed by *Macbeth* done by Roman Polanski.

You've been called the Stephen Spielberg of Hong Kong.

I've heard that. But I don't know – it's unfair to him, I think (laughs). It's unfair to me too: he's so rich.

I understand Tsui Hark is a name you invented.

My name was Tsui Man-kong. When I went to school in Texas, they called me King Kong.

Is that why you changed it?

I never liked my name. I thought it was too soft. I changed it to Hark, which means overcoming.

Filmography

1979 The Butterfly Murders (director)
1980 We're Going to Eat You (director)
1980 Dangerous Encounter of the First Kind (director)
1981 All the Wrong Clues . . . For the Right Solution (director)
1983 Zu: Warriors from the Magic Mountain (director)
1983 All the Wrong Spies (actor, production designer)
1984 Aces Go Places III: Our Man from Bond Street (director)
1985 Working Class (director, actor)
1984 Shanghai Blues (director)
1985 Run, Tiger, Run (actor)
1985 Yes, Madam! (actor)
1986 A Better Tomorrow (producer)
1986 Peking Opera Blues (director, producer)
1987 Final Victory (actor)
1987 A Chinese Ghost Story (producer)
1987 A Better Tomorrow II (producer)
1987 Just Heroes (producer)
1988 I Love Maria (producer, actor)

1988 Laser Man (producer)

1988 The Big Heat (producer)

1988 Diary of a Big Man (producer)

1988 Gunmen (producer)

1989 The Killer (producer)

1989 Deception (producer)

1989 Spy Games (producer)

1989 A Better Tomorrow III: Love and Death in Saigon (director, producer)

1989 The Terracotta Warrior (producer)

1990 Swordsman (producer, co-director)

1990 A Chinese Ghost Story II (producer)

1990 The Raid (producer, actor)

1991 Once upon a Time in China (director, producer)

1991 A Chinese Ghost Story III (producer)

1991 The Master (director, producer)

1991 The Banquet (director)

1992 Once upon a Time in China II (director, producer)

1992 Dragon Inn (producer)

1992 King of Chess (co-director, producer)

1992 Once upon a Time in China III (director, producer)

1992 Swordsman II (producer)

1992 The Wicked City (producer)

1992 Twin Dragons (co-director)

1993 East Is Red (producer)

1993 Green Snake (director, producer)

1993 Iron Monkey (producer)

1993 Once upon a Time in China IV (producer)

1993 The Magic Crane (producer)

1994 Burning Paradise (producer)

1994 Once upon a Time in China V (director, producer)

1994 The Lovers (director)

1995 Love in the Time of Twilight (director, producer)

1995 The Blade (director)

1995 The Chinese Feast (director)

1996 Black Mask (producer)

1996 Shanghai Grand (producer)

1996 Tri-Star (director, producer)

1997 Once upon a Time in China and America (co-producer)
1997 Double Team (director)

ANTHONY WONG, Actor
Wong Chow-sun
Born Hong Kong, 1961

Anthony Wong in *Young and Dangerous II*

Anthony Wong is the bad boy of the Hong Kong cinema, known for his outrageous roles in Category III movies, including the one that netted him a Hong Kong Film Award for Best Actor – the vengeful cook in *Bunman: The Untold Story* who bakes his victims into pork buns. Wong is an anomaly, a Hong Kong film star with formal training as a stage actor; and while he makes a lot of movies of varying quality, he has strong ideas about his craft – too strong, he says, for many Hong Kong directors, who accuse him of having a bad attitude. Though he is probably best known to American audiences as the central villain in John Woo's *Hard-Boiled*, he is a fan of neither the movie nor Woo. "We don't have enough communication," Wong complained of Woo during an interview, for which he sported a leather jacket, a Kiss T-shirt, a stubbly beard, and a filter-less cigarette. "He don't trust the actor – all except Chow Yun-fat."

Wong says he had to struggle all his life because he is Eurasian, an unloved species in the Chinese-speaking part of the world. His father, who was British, disappeared when Wong was a boy, and his Chinese mother sent him to boarding school. "When I was in school, nobody want to play with me," Wong says, "and even when I first joined the film industry, nobody give me a chance, because I look like a *gweilo*" – the pejorative Cantonese term for a white person. "Chinese, they get so many trouble from the foreigner in the history, so if they get someone look like a foreigner, it's their chance to release the emotion."

Wong was twenty-one and unemployed when a friend dragged him along for an audition at ATV, a Hong Kong television station, which had a training program for actors. The friend flunked the audition, but Wong was accepted. After three years, however, Wong decided he wasn't learning his craft properly, so he enrolled at Hong Kong's élite Academy for the Performing Arts. There, he starred in a number of plays, including *Cyrano de Bergerac* and *Oedipus Rex*, translated into Chinese. (It remains his ambition, he says, to play Edmund in *King Lear*.) Upon graduating, he returned to television acting, at station TVB, and soon made the transition into films.

Wong says he often gets into arguments with directors about the motivation of the characters he's been hired to play, a discussion as rare in the Hong Kong movie industry as it is common in Hollywood. "I like to find out some psychology," he says. "But most directors don't know what this mean. If they tell you to move to another place, and you ask, 'What is the motivation?' they say, 'You have feet. You can walk. That's the motivation.' I tell them, 'I'm an artist, not a soldier.' " Wong says his most satisfactory film-acting experiences have been with director Herman Yau, in *Bunman* and *Taxi Hunter*, in which he plays a vigilante who kills cab drivers, and with Johnny To in the comic-book-styled *The Heroic Trio*, and its sequel.

Wong has lately turned his own hand to directing, and he invited me to a screening of his début effort, an eerie suspense picture

called *New Tenant*, which starred himself and his then love
interest, Dolphin Chan, a young video disk-jockey with no prior
film experience. (They have since split up.) Afterward, at a
luncheon for the cast and crew, Wong asked for an assessment,
and, straining to think of something intelligent, I said *New Tenant*
reminded me in spots of a Fassbinder film, which seemed to please
him immensely. Presently, one of the luncheon guests declared of
John Woo, "The only difference between one of his movies and
another is the amount of artillery expended." Wong smiled. "That's
right," he said. "That's right."

Selected Filmography

1989 News Attack
1991 Angel Hunter
1992 Full Contact
1992 Hard-Boiled
1992 Madame City Hunter
1992 Now You See Love . . . Now You Don't
1992 Retribution Sight Unseen
1993 Bunman: The Untold Story
1993 Daughter of Darkness
1993 Fight Back to School III
1993 The Heroic Trio
1993 Executioners
1993 Legal Innocence
1993 Love to Kill
1993 Mad Monk
1993 Master Wong vs. Master Wong
1993 A Moment of Romance II
1993 Organized Crime and Triad Bureau
1993 Taxi Hunter
1993 The Tiger's Legend of Canton
1993 Underground Banker
1994 Awakening
1994 Brother of Darkness
1994 A Gleam of Hope
1994 Now You See Me, Now You Don't

1994 Oh! My Three Guys (cameo)
1994 Rock 'n Roll Cop
1995 The Day that Doesn't Exist
1995 New Tenant (also: director)
1995 Our Neighbor Detective
1995 World of Treasure
1996 Big Bullet
1996 Black Mask
1996 Ebola Syndrome
1996 Mongkok Story
1996 Top Banana Club (also: director)
1996 Young and Dangerous II
1996 Young and Dangerous III
1997 Armageddon

WONG JING, Director, Producer, Writer, Actor
Born Hong Kong, 1956

Wong Jing is Hong Kong's king of schlock, an unabashedly commercial film-maker whose output is prodigious in the extreme. One of his recent films – a hit, no less – was created from start to finish in less than three weeks. Wong depends heavily on assistants to maintain his pace, and in a number of cases, they, rather than he, probably deserve the directing credit. The character actor Dennis Chan, for instance, spent more time yelling "Action!" and "Cut!" on the set of *Holy Weapon*, Wong Jing's all-star martial-arts romp, than Wong, who was simultaneously directing another movie. I asked Chan why anyone would direct two movies at a time, and the question seemed to take him aback. "This is Hong Kong," he said. "You have to make use of every second. If you can make two dollars, why make one?" (For more information on Wong Jing and his oeuvre, please consult pages 48–9.)

Selected Filmography

1981 Challenge of the Gamesters (director)
1984 The Frog Prince (director)
1987 The Romancing Star (director)
1988 Mr. Possessed (director, actor)

Wong Jing

1989 Casino Raiders (director)
1989 God of Gamblers (director)
1990 God of Gamblers II (director)
1990 The Last Blood (director)
1991 Dances with the Dragon (director)
1991 God of Gamblers III: Back to Shanghai (director)
1991 Money Maker (director, producer, actor)
1991 Tricky Brains (director)
1992 Casino Tycoon (director)
1992 Casino Tycoon II (director, producer)
1992 Naked Killer (producer, writer)
1992 Royal Tramp (director)
1992 Royal Tramp II (director)
1993 Boys Are Easy (director, producer, writer)
1993 City Hunter (director)
1993 Fight Back to School III (director)
1993 Flying Dagger (producer)
1993 Future Cops (director)

1993 Holy Weapon (director)
1993 Kung Fu Cult Master (director)
1993 Last Hero in China (director)
1993 Legend of the Liquid Sword (director, producer)
1993 Millionaire Cop (director, producer)
1993 Raped by an Angel (producer, writer)
1993 The Last Hero in China (director)
1994 God of Gamblers' Return (director, writer)
1994 Hail the Judge (director, writer)
1994 Modern Romance (director, producer)
1994 New Legend of Shaolin (director, writer)
1994 Return to a Better Tomorrow (director, writer)
1994 To Live and Die in Tsimshatsui (producer)
1994 Underground Banker (producer)
1994 Whatever You Want (director, writer)
1995 High Risk (director, producer, writer)
1995 Sixty Million Dollar Man (producer)
1996 Ebola Syndrome (producer)
1996 Sexy and Dangerous (producer)
1996 Young and Dangerous (producer)

WONG KAR-WAI, Director, Writer
Born Shanghai, 1958

The art-film director Wong Kar-wai emigrated with his family from Shanghai to Hong Kong at the age of five. He studied graphic design at Hong Kong Polytechnic, and dabbled in photography, before enrolling in 1980 in the training program for television-drama production at TVB. Within a year, he was writing scripts for a dramatic series called *Don't Look Now*, and meanwhile worked to develop another, more ambitious series, to be called *Five Easy Pieces*, about the experiences of five women in the 1950s and 1960s. Unfortunately, the project was shelved when it was deemed too expensive, and Wong was asked to produce situation comedies. He soon quit, and joined the newly formed movie studio Cinema City, as a screenwriter.

QUESTION: *Describe what Cinema City was like when you joined.*
WONG KAR-WAI (Speaking through an interpreter): It was basically

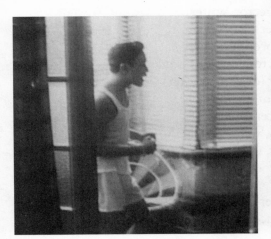

Days of Being Wild: Leslie Cheung   Wong Kar-wai

a new force in the industry, and they hired a lot of people out of TV. But you had to be able to do comedies. And every project was a group effort. Karl Maka, the head of Cinema City, had studied in the States, and he came back and introduced the studio system to Hong Kong. He was a big believer in statistics, and that everything had to be decided collectively. He had a room in an apartment, and all the seven heads of Cinema City [Maka, Dean Shek, Raymond Wong, Tsui Hark, Nansun Shi, Eric Tsang, and Teddy Robin Kwan] would meet there. We called them the Gang of Seven. You had to come in and get everything approved. Usually, they would meet after dinner, and adjourn the following morning. Each movie had nine reels, so they had nine pieces of paper. When you told them the story, they would judge you on comedy, on suspense, on gimmicks – they'd mark down how many of each. If there were not enough marks on a sheet of paper, they'd tell you which reel had a

Chungking Express: Faye Wong and Brigitte Lin

Fallen Angels: Michelle Reis

shortage. If a project was not approved in this creative workshop room, they believed it would be a flop.

How did you make out there?

Not very well. I didn't have a good relationship with Raymond Wong. At that time, Cinema City considered making films other than comedies, so they teamed me up with Ringo Lam, who wanted to do an action film. I practically lived in Ringo's apartment, trying to come up with a script idea. Christmas was approaching, and if we passed the script test with the Gang of Seven, we would get some money for the holiday. The meeting was on December 23rd. But we didn't pass – they wanted more comedy and more gimmicks – and so we got no money for Christmas. I was at Cinema City about a year, and never wrote a script. Raymond Wong was pissed off at me, and we parted company very happily.

What happened then?

I became a freelance scriptwriter. At that time, people in the industry had the impression that if you worked at Cinema City, you must be a great scriptwriter, but if you left the flock, you must be a bad sheep. So I began to work with film-makers who were not very successful, and from them I learned quite a lot of things about life. Cinema City's aim was to emulate Hollywood; but the people I met during my freelance days were interested in how you make a low-budget film in a quick period of time. A different kind of reality. I wrote a Category III film that was shot in Thailand – I never even saw it. And among the directors I worked with, there was one who was also a loanshark. He didn't want his crew to know he led a double life, but one time, people he had to collect money from saw him directing a movie. The film world is filled with these types of people, and some have a reputation for being tough and difficult. But once you start working with them, you find they are not really so tough. I treasure the life experiences of those years.

You recycled them.

I collected a lot of material. And eventually, I used some of it in collaboration with [new-wave director] Patrick Tam. He had never made a film like this, about the people of the lower caste. Our project did not get made at the time; it was made years later as *Final Victory*. It's one of my favorite scripts, although Patrick had his own treatment of the characters, and he departed from what I wrote. Still, I think it's a very satisfactory film.

And then, a year later, in 1988, you directed your first movie, As Tears Go By.

Patrick and I had conceived a trilogy, about two little bullies, who never succeeded in the criminal world. *Final Victory* was the third part, and *As Tears Go By* was the first part.

[*As Tears Go By* was a critical and commercial hit, but the second part of the trilogy was never made. Instead, Wong changed direction, and came out with his elliptical *Days of Being Wild*, which thrilled critics but not audiences. For more detail about this phase of Wong's career, please consult pages 50–52.]

You must have been prepared for the commercial failure of Days of Being Wild.

No, I felt it was going to be a very commercial movie. I thought at that time the gangster movie was approaching a low phase, and there was need for a romantic love story.

Was that film also based on your own experiences?

Yes. It's based on people I knew when I was young, in the 60s. When we first moved to Hong Kong, my father rented an apartment in the Tsimshatsui area, and he sublet two of the rooms. One of them went to a handsome young man, like Leslie Cheung's character in the movie, who always had girls hanging around, waiting for him. The other room went to someone like the cop played by Andy Lau. The film is in two parts. The first half takes place in 1960, and the second half is six years later. I wanted to capture the mood of that period, and show what happened to the first generation that grew up after the war.

I'm told that you purposely required your all-star cast members for Days of Being Wild *to do their scenes over and over again. Why?*

Because most Hong Kong actors come out of TV, and they're used to close-ups. I wanted to get a different kind of performance – not so self-aware. So I had to make them feel very tired.

Selected Filmography

1982 Once upon a Rainbow (writer)
1985 Chase a Fortune (writer)

1987 Final Victory (writer)
1988 As Tears Go By (director, writer)
1988 Haunted Cop Shop II (cameo)
1991 Days of Being Wild (director, writer)
1991 Saviour of the Soul (writer)
1994 Ashes of Time (director, writer)
1994 Chungking Express (director, writer)
1995 Fallen Angels (director, writer)
1997 Happy Together (director, writer)

JOHN WOO, Director, Producer, Writer
Wu Yu-sen
Born Canton, 1946

John Woo   *The Killer:* Chow Yun-fat

Bullet in the Head: Tony Leung Chiu-wai, Jacky Cheung, Waise Lee

Hard-Boiled: Tony Leung Chiu-wai

TERENCE CHANG, Producer, Manager
Chang Jia-tsun
Born Hong Kong, 1949

When the director John Woo made his move from Hong Kong to Los Angeles in 1992, his longtime friend and producer Terence Chang accompanied him there – to work, not to live. Chang, a Hong Kong native, had settled in Toronto in 1990, and he still calls the Canadian city his home. After *Broken Arrow,* the second Woo/Chang collaboration in the United States, became a hit, Woo bought a house in Calabasas, a wealthy Los Angeles suburb; Chang, however, continues to commute between Toronto and an apartment in West L.A. The two men are strikingly different personalities – Woo is soft-spoken and conciliatory, whereas Chang is outspoken, if not blunt.

Woo and Chang are plainly gratified by their success in the American film industry. (As this book went to press, they were in post-production for *Face/Off,* an action thriller starring John Travolta and Nicolas Cage.) But Woo is still a long way from achieving what he calls "my biggest dream" – the chance to make an historical epic on the grand scale of David Lean's *Lawrence of Arabia,* one of his favorite films. He has a subject in mind: the Chinese civil war that took place during the Ming Dynasty one thousand years ago. "My goal is that I establish my reputation and everything, and then I can get a much stronger support to make this film," he said during an interview, with Chang at his side. "Because this movie I assume need a huge budget."

When Chang was Woo's producer in Hong Kong, budgetary concerns were further from the director's thoughts. Indeed, while making his last Hong Kong film, *Hard-Boiled,* Woo was permitted to take a mad risk that would be inconceivable in a Hollywood action film. For the final section of the movie, the siege of an urban hospital, Woo shot a sequence of nearly three minutes' duration, full of gunfights, stunts, and explosions, in one continuous take. "In every one of my movie, I always like to do some kind of experiment," Woo said. "For that shot, we took two days to build the set, and then we rehearse several hundred times. Then we took two more days to try to shoot the shot. But always we failed. The timing is wrong, or the special effect doesn't go that well. I almost give up, but the crew and the stunt group and the actor, they all want to try it again. At last we got it done."

Terence Chang met John Woo in the mid 1970s at Golden Harvest, where Chang was a production manager, and Woo was a director of hit comedies. Chang had previously studied architecture at the University of Oregon and film at New York University. He left Golden Harvest after two years, without having had a chance to collaborate with Woo. After a stint in television, he worked in sales and distribution for movie producer Johnny Mak, and then became head of foreign sales for D&B, where he befriended the studio's biggest star, Michelle Yeoh. During his year and a half at D&B, Chang sold two of Yeoh's early movies in the marketplace at Cannes.

In 1986, Nansun Shi, who, at the time, ran Film Workshop for her husband, the director and producer Tsui Hark, asked Chang to take her place as general manager. Chang accepted, and found himself, after a decade, reunited with John Woo, who was under contract to Film Workshop as a director. When Woo subsequently got into a dispute with Tsui over their most famous collaboration, *The Killer*, Woo and Chang left Film Workshop together.

Today, Chang also manages the careers of Michelle Yeoh and Chow Yun-fat, who are both making the transition from Hong Kong to Hollywood. I questioned Chang about his gameplan for the two stars:

QUESTION: *It seems you've been taking a hard line as Chow Yun-fat's manager. I hear you turned down a number of Hollywood projects for him before signing off on* Replacement Killers.

TERENCE CHANG: If people want him, they have to be serious about him. Like *Aliens IV*, the writer, Joss Whedon, said he's a huge fan of Chow Yun-fat, and he wrote a part especially for him. But when I read the script, I was furious. He's in a lot of scenes, but always in the background, carrying a gun. Occasionally, he shoots some people. That's a part for Chow Yun-fat? I don't think so.

I understand that before Michelle was cast in the new James Bond movie, she was being considered for the American version of The Killer.

That's true. For several years, Tri-Star has had the rights to remake *The Killer*, but they couldn't do anything with it. The relationship of the killer and cop is hard to translate for an American audience. People think they are gay. So this producer at Tri-Star had a brilliant idea – why not have Michelle play the cop?

Is there a chance she still might do it?

I don't know. She's up for a lot of high-profile projects. Michelle has generated a lot of heat in a very short period of time.

Why won't you settle in Los Angeles?

My family is in Toronto, and I love it there. But I don't dislike L.A., actually. The first I knew of L.A. was from the books of Raymond Chandler. I thought it was romantic – the tall palm trees, the art deco buildings. I don't like the earthquakes. Something in the back of my mind says, this place is going to disappear. So I can never call L.A. my home.

It also seems fair to say that you're not the Hollywood type.

I'm not being sucked into this whole Hollywood thing. I always think of myself as an outsider. If somebody treats me badly, I say "fuck you" and move on.

You and John Woo were supposed to make Tears of the Sun *for Fox, an adventure film in the tropical rain forest. What happened?*

We pulled the plug. We decided we had enough. We spent eight months on the picture, and couldn't get the script right. And the picture was physically very demanding. The actors had to be in the water a lot of the time, wrestling with crocodiles, fighting off piranhas, falling down waterfalls. Some actors said, shoot it in the States, and then maybe I'll do it. American actors are spoiled.

Who did you try to cast?

We met with Woody Harrelson, Brad Pitt, Tommy Lee Jones. The list was long.

And then Broken Arrow *came along.*

We didn't develop *Broken Arrow*; they came to us with that project. It was an assignment to me.

Are you happy with the film?

Yeah, given what kind of film it is. It's a popcorn movie. John set out to achieve something, and he achieved it. Because after *Hard Target* [Woo's first American film, starring Jean-Claude Van Damme] a lot of people said, this is a Hong Kong movie in English.

Meaning John couldn't do an American film. And he was devastated by those kind of remarks. He said, I want to prove I can make a mainstream American film.

What are your expectations for Face/Off [*Woo's newest movie, starring John Travolta and Nicolas Cage*]?

I think it will be a solid film. John has never been so confident in himself.

Filmography
John Woo

1971 7 Blows of the Dragon (assistant director)
1972 Killer from Shantung (assistant director)
1972 Four Assassins (assistant director)
1973 Dynasty of Blood (assistant director)
1973 The Young Dragons (director)
1975 Games Gamblers Play (production manager)
1975 The Dragon Tamers (director, writer)
1975 Hand of Death (director, actor)
1975 Princess Chang Ping (director)
1976 The Private Eyes (production designer)
1977 Money Crazy (director, writer)
1977 Follow the Star (director, writer)
1977 Last Hurrah for Chivalry (director, writer)
1978 The Contract (production designer)
1977 Hello, Late Homecomers (co-director)
1977 From Riches to Rags (director, writer)
1981 Laughing Times (director)
1981 To Hell with the Devil (director)
1982 Plain Jane to the Rescue (director)
1984 The Time You Need a Friend (director)
1985 Run, Tiger, Run (director)
1985 Super Citizen (producer)
1985 Love Lonely Flower (producer)
1986 A Better Tomorrow (director, writer, actor)
1987 Heroes Shed No Tears (director)
1987 A Better Tomorrow II (director, writer)
1988 Starry Is the Night (cameo)
1989 The Killer (director, writer)

1989 Just Heroes (co-director)
1990 Bullet in the Head (director, producer, writer, cameo)
1991 Once a Thief (director, writer)
1991 Rebel from China (actor)
1992 Hard-Boiled (director, actor)
1994 Hard Target (director)
1995 Peace Hotel (producer)
1996 Somebody up There Likes Me (producer)
1996 Broken Arrow (director)
1997 Face/Off (director)

Filmography
Terence Chang

1979 Itchy Fingers (production manager)
1979 Tower of Death (production manager)
1981 Lonely 15 (producer)
1982 Dragon Force (producer)
1983 Everlasting Love (producer)
1984 Crazy 17 (producer)
1984 Double Decker (producer)
1985 Escape from Coral Cove (director)
1985 The Young Ones (writer)
1989 A Better Tomorrow III: Love and Death in Saigon
     (production executive)
1989 Deception (production executive)
1989 Gunmen (production executive)
1989 The Killer (production executive)
1990 A Chinese Ghost Story II (production executive)
1990 Spy Games (production executive)
1990 Swordsman (production executive)
1990 Bullet in the Head (executive producer)
1991 Once a Thief (producer)
1992 Hard-Boiled (producer)
1992 Now You See Love . . . Now You Don't (producer, cameo)
1994 Hard Target (co-producer)
1996 Broken Arrow (co-producer)
1997 Face/Off (co-producer)

Terence Chang

SIMON YAM, Actor
Yam Tat-wah
Born Hong Kong, 1955

Many fans of the Hong Kong cinema associate Category III star
Simon Yam with one type of role – as he puts it, "the bad guy, very
psychotic." A former model who in 1996 posed semi-nude for a
book of photographs, he has played, for example, a serial killer and
rapist (*Dr. Lamb*), a murderous homosexual crime boss (*Full
Contact*), and a deranged Vietcong mercenary (*Run and Kill*). In
person, Yam is a charming man who likes to talk about his hobbies
(painting and photography), his quiet home by the sea in Clearwater Bay, and his charity work with children. "I got ten child in
Bangkok, so poor I adopt them," he says.

Yam was eleven when his own father died, and he grew up poor
himself. He paid his way through secondary school by posing for
print ads – more than a hundred, he believes – and, in the mid-

Simon Yam

1970s, enrolled in the training program for actors at TVB. One of his classmates, Chow Yun-fat, performed with him in at least ten different series. By 1978, Yam says he had become "very famous" for his role in a soap opera called *Home Breaker*. He complains, however, that his strict contract with TVB forced him to turn down parts in movies and commercials, and he angrily quit the network in 1989. "Like an orange, they squeeze you, and the juice is belong to TVB, and the dry orange is belong to you," he says.

Now ostensibly a free agent, Yam soon became a favorite target of Hong Kong gangsters, rife in the movie business, who, he says, "force me to make some movies I don't like." Though Yam had signed up with a "very famous manager," even his handler could offer him no protection from the triads. "Hong Kong is too small, and they can get you very easy," he says. "That's why I say there's no good manager in Hong Kong, and now I handle by myself."

Along with his many low-budget exploitation movies, Yam has worked with some of Hong Kong's best-known film-makers. Ringo Lam directed him in *Full Contact*, and John Woo cast him as a suave ex-CIA agent in *Bullet in the Head*, a film that many consider to be Woo's finest. "Ringo Lam and John Woo is perfect director – they know how to put the actor very deeply inside the role," Yam says, adding, however, that both men are "crazy." For one scene in *Full Contact*, he claims, Lam asked him to shoot a real gun. "I say, 'No way.' " Woo, meanwhile, nearly got him killed in the jungles of Thailand, during the filming of *Bullet in the Head*. "John Woo like everything big, so he put the big bomb in the trees, and when everything is blow up, I was in the middle, encircled by fire," he recalls. "I burned all my hair. John Woo said, 'Good, good, good! Are you OK?' Then he smiled, because very good shot."

Selected Filmography

1985 Goodbye Mama
1988 Fatal Termination
1988 Tiger Cage
1989 Burning Ambition
1989 Chinese Cop-Out
1990 Bullet in the Head
1990 Killer's Romance
1990 Return Engagement
1990 Sea Wolves
1991 Black Cat
1991 Bullet for Hire
1991 Gigolo and Whore
1991 Great Pretenders
1991 Powerful Four
1991 Queen's High
1992 Dr. Lamb
1992 Full Contact
1992 Gun-N-Rose
1992 The Killer's Love
1992 Naked Killer

1992 The Night Rider
1992 Once upon a Time a Hero in China
1993 Don't Stop My Crazy Love for You
1993 The Final Judgement
1993 First Shot
1993 Future Cops
1993 Holy Weapon
1993 Insanity
1993 Love Among the Triad
1993 Prince of Portland Street
1993 Raped by an Angel
1993 Rose, Rose I Love You
1993 Run and Kill
1993 The Black Panther Warriors
1994 A Day Without Policemen
1993 The Incorruptible
1994 Awakening
1994 Crossings
1994 Crystal Fortune Run
1994 The Devil's Box
1994 Drunken Master III
1994 Tiger of Wanchai
1994 The True Hero
1995 Because of Lies
1995 Dragon Killer
1995 Farewell My Dearest
1995 Ghostly Bus
1995 Legendary Couple
1995 Love, Guns and Glass
1995 Man Wanted
1995 Passion 1995
1995 Police Confidential
1995 Twist
1996 All of a Sudden
1996 Bloody Friday
1996 The King of Robbery
1996 Scarred Memory
1996 Street Angels

1996 To Be No. 1
1996 Young and Dangerous
1996 Young and Dangerous II
1996 Young and Dangerous III

MICHELLE YEOH, Actress
Yeoh Chu-kheng
Born Malaysia, 1962

Michelle Yeoh in *Tai Chi Master*

Considering that she nearly lost her life on the set of her most
recent Hong Kong movie (see page 24), Michelle Yeoh has been
having a run of good fortune. In October 1996, not long after
Miramax released a dubbed version of *Supercop*, the action film
that paired her with Jackie Chan, she met with the producers of the
James Bond series, who were considering casting her as Bond's
sidekick in the forthcoming *Tomorrow Never Dies* (currently
scheduled for Christmas 1997 release). Yeoh submitted to her first-
ever screen test – with Pierce Brosnan, who plays Bond – and
landed the part. "A very nice surprise," she says. It will be the first

Michelle Yeoh (photo by Butch Belair)

English-language movie for the Malaysian-born Yeoh, who speaks
better English than Cantonese. "For once," she says, "I can actually
read my own lines without someone telling me what I'm supposed
to be saying."

Filmography

1984 The Owl vs. Bumbo
1985 Twinkle, Twinkle Lucky Stars (cameo)
1985 Yes, Madam!
1986 Royal Warriors
1987 Magnificent Warriors
1987 Easy Money
1992 Supercop

1993 The Heroic Trio
1993 Butterfly and Sword
1993 Executioners
1993 Holy Weapon
1993 Project S
1993 Tai Chi Master
1993 Wing Chun
1994 Wonder Seven
1996 The Soong Sisters
1996 Ah Kam: The Story of a Stuntwoman
1997 Tomorrow Never Dies

YIM HO, Director, Writer
Born Hong Kong, 1952

Yim Ho

Like a number of other important film-makers of his generation –
the so-called new-wave directors of Hong Kong – Yim Ho was
educated in the West, and got his professional start at the Hong
Kong television station TVB. His first movie, *The Extras*, was a hit

urban comedy about extras who work in motion pictures. He directed two less successful comedies, for Golden Harvest, before switching to serious drama in 1984, with *Homecoming*, which gained five Hong Kong Film Awards, including Best Picture, Best Director, and Best Screenplay. Ten years later, Yim's drama *The Day the Sun Turned Cold* took the Grand Prize at the Tokyo Film Festival, and he won Best Director at the festival in Berlin for his subsequent *The Sun Has Ears*. Meanwhile, he has published two prose collections, and directed plays – his Cantonese adaptation of Eugene O'Neill's *Desire Under the Elms* was staged in 1983 to enthusiastic reviews.

QUESTION: *You were brought up to be a good little soldier of Chairman Mao, I understand.*

YIM HO: My parents were pro-Communist, and so was I. I went to a pro-Communist school in Hong Kong, and I joined in the riots of 1967. For me, the whole thing stopped with the Cultural Revolution. My mother was the last holdout; she lasted until Tiananmen Square. She cried in front of the TV screen, and that was the end of pro-Communist.

Were you allowed to see Western movies as a child?

I still remember *The Sound of Music.* I went back to school and told my friend there was nothing capitalistic about it. It's a great film teaching you how to learn your ABCs. My little friend told my teacher, and she took me aside and said, "Don't see that movie again."

What sort of career had your education prepared you for?

After high school, I didn't know what to do. I was given a job in a bank, but I can't make out the credit from the debit even now, and I was constantly making mistakes. Instead of bringing home a salary, I had to bring back money to the bank to pay the difference. Then a director friend called Leong Po-chih told me about the London Film School. I applied and got in.

Why film school?

From my childhood, I was very keen on writing. My father was a writer as well as a newspaper editor. He had to write fiction all the time to support us, because he had a large family – I have eight brothers and sisters – and his salary was very low. I saw his back all the time, because to the day he died, he never got his own study room. He couldn't afford it, poor guy. After he died, the only thing he left us was his false teeth and beat-up glasses, and the piles of books he wrote. I haven't gone through every one of them. But I ate them, and they became my blood.

I presume you made student films in London.

The first was a one-minute film. The character was supposed to be a pianist, and when he sat down in front of the piano, the lid went down on him. There was no sound. The students all said, "What happened to Yim Ho? He's out of his mind."

After film school, you came back to Hong Kong?

I got a job at TVB as a screenwriter. The first drama I wrote was for Ann Hui. We were on the same team. Then I kept writing more scripts, and directing them as well. Police stories, stories about social workers. On and off for three years. Then I joined a production company called Film Force. We made one movie, *The Extras*, which I wrote with Philip Chan, and directed. It was quite a success – one of the top ten at the box office that year. After that, I started making movies for Golden Harvest. They were not very successful.

How long did that last?

Two years. After that, my father passed away and that was the turning point in my career. All that old stuff I felt came back to me – what was the significance of life, where do people go after death? Stuff like that. So I was determined to make a film that I really wanted to make. I went to Xia Ming [the producer of Ann Hui's *Boat People*] and said, "I'm not taking any director's fees, and I will raise one third of the financing to make this film." It was called *Homecoming*. It didn't make big money, but it was very well received.

From then on, Yim Ho has been called an art-film director.

What can I do? The fact is, ironically, when I set out to make *Homecoming*, I told everyone, I'm going to do a film which is a popular as well as a quality movie. But in the end, people saw the movie and felt sad and cried.

Your movie Red Dust *was also set in mainland China. Not to mention your award-winning* The Day the Sun Turned Cold.

I was always questioned by Hong Kong journalists why I keep

making movies in China and not in Hong Kong. I told them I don't
have a particular territory to make a movie. *Red Dust* was written
by myself and San Mao, a very popular writer in Hong Kong, as
well as Taiwan and mainland China. The script was written after
Tiananmen Square, so everybody was hot and angry, and that was
also the temperament of the film. Maybe too angry.

Red Dust *is based somewhat on the life of the Chinese novelist
Eileen Chang?*

Yes. And her husband was supposedly a traitor who worked for the
Japanese. But in the film, I portrayed him as someone who has no
control over his own fate. Which Chinese film-makers are not
allowed to do – you have to present this kind of person as a villain.
For allowing me to make *Red Dust* in China, some of the top
officials in the film bureau were forced to sit down and write a lot
of self-criticism.

*San Mao, your co-author, later killed herself. Can you talk about
that?*

Well, she was a very temperamental person. When she was
depressed she used to abuse herself – like beating herself, cutting
herself. And she was feeling depressed over aging, and also – I'm
purely guessing – over her failure to get a Golden Horse award
[Taiwan's equivalent of an Oscar]. She was alone in her room at
midnight, and she hung her belt over the shower rim, and put her
head in it, sitting on the toilet. With a little effort, she could lift her
head and be free, but she was too depressed, and could not do it.
She was gone. So she never committed suicide. I know her so well.
If she wanted to commit suicide, she write a lot of things to explain
why she died, and she would dress herself in a real pretty dress and
clean up her room. But she was in a nightgown, she didn't have her
makeup, she was in the toilet, and nothing was pretty. It couldn't be
a suicide.

How did you learn about her death?

I received this phone call from a journalist who said, "San Mao
killed herself over you." I said, "Are you kidding? Why over me?"
There were rumors we had a romance. I can assure you this is all
rumors, we never had anything between us.

*On another unhappy note, you had a falling-out with Tsui Hark
over the movie* King of Chess, *which you and he directed.*

Tsui Hark came up with the idea of marrying two stories under the same title in one movie. And, to cut it short, in the middle of it, we had an artistic argument, so he went ahead and finished the rest of the film without notifying me. He never apologized to me, not until many years later. After many years we met in a disco, and he said, "I was so young – too young and too consumed in energy." That was all he said.

Filmography

1979 The Extras
1980 The Happenings
1981 Wedding Bells, Wedding Belles
1984 Homecoming
1987 Buddha's Lock
1990 Red Dust (also: co-writer, actor)
1992 King of Chess (co-director, co-writer, actor)
1994 The Day the Sun Turned Cold (also: co-producer, writer)
1995 The Sun Has Ears
1996 Kitchen

RONNY YU, Director, Producer
Yu Yan-tai
Born Hong Kong, 1950

Director Ronny Yu is known to Hong Kong film fans primarily for one movie, *The Bride with White Hair*, a romantic swashbuckler set during the Ming Dynasty, which he freely adapted from a famous sword-and-sorcery novel. The movie stirred up interest in Hollywood after it won the Grand Prize at the Fantastica film festival in Paris. Before long, Yu had signed a deal to direct *Warriors of Virtue*, an action fantasy about a boy and five kung-fu kangaroos pitted against an evil warlord, for MGM.

Yu says he's been a fantasist ever since contracting polio at the age of nine months: unable to play with other children, he created an imaginary universe for himself at home. "The dining table was my fortress against the Indians," he recalls. Meanwhile, his father, a prominent businessman, took him to see American movies, and Yu grew up hooked on Westerns by Howard Hawks and John Ford.

Ronny Yu (right) directing *Warriors of Virtue*

The transition to English-language films has been a natural one for Yu, who was educated mainly in the United States, and today makes his home in Sydney. He attended the University of Southern California, and got an MBA at Ohio University, before returning to Hong Kong, in 1976, as production manager of his first movie, *Jumping Ash*, written by former Hong Kong police detective Philip Chan. Three years later, Chan persuaded Yu to leave his job in the news department of ABC Television in New York to co-direct a crime drama called *The Servant*. Yu went on to direct the late Brandon Lee in *Legacy of Rage*, and became the protégé of Raymond Wong, one of the founders of Cinema City. He picks up the story from there:

QUESTION: *Raymond Wong, I take it, was crucial to your career.*
RONNY YU: He's my mentor, my big brother. He keeps saying, "Ronny, when you start a film, do you have a fire inside? Are you dying to tell the story? If not, then don't do it." It was Raymond who showed me the novel that became *The Bride with White Hair*. *You changed the plot quite a bit.*

I thought the novel was too slow, too complicated. So I tracked down the author [Liang Yu-sheng]. He was seventy-something years old, and living in Sydney. I said, "Listen, your book was such a popular novel in the 50s. But I need to make major changes, and I'm asking for your permission." He said, "Change whatever you want, but just don't fuck it up."

I understand that the entire movie was filmed in the nighttime.

That's true. We filmed it during the summer, and it was so hot that, with all those heavy costumes, there was no way the actors could function. So we shot at night, and used lighting to create our day scenes.

Tell me about your directorial début, The Servants.

I was working as a trainee at ABC Television, in the States, with no thought of becoming a film-maker, when Philip Chan called me. He had quit the police department, and he wanted to be an actor. He came up with this cop story – one cop is crooked, and the other is loyal. He was going to play the crooked one. I came back to Hong Kong, and we wrote the script together. But we couldn't find a director – everybody told us our script sucks. Finally, Philip said we should direct it. But I had no training; I don't know anything about the camera. So we found the best cameraman, this guy from England, and figured we would just bullshit the actors. Then the nightmare begins. The first day of filming, there are sixty-some people standing around, and the man from England turns to me and says, "Mr. Director, where do you want to put the camera?" I said, "What do you mean?" All of a sudden, everyone is looking at me. So I just told him, "Put it here." Then the second question, he really messed me up. He said, "What lens do you want?" "What *lens?*" "Yes," he said. "Thirty-five? Fifty?" Somehow, we finished the day's work, and then my editor gave me a book of film grammar. I read it that evening, and the next morning we started shooting again. That's how I made it.

Filmography

1976 Jumping Ash (production manager)
1977 Foxbat (production manager)
1979 The Servants (co-director)

1979 The Extras (producer)
1980 The Saviour (director)
1982 The Postman Strikes Back (director)
1983 The Trail (director)
1984 The Occupant (director)
1985 Dear Mummy (director)
1985 Eight in the Family (producer)
1986 Legacy of Rage (director)
1986 It's a Mad, Mad World I (producer)
1987 It's a Mad, Mad World II (producer)
1987 Lover (producer)
1988 Bless This House (director)
1988 Chicken and Duck Talk (producer)
1988 The Girl Next Door (producer)
1989 The Deadly Sin (director)
1990 China White (director)
1991 Great Pretenders (director)
1992 Once upon a Time a Hero in China (co-producer)
1992 Shogun and Little Kitchen (director)
1992 Summer Lover (director)
1993 All's Well, Ends Well II (producer)
1993 Cohabitation (producer)
1993 The Incorruptible (producer)
1993 Master Wong vs. Master Wong (co-producer)
1993 The Bride with White Hair (also: producer)
1993 The Bride with White Hair II (co-director, producer)
1994 Satin Steel (producer)
1995 Phantom Lover (director)
1997 Warriors of Virtue (director)

3 Plot Summaries

Hong Kong Movies from the New Wave to the Present

Barry Long

What follows are plot summaries of more than three hundred Hong Kong movies over a two-decade period ending in 1996 – the cutoff point for this edition of this book. The modern Hong Kong cinema dates from the 1970s, with the emergence of the so-called "new wave" – movies made by a talented corps of directors and writers, many of whom got their start in Hong Kong television – and with the reemergence of the Cantonese language, which had for some years been supplanted by Mandarin. For the most part, I have tried to withhold judgment on the relative merits of these movies; my ratings and reviews, along with those of eleven other critics, can be found in the chapter that follows this one.

Nevertheless, every film in this survey was selected for a reason, and not just because it falls within the new-wave-to-present timeframe. In most cases, the reason is that I believe the movie is at least worthy of a look; in some cases, however, the movie is included to round off the filmography of an important director or star (example: John Woo's subpar *Just Heroes*); or because it is a sequel to a worthwhile film.

For each film, I have provided the Chinese title, which may prove useful to anyone attempting to rent or buy videos or laser disks from Chinese-speaking establishments; and in every case, I have listed the year of release, and the names of the director, and the principal cast members. If the movie had a producer, writer, action director, or cinematographer of note, I have endeavored to list that person as well, though the names of less notable co-producers are generally omitted. Movie personnel are usually identified by their anglicized names (e.g., Brigitte Lin, rather than Lin Ching-hsia), if they have one.

Contents

THE BIG HEAT
BLACK CAT
BLACK CAT II: THE ASSASSINATION OF PRESIDENT YELTSIN
THE BLACK PANTHER WARRIORS
THE BLADE
THE BLUE JEAN MONSTER
BOAT PEOPLE
THE BODYGUARD FROM BEIJING
BOYS ARE EASY
THE BRIDE WITH WHITE HAIR
THE BRIDE WITH WHITE HAIR II
BUGIS STREET
BULLET IN THE HEAD
BUNMAN: THE UNTOLD STORY
BURNING AMBITION
BURNING PARADISE
BUTTERFLY AND SWORD
BUTTERFLY LOVERS (*see* THE LOVERS)
BUTTERFLY MURDERS
BY HOOK OR BY CROOK

C

CAGEMAN
THE CANTON GODFATHER (*see* MIRACLES)
THE CASE OF THE COLD FISH
CASINO RAIDERS
CENTER STAGE (*aka* ACTRESS)
C'EST LA VIE, MON CHERIE
CHERRY BLOSSOMS
CHEZ 'N HAM
CHICKEN AND DUCK TALK
CHINA DRAGON
THE CHINESE FEAST
THE CHINESE GHOSTBUSTER
A CHINESE GHOST STORY
A CHINESE GHOST STORY II
A CHINESE GHOST STORY III
A CHINESE ODYSSEY I: PANDORA'S BOX

LOVING YOU

M
MACK THE KNIFE (*aka* DOCTOR MACK)
MAGIC COP
THE MAGIC CRANE
THE MAGNIFICENT BUTCHER
MAGNIFICENT WARRIORS
MIRACLES (*aka* THE CANTON GODFATHER; MR. CANTON AND
    LADY ROSE)
A MOMENT OF ROMANCE
A MOMENT OF ROMANCE II
A MOMENT OF ROMANCE III
MONEY CRAZY
MOON WARRIORS
MR. BOO (*see* THE PRIVATE EYES)
MR. CANTON AND LADY ROSE (*see* MIRACLES)
MR. VAMPIRE
MURDER
MY AMERICAN GRANDSON
MY FATHER IS A HERO
MY HEART IS THAT ETERNAL ROSE

N
NAKED KILLER
NEW LEGEND OF SHAOLIN
NEW TENANT
NIGHT CALLER
NOMAD
NOW YOU SEE LOVE . . . NOW YOU DON'T

O
OH! MY THREE GUYS
ONCE A COP (*see* PROJECT S)
ONCE A THIEF
ONCE IN A LIFETIME
ONCE UPON A TIME IN CHINA
ONCE UPON A TIME IN CHINA II

R

RAINING IN THE MOUNTAIN

RED DUST

RED ROSE, WHITE ROSE

RED TO KILL

REINCARNATION OF GOLDEN LOTUS

REMAINS OF A WOMAN

RETRIBUTION SIGHT UNSEEN

THE RETURNING

RETURN TO A BETTER TOMORROW

ROBOFORCE (*see* I LOVE MARIA)

ROBOTRIX

ROCK 'N ROLL COP

ROMANCE OF BOOK AND SWORD

ROMANCE OF BOOK AND SWORD II (*see* PRINCESS FRAGRANCE)

ROOF WITH A VIEW

ROSE, ROSE I LOVE YOU

ROUGE

ROYAL TRAMP

ROYAL TRAMP II

ROYAL WARRIORS (*aka* IN THE LINE OF DUTY II)

RUMBLE IN THE BRONX

RUN AND KILL

S

SAVIOUR OF THE SOUL

SCHOOL ON FIRE

THE SECRET

SECURITY UNLIMITED

SEMI-GODS AND SEMI-DEVILS

SEX AND ZEN

SEXY AND DANGEROUS

SHANGHAI BLUES

SLAVE OF THE SWORD

SOMEBODY UP THERE LIKES ME

SONG OF THE EXILE

SOUL

THE SPOOKY BUNCH

TWIN DRAGONS
TWINKLE, TWINKLE LUCKY STARS

U

UMBRELLA STORY
UNDERGROUND BANKER

W

WEB OF DECEPTION (*see* DECEPTION)
WE'RE GOING TO EAT YOU
WHAT A WONDERFUL WORLD
WHAT PRICE SURVIVAL
WHEELS ON MEALS
THE WICKED CITY
WILD SEARCH
WING CHUN
WINNERS AND SINNERS
WITCH FROM NEPAL (*aka* A TOUCH OF LOVE)
WONDER SEVEN

Y

YES, MADAM! (*aka* IN THE LINE OF DUTY)
YOUNG AND DANGEROUS
YOUNG AND DANGEROUS II
YOUNG AND DANGEROUS III

Z

ZODIAC KILLERS
ZU: WARRIORS FROM THE MAGIC MOUNTAIN

92 LEGENDARY LA ROSE NOIRE
92 黑玫瑰對黑玫瑰
Year: 1992
Director: Jeff Lau
Stars: Tony Leung (Ka-fai), Teresa Mo, Fung Bo-bo, Maggie Siu

Fearful of being implicated in a gangland slaying, a young woman tries to confuse the police by leaving a note signed "the Black Rose," the name of a crime-fighting heroine from a 1960s movie serial. Unfortunately, there really is a Black Rose – and she's none too pleased about being framed for murder. A well-regarded pastiche of the Cantonese cinema of the 60s, full of references to period musicals, melodramas, comedies, and action films.

A

ACES GO PLACES
最佳拍檔
Year: 1982
Director: Eric Tsang
Producers: Karl Maka and Dean Shek
Writer: Raymond Wong
Stars: Sam Hui, Karl Maka, Sylvia Chang

The first in a popular comedy series, combining slapstick, martial arts, and stunt work. Sam Hui is a debonair thief who finds himself running for his life after he steals some diamonds from the Mafia (a device borrowed by Jackie Chan for *Rumble in the Bronx*). To thwart his Mob pursuers, Hui must team up with an unlikely pair of cops – Kodijack, a New York City detective (Karl Maka) and Hot Tongue, a Chinese police officer (Sylvia Chang).

ACES GO PLACES II
最佳拍檔大顯神通
Year: 1983
Director: Eric Tsang
Producers: Karl Maka and Raymond Wong
Stars: Sam Hui, Karl Maka, Sylvia Chang

A mad scientist is dead set on eliminating both Sam Hui and Karl

Maka ("they're annoying"); and so begins a series of mishaps. Hui and Maka are framed for several crimes – including diamond theft, of course – and find themselves running from mobsters and lawmen. Among the latter is a Clint Eastwood knockoff named Filthy Harry. Both the opening and closing sequences involve spectacular battles against giant versions of a popular toy robot.

ACES GO PLACES III: OUR MAN FROM BOND STREET
最佳拍檔：女皇密令
Year: 1984
Director: Tsui Hark
Producer and Writer: Raymond Wong
Stars: Sam Hui, Karl Maka, Sylvia Chang

A James Bond spoof, complete with two Bond villains – Jaws and Oddjob – recreated by the original actors, Richard Kiel and Harold Sakata. (Peter Graves of *Mission Impossible* is thrown in for good measure.) The film opens with a fight atop the Eiffel Tower, though it soon moves into more familar territory, as Sam Hui once again attempts to steal a diamond. The director, Tsui Hark, a former angry young man of the Hong Kong new wave, had already made one madcap comedy (*All the Wrong Clues*), but the huge commercial success of this film in Hong Kong signaled his passage to the mainstream.

ACTRESS (*see* CENTER STAGE)

AH YING
半邊人
Year: 1982
Director: Allen Fong
Stars: Hui So-ying, Peter Wang, Cheng Chi-hung, Yao Lin-shum

An art-house favorite, concerning a young woman, Ah Ying, who works at her family fish stand. Discontented with her home life and neglectful boyfriend, she joins an acting class run by a professor who, as it happens, is at work on the script of a film that is supposed to document the lives of ordinary people. A friendship blossoms between teacher and student, and he begins to delve into her life for inspiration.

ALL FOR THE WINNER
賭聖
Year: 1990
Directors: Corey Yuen and Jeff Lau
Producer: Corey Yuen
Writer: Jeff Lau
Stars: Stephen Chiau, Cheung Man, Ng Man-tat, Sandra Ng

Comic star Stephen Chiau plays Mao, a mainland Chinese bumpkin with X-ray vision. During a visit to Hong Kong, his Uncle Greedy puts Mao's supernatural powers to use at the gaming tables; all goes smoothly until Mao's gangster girlfriend is kidnapped by the bad buys, leaving Mao an emotional wreck. This spoof of *God of Gamblers*, the smash hit of 1989, proved as popular at the box office as the movie it parodies.

ALL NIGHT LONG
夜瘋狂
Year: 1989
Director: Peter Mak
Stars: Carol Cheng, Elizabeth Lee, Wu Ma

Black comedy in the manner of Martin Scorsese's *After Hours*, from which this film appropriates plot elements and music. Carol Cheng plays a bored schoolteacher whose nighttime stroll turns into a series of life-threatening mishaps. She ultimately ends up the hostage of some greedy women in a convenience store, where a fatally wounded gangster has left behind the proceeds of an armored-car robbery.

ALL'S WELL, ENDS WELL
家有喜事
Year: 1992
Director: Clifton Ko
Producer: Raymond Wong
Stars: Stephen Chiau, Leslie Cheung, Raymond Wong, Sandra Ng,
Maggie Cheung, Teresa Mo

A madcap farce, concerning the exploits of three brothers: a
philandering husband; an effeminate man in a love/hate relationship with his butch cousin; and a womanizing disk-jockey, whose
current love interest is obsessed with Hollywood movies. Stephen
Chiau and Maggie Cheung, as the DJ and his amour, upstage the
rest of the cast in a series of parodies of American films such as
Pretty Woman and *Terminator 2*.

ALL THE WRONG CLUES . . . FOR THE RIGHT SOLUTION
鬼馬智多星
Year: 1981
Director: Tsui Hark
Producers: Karl Maka and Dean Shek
Writers: Roy Szeto and Raymond Wong
Stars: George Lam, Teddy Robin Kwan, Karl Maka, Wong Tso-sze,
Carol Cheng (cameo), Eric Tsang (cameo)

After the blood-soaked nihilism of *Dangerous Encounter of the
First Kind*, the director Tsui Hark unexpectedly made this
slapstick-filled spoof of the American gangster film of the 1940s.
(The movie just as unexpectedly won him a Golden Horse award –
Taiwan's Oscar – for Best Director.) George Lam plays a private
dick who finds his life turned upside down when the girlfriend of
Al Capone (Karl Maka) – a woman Lam has never met before –
tries to elope with him.

ALWAYS ON MY MIND
搶錢夫妻
Year: 1993
Director: Jacob Cheung
Writer: James Yuen
Stars: Michael Hui, Josephine Siao, Chan Siu-ha, John Tang

Comedian Michael Hui plays a TV personality with cancer who exploits his illness to improve ratings, all the while persuading his wife and children that it's a publicity stunt. Though billed as a comedy, the film focuses on middle-class concerns in a fairly realistic manner; it won good reviews but did poorly at the box office, prompting Hui to state that he would never again deviate from his traditionally more lighthearted fare.

AN AMOROUS WOMAN OF THE TANG DYNASTY
唐朝豪放女
Year: 1984
Director and Writer: Eddie Fong
Producer: Mona Fong
Stars: Pat Ha, Alex Man, Zhang Gouzhu

Classic new-wave film, based on the life of the Tang Dynasty poet Lady Yu, who seduced a wide variety of men and women. Considered shocking for its abundant nudity, the movie attempts to recreate with painstaking detail the look of ancient China. The original Taiwanese print ran over three hours, while the version currently available is less than two.

ANGEL (aka IRON ANGELS)
天使行動
Year: 1987
Directors: Raymond Leung, Leung Siu-ming, and Ivan Lai
Supervisor: Teresa Woo
Stars: Moon Lee, Alex Fong, Elaine Lui, Yukari Oshima, Hideki Saijo, David Chiang

The Angels are an espionage team called upon to stop a beautiful but deadly drug and gold smuggler (Yukari Oshima). The female

Angels (Moon Lee, Elaine Lui) are adept at martial arts, and also employ secret weapons – bracelets that shoot acid, and shirt buttons that are actually tiny bombs, for instance – to combat their foes. Moon Lee made her name as an action star in this movie.

ANGEL II
天使行動 II 之火鳳蛟龍
Year: 1988
Director: Teresa Woo
Action Director: Stanley Tong
Stars: Moon Lee, Alex Fong, Elaine Lui, Kharina Isa

The Angels are on vacation in Malaysia, where Alex Fong bumps into an old school friend who has become a Hitler-worshipping maniac with grand plans for world domination. Before his character flaw is discovered, Elaine Lui falls for him, and it is up to the other Angels – with the aid of a local transsexual – to rescue her from the madman's clutches. Despite the Mel Brooks plot, the film takes itself seriously.

ANGEL III
天使行動 III
Year: 1989
Director: Teresa Woo
Assistant Director: Stanley Tong
Stars: Moon Lee, Alex Fong, Ralph Chen, Kharina Isa

The third outing finds Moon Lee working undercover among a group of kamikaze assassins, though the plot is secondary to the action sequences, which include car chases and an extended bout of kickboxing. In the finale, two of the male Angels, armed with machine guns and flying around in jet packs, wipe out a small army.

ARMOUR OF GOD

龍兄虎弟

Year: 1986

Director: Jackie Chan and Eric Tsang (uncredited)

Assistant Director: Stanley Kwan

Producer: Leonard Ho

Stars: Jackie Chan, Rosamund Kwan, Alan Tam

Jackie Chan is Asian Hawk, a Chinese version of Indiana Jones, in this goofy adventure film whose making nearly cost Chan his life. After Chan steals the "sword of God" from an African tribe, a villainous cult kidnaps his ex-girlfriend; the ransom is the sword, plus the rest of the magical collection of armor from which it came. Chan does less stunt work than usual, though the memorable finale finds him leaping onto an airborne hot-air balloon.

ARMOUR OF GOD II (*see* OPERATION CONDOR)

ARREST THE RESTLESS

藍江傳之反飛組風雲

Year: 1992

Director: Lawrence Ah Mon

Producers: Jimmy Heung and Charles Heung

Stars: Leslie Cheung, Charles Heung, Vivian Chow, Deannie Yip

Set during the 1950s, this film recounts the story of suave but small-time triad (Leslie Cheung) who finds himself in deep trouble after offending another young tough whose father is one of Hong Kong's richest businessman. The incorruptible cop who comes to Cheung's aid is played by Charles Heung, the powerful movie producer whose father founded the Sun Yee On, Hong Kong's largest criminal society.

ASHES OF TIME
東邪西毒
Year: 1994
Director and Writer: Wong Kar-wai
Producer: Tsai Sung-lin
Action Director: Sammo Hung
Cinematographer: Christopher Doyle
Stars: Leslie Cheung, Tony Leung (Ka-fai), Brigitte Lin, Tony Leung (Chiu-wai), Carina Lau, Jacky Cheung, Maggie Cheung, Charlie Yeung

This controversial art-house swashbuckler, peopled with characters from the classic Louis Cha novel *The Eagle Shooting Heroes*, failed commercially, despite a cast that includes eight of the biggest stars of the Hong Kong cinema. Leslie Cheung plays a loner who lines up work for assassins-for-hire; Tony Leung Ka-fai is a young swordsman with a knack for making enemies; and Maggie Cheung portrays the woman in the hearts of both men who sets the story in motion with her "wine of forgetfulness." Exquisitely photographed in the Yuli desert of mainland China, the film's narrative unfolds entirely out of sequence – a device that many viewers find maddening. The movie won multiple awards from the Hong Kong Film Critics Society, including Best Picture of 1994, and picked up a Golden Horse for its cinematography.

ASIAN COPS: HIGH VOLTAGE
高壓線
Year: 1995
Director: Andrew Kam
Action: Donnie Yen
Stars: Donnie Yen, Edu Manzano, Roy Cheung, Lily Lee

This Hong Kong and Filipino co-production finds Donnie Yen as an unconventional cop assigned to escort a dangerous criminal who has been extradited to the Philippines. Once there, the criminal manages a daring escape, and Yen is forced to team up with a local policeman. The pursuit leads the two lawmen to the villainous Roy Cheung, with whom they both have an old score to settle. Slickly directed, with bone-crunching fight choreography.

AS TEARS GO BY

旺角卡門

Year: 1988

Director and Writer: Wong Kar-wai

Producer: Alan Tang

Stars: Andy Lau, Maggie Cheung, Jacky Cheung, Alex Man

Wong Kar-wai, Hong Kong's leading art-film director of the moment, made his directorial début with this unromanticized gangster story. Ah Wah, a triad in Hong Kong's rough Mongkok district, plays the protective big brother to Fly, his younger friend in the crime syndicate – a role made more difficult by Fly's penchant for screwing up badly. Ah Wah's life is further complicated by his budding romance with a distant cousin who wants him to give up his violent lifestyle. The movie was a career breakthrough for the lovely Maggie Cheung – the cousin – who previously had not been regarded as a serious actress.

AU REVOIR, MON AMOUR

何日君再來

Year: 1991

Director: Tony Au

Stars: Anita Mui, Tony Leung (Ka-fai), Carrie Ng, Kenneth Tsang

Epic love story set against the Japanese occupation of Shanghai. Anita Mui plays a torch singer who is romanced by a member of the Chinese resistance, as well as a not-unsympathetic Japanese man. Former set designer Tony Au creates a lush period film complete with musical numbers – courtesy of Mui, a pop star in real life – and action scenes.

AUTUMN MOON
秋月
Year: 1992
Director: Clara Law
Producers: Clara Law and Eddie Fong
Writer: Eddie Fong
Stars: Masatoshi Nagase, Li Pui-wai, Choi Siu-wan

Clara Law's most intimate film concerns the unlikely friendship between a teenage girl from Hong Kong and a slightly older Japanese man who meet on vacation and communicate mostly in broken English. The girl is discovering first love, while trying to cope with the prospect of emigrating to Canada, and her grand-mother's failing health; the man is a sexual compulsive unable to remember – much less form attachments to – the women he has known. Fine cinematography and a smart script by the director Eddie Fong (Law's husband) set this film apart from the average drama.

AN AUTUMN'S TALE
秋天的童話 （流氓大亨）
Year: 1987
Director: Mabel Cheung
Producer: John Sham
Writer: Alex Law
Stars: Chow Yun-fat, Cherie Chung, Chan Bak-cheung, Gigi Wong

Chow Yun-fat often mentions this bittersweet love story, filmed in New York, as one of his personal favorites. Cherie Cheung is a young woman who moves to New York from Hong Kong to join her boyfriend, only to discover that he has a new love interest. She finds solace in her friendship with a distant cousin (Chow Yun-fat), a rambunctious gypsy cab driver, but, because of Chow's inferior class status, she retreats when that friendship begins to turn romantic.

AWAKENING
鬼迷心竅
Year: 1994
Director: Cha Chuen-yi
Stars: Anthony Wong, Simon Yam, Carman Lee

The two leading male stars of the Category III genre – Hong Kong's equivalent of NC-17 – team up in this surreal horror film. An oversexed Taoist priest (Anthony Wong) becomes the target of a ghost (Simon Yam) whose wife and child ostensibly died as a consequence of the priest's fraudulent fortune-telling. Yam's diabolical scheme of revenge ultimately reduces Wong to the cross-dressing lover of a transsexual.

B

THE BAREFOOTED KID
赤腳小子
Year: 1993
Director: Johnny To
Action Director: Lau Kar-leung
Stars: Aaron Kwok, Maggie Cheung, Ti Lung, Wu Chien-lien

Aaron Kwok plays a young peasant, skilled in martial arts, who finds work in a textile factory run by Maggie Cheung, and who becomes a naïve pawn in a scheme to destroy her business. The film boasts exceptional fight choreography, and pays more attention to emotion than the average kung-fu film.

THE BEASTS
山狗
Year: 1980
Director: Dennis Yu
Assistant Director: Stanley Kwan
Producer: Teddy Robin Kwan
Co-Writer: Eddie Fong
Art Director: Tony Au
Stars: Chan Sing, Kent Cheng

An amalgam of *Last House on the Left* and *The Texas Chainsaw*

Massacre, made by some of the leading figures of the Hong Kong new wave. Teenagers on a hiking trip stumble upon a small town terrorized by a gang of rapist-murderers (amiably called "The Disco Boys"); the teens are picked off one by one, until the father of a raped girl shows up to exact revenge. An extremely grim movie that would probably be unwatchable in less talented hands.

BEFORE DAWN
第 8 點
Year: 1983
Director: Clarence Fok
Stars: Deannie Yip, Guk Fung, Loletta Lee

The police are searching for a serial killer of gay men in Hong Kong when their attention is drawn to a troubled young man, the son of a prostitute. The story focuses less on the murders than on Hong Kong's gay subculture, and the young man's confused identity. While this movie lacks the hyperactive style of Clarence Fok's later films – *Naked Killer*, for one – it exemplifies his fascination for sexual politics.

A BETTER TOMORROW
英雄本色
Year: 1986
Director and Writer: John Woo
Producer: Tsui Hark
Stars: Chow Yun-fat, Ti Lung, Leslie Cheung, Emily Chu, Waise Lee, John Woo, Tsui Hark (cameo)

This is the film that established John Woo as the king of the Hong Kong gunplay picture, and made a superstar of the actor Chow Yun-fat. Chow plays counterfeiter Mark Gor, whose partner, Ho, has a younger brother, Kit, in the police force. Kit knows nothing of Ho's life of crime until a gangland doublecross results in the death of their father; the younger man's love for his big brother turns to hatred, until the two of them, along with Mark, are drawn into a violent showdown against the syndicate.

A BETTER TOMORROW II

英雄本色 II

Year: 1987

Director and Writer: John Woo

Producer: Tsui Hark

Action Director: Ching Siu-tung

Stars: Chow Yun-fat, Dean Shek, Ti Lung, Leslie Cheung, Emily Chu

Chow Yun-fat, who got bumped off in Part I, returns as Mark's twin brother, Ken, the owner of a Chinese restaurant in Brooklyn (where the movie was partly shot). Kit, the police officer, has gone undercover; soon he is joined by his brother, Ho, and Ken, in another showdown against the syndicate. John Woo and producer Tsui Hark struggled for control of the movie; Tsui insisted that the story focus on the character played by Dean Shek, who, in the film, is betrayed by his bosses – just as Shek was betrayed in real life, in Tsui's assessment, by his partners at Cinema City. Woo, who had something else in mind, has essentially disowned the movie, apart from the prolonged gun battle at the end.

A BETTER TOMORROW III: LOVE AND DEATH IN SAIGON

英雄本色 III

Year: 1989

Director and Producer: Tsui Hark

Stars: Chow Yun-fat, Anita Mui, Tony Leung (Ka-fai), Saburo Tokito

Tsui Hark took over the reins completely for the final installment of the series, which was shot on location in Saigon, and which, in its feminism, departs radically from Woo's approach to storytelling. In this prequel to Part I, set in 1974, a young Mark Gor tries to help his father and best friend escape from Vietnam. Mark, not yet the tough guy, meets up with femme fatale Anita Mui, who teaches him how to shoot a gun, among other things. The movie's sense of desperation was undoubtedly heightened by the Tiananmen Square Massacre, which occured just before the start of production.

THE BIG HEAT
城市特警
Year: 1988
Directors: Johnny To and Andrew Kam
Producer: Tsui Hark
Executive Producer: Raymond Wong
Writer: Gordon Chan
Stars: Waise Lee, Philip Kwok, Joey Wong, Chu Kong, Matthew Wong

Waise Lee is a cop with a problem: a job-related accident has left his right hand barely functional. Just as he is about to quit the force, he finds out that his former partner has been brutally murdered, leading him to take on one last case. The movie's unflinching violence – including scenes of decapitation, crushed bones, severed fingers, and bodies on fire – is remarkable even by Hong Kong standards.

BLACK CAT
黑貓
Year: 1991
Director: Stephen Shin
Producers: Stephen Shin and Dickson Poon
Stars: Jade Leung, Simon Yam, Thomas Lam

In this unabashed rip-off of Luc Besson's *La Femme Nikita*, Jade Leung stars as a young drifter who is sentenced to death for committing a number of murders. Simon Yam is the CIA agent who offers her a second chance if she becomes a computer-controlled assassin.

BLACK CAT II: THE ASSASSINATION OF PRESIDENT
YELTSIN
黑貓 II
Year: 1992
Director: Stephen Shin
Producers: Stephen Shin and Dickson Poon
Stars: Jade Leung, Robin Shou

The sequel finds the Black Cat with a new and improved computer
chip in her head, and a new and improbable assignment: to prevent
Boris Yeltsin from being assassinated. Shot on location in Russia,
the movie lacks the grittiness of Part I, and plays more like a James
Bond film.

THE BLACK PANTHER WARRIORS
黑豹天下
Year: 1993
Director: Clarence Fok
Stars: Alan Tang, Brigitte Lin, Tony Leung (Ka-fai), Simon Yam,
Carrie Ng, Elsie Chan, Yuen Wah, Dicky Cheung

The veteran actor Alan Tang (who produced Wong Kar-wai's first
two films) and Brigitte Lin star as the leaders of a group of
mercenaries hired to steal a file from a high-tech police station.
Complications ensue when it is revealed that Tang's evil brother is
trying to doublecross him. This comic book of a movie is no less
outlandish than Clarence Fok's better-known *Naked Killer*, though
a good deal more disjointed – the production went through six
cinematographers, and Fok threatened to quit himself because of
difficulties in scheduling shoots with all the film's stars.

THE BLADE
刀
Year: 1995
Director: Tsui Hark
Stars: Zhao Wen-zhou, Valerie Chow, Xiong Xin-xin, Austin Wai,
Chan Ho, Sang Ni

Dark and visually compelling, *The Blade* is Tsui Hark's answer to

Wong Kar-wai's existential sword epic *Ashes of Time* – not to mention a remake of the Shaw Brothers classic *The One-Armed Swordsman*. On (Zhao Wen-zhou) uncovers the long-buried secret of his father's brutal murder by Lung, and sets out for vengeance, only to lose an arm after falling into a trap set by bandits. Nursed back to health by a nameless young orphan, On must master the art of one-armed swordfighting, or, like his father, fall victim to Lung's treachery.

THE BLUE JEAN MONSTER
著牛仔褲的鍾馗
Year: 1991
Director: Ivan Lai
Stars: Shing Fui-on, Gloria Yip, Pauline Wong, Amy Yip

Shing Fui-on (an actor whose distended features have earned him the nickname "Big Sillyhead") plays a good cop who is brutally murdered, and comes back to life with the aid of a lightning bolt. He vows he will not die again until his pregnant wife gives birth and he tracks down the men who killed him. Meanwhile, he must hide from his wife his numerous graphic wounds – not to mention that his body is decomposing. A funny and quite deliberately tasteless film.

BOAT PEOPLE
投奔怒海
Year: 1982
Director: Ann Hui
Assistant Director: Stanley Kwan
Art Director: Tony Au
Stars: George Lam, Season Ma, Cora Miao, Andy Lau

A pro-Communist Japanese photojournalist (George Lam) travels to Vietnam several years after the Communist victory. At first he is blithely taken in by the official image of happy Vietnamese, but soon sets off on his own to discover the harsh realities of day-to-day life. He befriends a young girl (Season Ma) and her family, and his good intentions lead to their undoing as they fall under the scrutiny of the authorities. Meanwhile, Lam crosses paths with a young Vietnamese man (the pop star Andy Lau, in one of his earliest movie roles) who is sent to a "New Economic Zone" – a polite term for an internment camp in which prisoners spend their days digging up live mines. This harrowing, violent film has been read as a none-too-subtle indictment of mainland China; not coincidentally, all the Communist officials are played by mainland Chinese actors.

THE BODYGUARD FROM BEIJING
中南海保鑣
Year: 1994
Director: Corey Yuen
Stars: Jet Li, Christy Cheung, Kent Cheng, Ngai Sing

A Chinese version of *The Bodyguard*, with Jet Li in the Kevin Costner role. Christy Cheung is a spoiled millionairess who is assigned a bodyguard by the mainland Chinese military after witnessing a gangland murder. Though at first annoyed by the straitlaced Li, Cheung soon finds herself falling for him. The final twenty minutes of the film consist of nonstop martial-arts action.

BOYS ARE EASY
追男仔
Year: 1993
Director: Wong Jing
Stars: Brigitte Lin, Maggie Cheung, Chingmy Yau, Tony Leung (Ka-fai), Dior Cheng, Jacky Cheung, Sandra Ng, Jimmy Lin, Richard Ng, Shing Fui-on, Ken Lo, Ha Ping

The father of three unwed young women fakes a terminal illness in hopes of getting them to marry – his last wish – but each of the single-minded daughters concocts a phony relationship so that the old man can die in peace. Brigitte Lin, a butch policewoman, hires male prostitute and self-styled "king of karaoke" Tony Leung; Maggie Cheung recruits small-time triad Jacky Cheung (who, unknown to her, is out to kill her cop sister); and Chingmy Yau, a successful doctor, attracts an innocent young man by pretending to be a call girl. Sandra Ng rounds out the all-star cast as the father's gold-digging pen pal.

THE BRIDE WITH WHITE HAIR
白髮魔女傳
Year: 1993
Director: Ronny Yu
Producers: Raymond Wong and Michael Wong
Executive Producers: Ronny Yu and Clifton Ko
Stars: Leslie Cheung, Brigitte Lin, Elaine Lui, Yammie Nam, Francis Ng

This popular and artfully crafted film finds Leslie Cheung as a reluctant swordsman sent to destroy an evil cult headed by sadistic male and female Siamese twins. Conflict ensues when Cheung falls for the cult's prime assassin, the Wolf Woman, played by the Taiwanese actress Brigitte Lin. As the two lovers try to escape the tumult, they are both betrayed, leading to a tragic conclusion. Based on a Chinese folk tale.

THE BRIDE WITH WHITE HAIR II
白髮魔女傳 II
Year: 1993
Directors: David Wu and Ronny Yu (uncredited)
Producer: Ronny Yu
Stars: Brigitte Lin, Christy Cheung, Leslie Cheung (cameo)

Left abandoned and bitter in the first installment, Brigitte Lin, now a white-haired witch, heads an all-female cult bent on destroying the eight martial-arts clans from which her former lover, Leslie Cheung, had come. Her own cult comes under attack by a man whose bride has been kidnapped by Lin. Cheung, meanwhile, sits atop a snow-covered mountain, waiting for the mystical flower to bloom that can restore Lin's beauty.

BUGIS STREET
妖街皇后
Year: 1995
Director: Yeung Fan
Stars: Hiep Thi-lee, Michael Lam

In 1960s Singapore, an innocent young woman (Hiep Thi-lee, who starred in Oliver Stone's *Heaven and Earth*) comes to work at a hotel on Bugis Street, a thoroughfare notorious for its drag-queen prostitutes. Horrified at first, the woman soon strikes up a friendship with a few of the drag queens, and shares in their triumphs and heartbreaks. After suffering her own disappointment with a rich former boyfriend, the woman has a brief affair with one of the male prostitutes. A film that is more artful than exploitative.

BULLET IN THE HEAD
喋血街頭
Year: 1990
Director, Producer, and Writer: John Woo
Executive Producer: Terence Chang
Stars: Tony Leung (Chiu-wai), Jacky Cheung, Waise Lee, Simon Yam, Fennie Yuen, Yolinda Yan, John Woo (cameo)

John Woo's most uncomfortably violent film concerns three buddies on the lam from 1968 Hong Kong who end up in war-torn Vietnam, where they meet a variety of violent circumstances that test their moral character and the bonds of brotherhood. Their friendship is ultimately doomed when, with the aid of a suave ex-CIA agent, they obtain a case of gold bullion. An epic movie that has been compared, not inaptly, to *The Deer Hunter*, particularly for its harrowing scenes in a Vietcong internment camp. While the international print runs well over two hours, the commonly available video and laser disk versions are almost half an hour shorter.

BUNMAN: THE UNTOLD STORY
八仙飯店之人肉叉燒包
Year: 1993
Director: Herman Yau
Producer: Danny Lee
Stars: Anthony Wong, Danny Lee, Shing Fui-on, Emily Kwan, Lee Wah-yuet, Parkman Wong

Grisly Category III movie with shades of *Sweeney Todd*, though supposedly based on a true story. In Macao, a mentally unbalanced chef murders his boss and the boss's family to get ownership of their restaurant. When suspicious co-workers threaten to expose his guilt, he murders them, too – and disposes of the bodies by baking them into meat pies. Anthony Wong, as the chef, won Best Actor at the Hong Kong Film Awards for his chilling performance.

BURNING AMBITION
龍之爭霸
Year: 1989
Director and Producer: Frankie Chan
Stars: Simon Yam, Yukari Oshima, Frankie Chan, Hui Ying-hung, Roy Chiao, Eddie Ko, Robin Shou, Jeff Falcon

When a triad patriarch is killed at the hands of a rival, two crime families go to war. Each killing leads to another, until one family, its ranks depleted, calls in a group of Caucasian martial artists from Holland. Though the gunplay and fight choreography are fast and furious – in one scene, a woman fights off enemies with the glass shards embedded in her bare feet – the movie is rather grim, and leaves the viewer at a loss over whom, if anyone, to root for.

BURNING PARADISE
火燒紅蓮寺
Year: 1993
Director: Ringo Lam
Producer: Tsui Hark
Stars: Willie Chi, Wong Kam-kong, Carman Lee, Lee Tien-san

Ringo Lam brings his urban cynicism to his first period film, a radical retelling of the story of the legendary Shaolin patriot Fong Sai-yuk. Held captive in the notorious Red Lotus Temple, Master Fong faces a wide variety of deadly booby traps, and the wrath of an old Ming tyrant who, convinced of the meaninglessness of life, plays out his sadistic fantasies on his captives.

BUTTERFLY AND SWORD
新流星蝴蝶劍
Year: 1993
Director: Michael Mak
Producer: Wu Ton
Action Director: Ching Siu-tung
Stars: Michelle Yeoh, Tony Leung (Chiu-wai), Joey Wong, Donnie Yen, Jimmy Lin

Michelle Yeoh and Tony Leung lead a gang of martial-arts warriors at the service of an old, dying eunuch, who pits the gang against a rival clan. Yeoh sends Leung undercover before resorting to an all-out frontal attack. Produced by a Taiwanese triad, this movie is based on Gu Long's classic novel, *Comet Butterfly and Sword*, previously adapted for the screen by the Shaw Brothers in the early 1980s.

BUTTERFLY LOVERS (*see* THE LOVERS)

BUTTERFLY MURDERS
蝶變
Year: 1979
Director: Tsui Hark
Assistant Director: Lawrence Ah Mon
Stars: Lau Siu-ming, Michelle Chan, Wong Shee-tong, Cheong Kwok-chu, Mai Suet, Tsui Siu-keung, Eddie Ko

Tsui Hark's directorial début is a swordplay and horror film, with touches of Edgar Allan Poe's *Masque of the Red Death*. The castle of Lord Shum is a nesting place for a flock of killer butterflies; when swordsmen arrive to investigate, they are trapped in an underground labyrinth, and left to the mercy of the butterflies and a seemingly invincible armor-clad assassin. Claustrophobic and devoid of humor, the movie features some impressive action sequences.

BY HOOK OR BY CROOK
咸魚翻生
Year: 1980
Director: Karl Maka
Action Director: Sammo Hung
Writer: Raymond Wong
Stars: Sammo Hung, Wu Ma, Dean Shek, Karl Maka, Lam Ching-ying, Eric Tsang

In this surreal martial-arts comedy, Sammo Hung is a novice do-gooder impersonating his Robin Hood-like hero, the Flower Kid. With the help of Dean Shek (doing an inexplicable Jerry Lewis impersonation), Hung finds the real Flower Kid, who has become a wimp in need of a drastic makeover to restore his former glory. The last reel contains a series of fight scenes that show Hung at his wittiest and most acrobatic.

C

CAGEMAN
籠民
Year: 1992
Director: Jacob Cheung
Stars: Roy Chiao, Michael Lee, Wong Ka-kui, Teddy Robin Kwan, Dennis Chan

Loosely styled after the 1973 Shaw Brothers classic *The House of 72 Tenants*, this film tells the story of a group of men who cope with the housing shortage in present-day Hong Kong by inhabiting a building in which each man lives in a small cage. Trouble ensues when politicians and the landlord conspire to tear down the building. Though the film is devoid of sex and violence, it received a Category III rating, ostensibly for its coarse language, but more likely for its political content.

THE CANTON GODFATHER (*see* MIRACLES)

THE CASE OF THE COLD FISH
月黑風高
Year: 1995
Director: Jamie Luk
Producer: Danny Lee
Stars: Michael Wong, Michael Chow, Kwan Bo-wai, Valerie Chow,
Shing Fui-on, Danny Lee (cameo)

Atypical comedy that finds Amerasian Michael Wong as a Hong
Kong police officer investigating a small-town murder. The local
police, led by Michael Chow, have their own ways, and find the
presence of a big-city lawman most unwelcome. This film is
surprising in its gentle and even-handed way of making fun of
both the provincial police and the arrogant urban cop.

CASINO RAIDERS
至尊無上
Year: 1989
Directors and Writers: Wong Jing and Jimmy Heung
Producer: Jimmy Heung
Stars: Andy Lau, Alan Tam, Rosamund Kwan

When gambling ace Andy Lau and his best friend, Alan Tam, help a
casino bust a ring of Japanese cheats, they find themselves marked
for murder. More complications arise when Tam forsakes his friend
to marry a rich socialite; the heartbroken Lau tries to pull off one
last scam, with tragic results for all concerned. A grim portrait of
small-time gamblers, and the polar opposite of Wong Jing's
gambling action-comedies, such as *God of Gamblers*.

CENTER STAGE (*aka* ACTRESS)
阮玲玉
Year: 1991
Director: Stanley Kwan
Producer: Jackie Chan
Writers: Chiu Kong-chien and Peggy Chiao
Stars: Maggie Cheung, Tony Leung (Ka-fai), Waise Lee, Carina Lau

Biopic based on the life of the Chinese silent movie actress Ruan Ling-yu, who committed suicide before she was twenty-five. This Brechtian drama employs old film clips, interviews with Ruan's surviving friends and fellow actors, as well as with this movie's director, Stanley Kwan, and its cast members. Maggie Cheung won the Best Actress award at the Berlin Film Festival for her portrayal of the troubled movie star.

C'EST LA VIE, MON CHERIE
新不了情
Year: 1993
Director and Writer: Derek Yee
Stars: Anita Yuen, Lau Ching-wan, Carrie Ng, Carina Lau, Fung Bo-bo, Paul Chun

The tearjerker that launched Anita Yuen as a new superstar of the Hong Kong cinema, and won her the Best Actress prize at the Hong Kong Film Awards. (The movie clinched five other awards as well, including Best Picture.) Yuen plays a high-spirited young woman who falls for a down-at-the-heels saxophone player and reforms his life; the tables are turned when she develops bone cancer. Based on a popular film from 1961 called *Love Without End*, starring Lin Dai and Kwan Shan (Rosamund Kwan's father), and remade into a mod version in 1971 called *New Love Without End*.

CHERRY BLOSSOMS
郁達夫傳奇
Year: 1987
Director and Writer: Eddie Fong
Producer: Leonard Ho
Stars: Chow Yun-fat, Wong Kwok-ling, Fok Tak-wah, Muthumi Itakura, Sachiko Nakamura

Like Fong's *Kawashima Yoshiko*, this film deals with the Japanese occupation of China, and is based on a real historical figure – in this case, the Chinese writer Yu Dafu. Yu's masculine shortcomings cast him in sharp contrast to the militarized Japanese, whom this controversial movie in some ways appears to glorify. Chow Yun-fat appears briefly at the beginning and end of the film as Yu in old age, while Wong Kwok-ling portrays him during the occupation. Because of extensive recutting by the studio, Fong has essentially disowned the film.

CHEZ 'N HAM
芝士火腿
Year: 1993
Director: Blackie Ko
Stars: Dickie Cheung, Eric Tsang, Joey Wong, Cheung Man, Ng Man-tat, Blackie Ko

Irreverent comedy about two problem-fixers (Dicky Cheung and Eric Tsang) who are hired by a wealthy old man to bump off the daughter of his arch-rival. All seems to be going well when Cheung disguises himself as an orphaned twelve-year-old, and the young woman adopts him, but the murder plans are confounded by her kindness, and the pedophilic advances of her bodyguard.

CHICKEN AND DUCK TALK
雞同鴨講
Year: 1988
Director: Clifton Ko
Producer: Ronny Yu
Writers: Michael Hui and Clifton Ko
Stars: Michael Hui, Ricky Hui, Sylvia Chang, Lowell Lo

Popular Hui Brothers comedy in which an unsanitary roast-duck restaurant, owned by a tyrannical Michael Hui, is forced to compete with a gleaming, new fried-chicken franchise across the street. Tensions rise as the two eateries resort to dirty tricks in an attempt to run each other out of business, and reach a pinnacle when Michael's brother Ricky is recruited by the enemy restaurant – leading to a street brawl between the siblings, who are dressed in promotional chicken and duck costumes.

CHINA DRAGON
中國龍
Year: 1995
Director: Chu Yen-ping
Stars: Sik Siu-lung, Yip Chuen-chun, Kok Siu-man, Takeshi Kaneshiro, Ng Man-tat, Tsui Kam-kong

Cult director Chu Yen-ping (*Fantasy Mission Force*, *Golden Queen Commandos*) has carved out a sub-specialty as a director of children's action comedies, of which this is one. Tough tike Sik Siu-lung and the beautiful Yip Chuen-chun are Shaolin disciples who head to Hawaii for an annual competition of martial arts and supernatural powers. When the two youths acquire the key to a nuclear power plant, the evil Tsui Kam-kong attempts to kidnap them for his own nefarious purposes.

THE CHINESE FEAST

金玉滿堂

Year: 1995

Director: Tsui Hark

Stars: Leslie Cheung, Anita Yuen, Zhao Wen-zhou, Kenny Bee, Law Kar-ying, Xiong Xin-xin

After a string of box-office disappointments, Tsui Hark bounced back with this hit New Year's comedy. Leslie Cheung is a junior triad who becomes a chef, gets a job in a restaurant, and befriends the owner's teenybopper daughter (Anita Yuen). When an evil competitor forces Cheung's boss to bet his restaurant on a cooking contest, Cheung must find China's one-time greatest chef – now an emotional wreck – and get him back on his feet to save the day.

THE CHINESE GHOSTBUSTER

鍾馗嫁妹

Year: 1994

Director: Wu Ma

Stars: Wu Ma, Lam Ching-ying, Mark Cheng

A god of the underworld (Wu Ma), desperate to marry off his daughter, travels to earth with his devilish clan in order to bag her a groom – a young male prostitute. The intended seeks the help of a Taoist priest (Lam Ching-ying) to send the ghosts back to hell. Though set in contemporary times, the film contains more than a touch of Peking Opera influence.

A CHINESE GHOST STORY

倩女幽魂

Year: 1987

Director: Ching Siu-tung

Producer: Tsui Hark

Stars: Leslie Cheung, Joey Wong, Wu Ma

Ground-breaking fantasy based on the ghost stories of the popular Ming Dynasty writer Pu Song-ling, and on the 1958 film *The Enchanting Shadow*. Leslie Cheung plays a naïve young tax collector who takes shelter in a haunted temple and falls in love with a beautiful ghost (Joey Wong), herself the captive of a thousand-year-old tree demon with a life-sapping tongue. Coming to the couple's aid is a Taoist monk who battles the evil spirits with sword and scripture.

A CHINESE GHOST STORY II
倩女幽魂 II：人間道
Year: 1990
Director: Ching Siu-tung
Producer: Tsui Hark
Stars: Leslie Cheung, Joey Wong, Michelle Reis, Jacky Cheung, Waise Lee

Part II trades much of the romantic charm of the first installment for more action and special effects. Cheung meets up with a human lookalike of his former ghostly love, and is enlisted to help a group of swordsmen rescue her father from corrupt government officials. Along the way, they meet up with a mysterious monk, who is actually a giant centipede monster, intent on eating every human it comes across.

A CHINESE GHOST STORY III
倩女幽魂 III：道道道
Year: 1991
Director: Ching Siu-tung
Producer: Tsui Hark
Stars: Tony Leung (Chiu-wai), Joey Wong, Jacky Cheung, Nina Li Chi

Though Part III opens with the epigraph "One Hundred Years Later," it is more a remake of Part I than a sequel. Joey Wong returns as another ghost-woman whose soul is held captive by an evil tree demon. Tony Leung is the young monk who comes to her rescue. Heavy on special effects, including Leung's transformation in the finale into a flying golden Buddha.

A CHINESE ODYSSEY I: PANDORA'S BOX
西遊記第壹佰零壹回之月光寶盒
Year: 1995
Director: Jeff Lau
Action Director: Ching Siu-tung
Stars: Stephen Chiau, Karen Mok, Ng Man-tat, Yammie Nam,
Law Kar-ying

Stephen Chiau, the master of Cantonese *mo lai to* (makes no sense)
comedy, displays his range in this adaptation of the classic novel
Journey to the West. He plays a desert bandit whose life is turned
upside-down with the appearance of two evil sisters. They are
searching for the reincarnated Monkey King, so he can lead them
to his master, the Longevity Monk, whose flesh grants immortality.
Chiau, to his horror, begins to suspect that *he* is the Monkey King.

A CHINESE ODYSSEY II: CINDERELLA
西遊記大結局之仙履奇緣
Year: 1995
Director: Jeff Lau
Action Director: Ching Siu-tung
Stars: Stephen Chiau, Karen Mok, Law Kar-ying, Yammie Nam,
Ng Man-tat

A Pandora's box introduced in Part I plunges Stephen Chiau five
hundred years into the past. He must help rescue the Longevity
Monk from captivity, fight off the evil Bull King (and the advances
of his amorous wife), and come to grips with the fact that he is
indeed the reincarnated Monkey King.

CHUNGKING EXPRESS
重慶森林
Year: 1994
Director and Writer: Wong Kar-wai
Cinematographer: Christopher Doyle
Stars: Tony Leung (Chiu-wai), Faye Wong, Takeshi Kaneshiro,
Brigitte Lin, Valerie Chow

Two disconnected stories about Hong Kong policemen jilted by

their girlfriends. Takeshi Kaneshiro, in story No. 1, goes to a bar on
his birthday, determined to fall in love with the first woman he
meets, and picks up blonde-wigged heroin smuggler Brigitte Lin. In
the second story, Tony Leung's ex has dropped off his keys at a fast-
food joint, and he is too depressed to notice that the counter girl,
who has a crush on him, is subtly redecorating his apartment when
he isn't there. A plot summary, however, cannot do justice to this
much-admired film, which relies on atmosphere to convey its
message of urban alienation.

CITY HUNTER
城市獵人
Year: 1993
Director: Wong Jing
Stars: Jackie Chan, Chingmy Yau, Leon Lai, Goto Kumiko, Joey
Wong, Richard Norton

In this adaptation of a Japanese anime (animated film), Jackie Chan
is Roy Saeba, a private detective on the prowl for a missing heiress
aboard a cruise liner. This movie is pure Wong Jing, with many
trademark elements of Hong Kong's favorite director of schlock – a
god of gamblers, a sex-bomb woman detective, international
terrorists – as well as a parody of the Streetfighter video game.
Chan has made no secret of his loathing for this film. (Wong Jing
got his revenge in 1995 as writer and director of the devastating
Jackie Chan sendup *High Risk*.)

CITY ON FIRE
喋血城市
Year: 1987
Director: Ringo Lam
Producer: Karl Maka
Music: Teddy Robin Kwan
Stars: Chow Yun-fat, Roy Cheung, Carrie Ng, Danny Lee, Sun Yueh

A Hong Kong cop (Chow Yun-fat) goes undercover as a gun-
smuggler to infiltrate a gang that has staged a series of daring
robberies, then has an identity crisis when he develops a friendship
with one of the gangsters. Winner of Best Picture and Best Actor

(Chow) at the Hong Kong Film Awards, *City on Fire* gained international exposure when Quentin Tarantino appropriated the last section as the basis for *Reservoir Dogs*. The movie also marked the screen début of Carrie Ng.

CLOSE ENCOUNTERS OF THE SPOOKY KIND (*see* ENCOUNTERS OF THE SPOOKY KIND)

COMRADES, ALMOST A LOVE STORY
甜蜜蜜
Year: 1996
Director: Peter Chan
Stars: Leon Lai, Maggie Cheung, Eric Tsang, Christopher Doyle

Leon Lai plays a young Chinese immigrant who arrives friendless in Hong Kong with hopes of creating a new life for himself and his sweetheart back home. He meets Maggie Cheung, another mainlander who has more successfully adapted to the money culture of Hong Kong, and who soon takes up with a rich triad. Though Lai and Cheung fall in love, their romance is doomed – or so they think. Filmed partly in New York City, *Comrades* won nine prizes, including Best Picture, at the Hong Kong Film Awards.

CRAZY SAFARI
非洲和尚
Year: 1991
Director: Billy Chan
Producers: Charles Heung and Jimmy Heung
Stars: Lam Ching-ying, N!xau, Peter Chan, Sam Christopher Chan, Stephen Chiau (narration), Ng Man-tat (narration)

Sequel to *The Gods Must Be Crazy*, featuring its original bushman star, N!xau, with elements of the Hong Kong hit *Mr. Vampire*. A plane en route from Paris develops engine trouble, and its passengers, including a hopping vampire in the custody of a Taoist priest, bail out over the African savannah. The priest and the vampire join forces with local tribesmen to fight off some nasty Caucasians. A film that, in its blend of genres, could have come only from Hong Kong.

CRIME STORY
重案組
Year: 1993
Director: Kirk Wong
Action Director: Jackie Chan
Stars: Jackie Chan, Kent Cheung, Chung Fat, Ken Lo

The first part of Kirk Wong's police trilogy (followed by *Organized Crime and Triad Bureau* and *Rock 'n Roll Cop*) casts Jackie Chan in the role that finally bagged him a Best Actor trophy at the Golden Horse Film Awards. Chan plays a cop assigned to protect a real-estate billionaire from a kidnapping plot. When the tycoon is abducted nonetheless, Chan teams up with a senior police officer (Kent Cheng) to rescue him, only to discover that Cheng is working with the bad guys. Despite car chases, a few impressive stunts, and a (literally) incendiary finish, *Crime Story* is atypically somber for a Jackie Chan movie.

CROSSINGS
錯愛
Year: 1994
Director: Evans Chan
Stars: Anita Yuen, Simon Yam, Lindsay Chan

After the critical success of his *To Liv(e)*, Evans Chan shot this unusual drama in New York, with a Chinese and American cast. Anita Yuen lands in Manhattan to find her missing boyfriend who, it turns out, is a triad involved in prostitution and smuggling. Her search is cross-cut with the tale of a young Caucasian male's descent into madness because of his homosexuality – a subplot that makes more sense in the international print, which runs twelve minutes longer than the Hong Kong version.

D

DANGEROUS ENCOUNTER OF THE FIRST KIND (*aka* DON'T
   PLAY WITH FIRE)
第一類型危險
Year: 1980
Director: Tsui Hark
Action Director: Ching Siu-tung
Art Director: Tony Au
Stars: Robert Au, Paul Che, Lim Ching-chi, Lo Lieh, Bruce Barron

Tsui Hark's third feature, an exercise in nihilism and deliberately
shocking violence, is unlike any movie he has made before or since.
When three teenage boys plant a small bomb in a movie theater for
kicks, they attract the attention of an amoral woman, who
blackmails them into participating in acts of terrorism. After the
four steal a large sum of money from some ex-CIA mercenaries,
they are hunted down and slaughtered.

DAYS OF BEING DUMB
亞飛與亞基
Year: 1992
Director: Blackie Ko
Stars: Tony Leung (Chiu-wai), Jackie Cheung, Anita Yuen, Eric
   Tsang

An action-comedy about two would-be triads trying to find a gang.
Unfortunately, they are jinxes, and every crime boss who takes
them in dies under bizarre circumstances. The pair then decide to
become pimps, but are too smitten with their would-be prostitute
to put her to work. Like most Blackie Ko films, this one ends with a
powerhouse action scene.

DAYS OF BEING WILD

阿飛正傳

Year: 1991

Director and Writer: Wong Kar-wai

Producer: Alan Tang

Stars: Leslie Cheung, Maggie Cheung, Carina Lau, Andy Lau, Jacky Cheung, Rebecca Pan, Tony Leung (Chiu-wai) (cameo)

The film that launched Wong Kar-wai as Hong Kong's leading art-house director has always been more popular with critics (it swept the Hong Kong Film Awards, and ranks high in the poll conducted for this book) than with audiences. Set in Hong Kong in the 1960s, it tells the story of a violent young man (Leslie Cheung) who romances and dumps a pair of women, before heading off to the Philippines in search of his birth mother. Andy Lau plays a cop who befriends one of Cheung's castoff girlfriends; later on, as a sailor on leave, he meets up with Cheung in Manila. *Days of Being Wild* was meant to be the first of two parts, but because of the movie's financial failure, Part II, to have starred Tony Leung Chiu-wai as a gambler, was never completed.

THE DAY THAT DOESN'T EXIST

二月三十

Year: 1995

Directors: Wellson Chin and Ko Lam-pau

Stars: Anthony Wong, Dayo Wong, Sheila Chan, Lau Mei-kuen, Kenneth Chan, Bowie Lam, Yuen King-tan

A pair of loosely connected horror stories that involve automobile accidents. In the first segment, a man supposedly killed in a car crash on the eve of his wedding turns up alive a month later – or so his fiancée thinks, before suspecting him to be a ghost who preys on pregnant women for their fetuses. The second story involves a married man whose soul enters the body of a cannabalistic murderer after both men die in traffic accidents at the same location.

THE DAY THE SUN TURNED COLD
天國孽子
Year: 1994
Director and Writer: Yim Ho
Producers: Yim Ho and Ann Hui
Stars: Siqin Gowa, Tuo Zhong-hua, Ma Jing-wu, Wai Zhi

Award-winning drama (Best Picture and Best Director, Tokyo
International Film Festival) about a young man who returns to his
small hometown in northern China and reports to the police that
he suspects his mother fatally poisoned his father ten years earlier.
Flashbacks reveal that the young man loved his mother deeply, and
disdained his father, making his motives for reporting her
mysterious. Based on an actual case, and filmed in Mandarin,
with a mainland Chinese cast.

THE DEAD AND THE DEADLY
人嚇人
Year: 1982
Director: Wu Ma
Action Director and Producer: Sammo Hung
Writers: Sammo Hung and Barry Wong
Stars: Wu Ma, Sammo Hung, Lam Ching-ying, Cherie Chung,
Chung Fat

A classic kung-fu horror-comedy that finds Wu Ma faking his own
death in order to scam money from rich relatives, only to be killed
for real by his greedy wife. He returns as a ghost and possesses the
body of his best friend (Sammo Hung) to seek vengenance.

DECEPTION (*aka* WEB OF DECEPTION)
驚魂記
Year: 1989
Director: David Chung
Producer: Tsui Hark
Stars: Brigitte Lin, Joey Wong, Pauline Wong, Elizabeth Lee, Waise
Lee

Brigitte Lin is a corporate executive who is being blackmailed after she embezzles money from her company. The audience is let in on the blackmailer's identity early on, but Lin can't figure out whether it's her broker, her secretary, the secretary's roommate, or the roommate's evil twin sister. Eventually, all four suspects end up at Lin's secluded mansion. Perhaps the best example of a Hitchcock homage in the modern Hong Kong cinema.

DIRTY HO
爛頭何
Year: 1979
Director: Lau Kar-leung
Producer: Run Run Shaw
Stars: Gordon Liu, Young Wang Yu, Hui Ying-hung, Lo Lieh

In Lau Kar-leung's groundbreaking martial-arts comedy, the emperor of China is getting ready to choose a successor among his fourteen children, leaving the eleventh prince at the peril of the fourth prince, who thinks his brother is the favorite. With the help of the amiable rascal Dirty Ho, the eleventh prince fends off a team of would-be assassins, and fights his way back to the capital.

DOCTOR MACK (see MACK THE KNIFE)

DON'T PLAY WITH FIRE (see DANGEROUS ENCOUNTER OF THE FIRST KIND)

DRAGON FROM RUSSIA
紅牆飛龍
Year: 1990
Director: Clarence Fok
Producer: Dean Shek
Stars: Sam Hui, Maggie Cheung, Dean Shek, Carrie Ng, Nina Li Chi

The leader of the Eight Hundred Dragons cult kidnaps Sam Hui and erases his memory, turning him into a topnotch assassin; but when Hui encounters a woman he has known since childhood, he begins to recollect his past. Now he must decide whether to kill her or betray his leader. Loosely based on the Japanese comic book

Crying Freeman, this was the first ever Hong Kong movie filmed on location in Russia.

DRAGON INN
新龍門客棧
Year: 1992
Director: Raymond Lee
Producer: Tsui Hark
Production Designer: Ching Siu-tung
Stars: Brigitte Lin, Tony Leung (Ka-fai), Maggie Cheung, Donnie Yen

Remake of King Hu's 1967 swordplay classic *Dragon Gate Inn*. Two noble warriors (Tony Leung and Brigitte Lin) rescue the children of a general murdered by an evil eunuch, and, while fleeing through the desert, take refuge at the Dragon Inn. Trapped there by bad weather, the heroes play an elaborate game of cat and mouse when the eunuch's band of murderous swordsmen show up. Maggie Cheung shines as the opportunistic innkeeper.

DRAGONS FOREVER
飛龍猛將
Year: 1988
Director: Sammo Hung
Co-Writer: Gordon Chan
Stars: Jackie Chan, Sammo Hung, Yuen Biao, Pauline Yeung, Crystal Kwok, Yuen Wah, Corey Yuen, Deannie Yip

The last (so far) of six movies to feature the threesome of Jackie Chan, Sammo Hung, and Yuen Biao – who grew up together at a Peking Opera academy – and one of the most popular. When an industrialist is sued by a woman who claims his factory is poisoning her fish farm, he hires attorney Jackie Chan to get her off his back. Chan in turn recruits his old friends Hung and Yuen to spy on the woman; but when the three men discover that the industrialist is manufacturing narcotics, they switch sides and raid his factory.

DREAM LOVERS
夢中人
Year: 1986
Director: Tony Au
Stars: Chow Yun-fat, Brigitte Lin, Yeung Suet-yi, Elaine Kam

Romantic tragedy about two strangers in contemporary Hong Kong (Chow Yun-fat and Brigitte Lin) who were lovers two thousand years ago during the Qing Dynasty. When they meet, they are inexorably drawn to one another, much to the dismay of Chow's current girlfriend. The mood darkens as it begins to appear that they will be forced to pay for their past-life sins.

DR. LAMB
羔羊醫生
Year: 1992
Directors: Billy Tang and Danny Lee
Producer: Danny Lee
Stars: Simon Yam, Danny Lee, Kent Cheng

True horror story about a mentally disturbed taxi driver (Simon Yam) who kills and mutilates his nighttime female passsengers, and then takes photographs of their dead bodies. The story is told mostly in flashback after Yam has been captured by the police.

DRUNKEN MASTER
醉拳
Year: 1978
Director: Yuen Woo-ping
Stars: Jackie Chan, Yuen Siu-tien, Huang Cheng-li, Dean Shek

Jackie Chan became Asia's biggest movie star with this comic portrayal of the Cantonese folk hero Wong Fei-hung as a young ne'er-do-well. When Wong disgraces his family twice in one day, his father sends him to study martial arts with a wino uncle, Sam the Seed, notorious for working his students to death. Wong escapes his uncle's clutches, but after being trounced by a bully he comes back to train in earnest.

DRUNKEN MASTER II
醉拳 II
Year: 1994
Directors: Lau Kar-leung and Jackie Chan (uncredited)
Producer: Leonard Ho
Stars: Jackie Chan, Anita Mui, Ti Lung, Lau Kar-leung, Ken Lo, Andy Lau (cameo)

Jackie Chan's triumphant sequel, sixteen years later, to the period martial-arts film that made him a superstar. The evil British and their treasonous Chinese henchmen are planning to smuggle the emperor's jade seal and other art treasures out of Manchuria, unless Wong Fei-hung (Chan) can stop them with his drunken boxing – a style of fighting that works better for Wong when he is truly drunk. Though Chan was nearly forty when he completed this film, and fired his director midway through production, it is considered one of his peak achievements; by the end of the climactic action sequence, a showdown in a steel foundry, he has ingested industrial alcohol and is literally spitting fire. Anita Mui stands out as Chan's gambling, free-spirited stepmother.

DR. WAI IN "THE SCRIPTURE WITH NO WORDS"
冒險王
Year: 1996
Director: Ching Siu-tung
Stars: Jet Li, Rosamund Kwan, Takeshi Kaneshiro, Charlie Yeung, Ngai Sing, Billy Chow, Law Kar-ying

In this Hong Kong Walter Mitty tale, Jet Li is a timid writer of serial adventure stories whose wife wants a divorce. Seeking refuge in his fiction, he becomes the heroic Dr. Wai, who must overcome the evil Japanese and procure a secret box that can tell the future; his wife, meanwhile, is cast as a Japanese villainess who performs sadistic experiments on men. But Li is unable to complete the story by himself, and two of his spunky assistants take over, resulting in numerous plot twists.

DUEL TO THE DEATH

先死決

Year: 1983

Director: Ching Siu-tung

Stars: Tsui Siu-keung, Damian Lau, Eddie Ko

A martial-arts competition in ancient China is sabotaged by a ninja, who helps his fellow Japanese eliminate their Chinese foes one by one through treachery. The film is less about plot than it is an opportunity for the director to create a series of surreal set pieces, including an attack by ninjas attached to giant kites.

E

THE EAGLE SHOOTING HEROES

射鵰英雄之東成西就

Year: 1993

Director: Jeff Lau

Executive Producer: Wong Kar-wai

Action Director: Sammo Hung

Stars: Brigitte Lin, Leslie Cheung, Jacky Cheung, Carina Lau, Veronica Yip, Tony Leung (Chiu-wai), Tony Leung (Ka-fai), Kenny Bee, Joey Wong, Maggie Chueng

A martial-arts parody filmed as a companion piece to Wong Kar-wai's *Ashes of Time*, featuring most of the stars of that movie, and several other top names. When an evil prince tries to usurp the emperor's throne, which, in his absence, is held by the emperor's daughter, she seeks help from an eccentric assortment of swordsmen to set things right. There is no way to summarize the madcap plot, however, with its scenes of goofy martial arts, cross-dressing swordfighters, campy musical numbers, rubber-suited monsters, and mind-controlling centipedes.

EASTERN CONDORS
東方禿鷹
Year: 1986
Director: Sammo Hung
Stars: Sammo Hung, Yuen Biao, Yuen Wah, Lam Ching-ying, Joyce Godenzi, Billy Lau, Phillip Ko, James Tien, Dr. Haing S. Ngor

In Sammo Hung's turbocharged remake of *The Dirty Dozen*, a group of Asian convicts are offered freedom by their American handlers if they can destroy a munitions dump in wartime Vietnam. The mission is officially scrubbed just as the convicts are about to parachute into the Vietnamese jungle, but by then it's too late to turn back. Immensely popular with American audiences, despite its anti-Yankee theme, *Eastern Condors* is a high body-count affair, filled with gun battles, explosions, and some of Hung's best fight choreography.

EAST IS RED (*aka* SWORDSMAN III)
東方不敗 2 ：風雲再起
Year: 1993
Directors: Ching Siu-tung and Raymond Lee
Producer: Tsui Hark
Stars: Brigitte Lin, Yu Rong-guang, Joey Wong, Eddie Ko, Yuen King-tan

Brigitte Lin achieved superstardom for her portrayal of the androgynous villain Asia the Invincible in *Swordsman II*, so it was perhaps inevitable that Part III of the series would focus on her character. A soldier visits her grave, finds she is alive after all, and informs her that numerous Asia the Invincible impostors, including her former lover, Snow, are causing havoc in her name. Soon the real Asia is on a campaign to reclaim control of the world, with a Japanese submarine and a Spanish warship at her disposal.

EASY MONEY
通天大盜
Year: 1987
Director: Stephen Shin
Producer: Dickson Poon
Stars: Michelle Yeoh, George Lam, Kent Cheng

Physically exhausted from shooting *Magnificent Warriors*, Michelle Yeoh opted for a non-action film – her last before her three-year marriage to Dickson Poon, and corresponding absence from movie-making. In this reverse-gender remake of *The Thomas Crown Affair*, Yeoh plays a self-named character – a rich socialite who gets her kicks by staging complicated robberies – and George Lam is the insurance investigator who falls for her.

EIGHT-DIAGRAM POLE FIGHTER
五郎八卦棍
Year: 1984
Director: Lau Kar-leung
Producer: Mona Fong
Stars: Fu Sheng, Gordon Liu, Hui Ying-hung, Lilly Li, Lau Kar-leung, Young Wang Yu, Philip Ko

When patriotic General Yang and five of his seven sons are massacred through the treachery of a jealous rival, the two surviving brothers seek vengeance. One brother (Fu Sheng) returns home, while the other (Gordon Liu) joins a monastery, where he learns the powerful eight-diagram pole-fighting technique that he ultimately uses to vanquish his foes. This was not only Lau Kar-leung's last film for Shaw Brothers, but the final screen performance of Fu Sheng, who was killed in a car accident during production.

THE EIGHTH HAPPINESS

八星報喜

Year: 1988

Director: Johnny To

Producer and Co-Writer: Raymond Wong

Stars: Chow Yun-fat, Raymond Wong, Jacky Cheung, Cherie Chung, Fung Bo-bo, Fennie Yuen, Carol Cheng

Another comedy for the Chinese Lunar New Year from Raymond Wong, in the spirit of his *All's Well, Ends Well*, concerning the amorous adventures of three brothers. Chow Yun-fat's ploy to pick up girls – posing as a homosexual – is oddly successful, and so is Raymond Wong's: hosting a patronizing cooking show called "Mainly for Women." Jacky Cheung, as the youngest brother, however, must contend with the sword-wielding mother and ping-pong-racquet-wielding boyfriend of his current love interest.

ENCOUNTERS OF THE SPOOKY KIND (*aka* CLOSE ENCOUN-
   TERS OF THE SPOOKY KIND)

鬼打鬼

Year: 1980

Director: Sammo Hung

Producer: Raymond Chow

Writers: Sammo Hung and Huang Ying

Stars: Sammo Hung, Lam Ching-ying, Wu Ma, Chung Fat, Chan Lung, Wong Ha

Classic martial-arts horror-comedy that spawned an entire genre (spin-offs include *The Dead and the Deadly* and the *Mr. Vampire* series). Sammo Hung's adulterous wife and her lover plot to kill him through witchcraft, and hire an evil *fat-si*, or black-magic priest, for the purpose; but Hung has a good *fat-si* working to save him. The two priests wage an epic battle, using corpses and the living possessed as their soldiers.

ENCOUNTERS OF THE SPOOKY KIND II (*aka* SPOOKY
    ENCOUNTERS)
鬼咬鬼
Year: 1989
Director: Ricky Lau
Stars: Sammo Hung, Lam Ching-ying, Wu Ma

An unrelated sequel that finds Sammo Hung as another bumbling
nice guy. This time he is romantically interested in a young
waitress, but her father wants to marry her off to a rich bully,
with an evil *fat-si* at his disposal. Hung once again enlists the aid of
a good *fat-si*, and soon finds himself embroiled in a supernatural
battle against zombies, snake people, and kung-fu mummies.

EROTIC GHOST STORY
聊齋豔譚
Year: 1990
Director: Lan Nai-kai
Stars: Amy Yip, Man So, Tan Lap-man

A soft-porn derivative of *The Witches of Eastwick*. If three young
fox fairies (including the double-D Amy Yip) can avoid carnal
relations for one month, they will achieve immortality. All goes
well until a mysterious handsome scholar – actually a powerful sex
demon – shows up and seduces them one by one, causing them to
sprout fox hair.

EVEN MOUNTAINS MEET
情天霹靂之下集大結局
Year: 1993
Director: Lawrence Ah Mon
Stars: Dicky Cheung, Ng Man-tat, Fung Bo-bo, Michael Chow,
Dik Bo-lai, Wong Wan-si, Pauline Yeung

A comic homage to the Cantonese musicals and ghost stories of the
1960s, in the tradition of *92 Legendary La Rose Noire*. A prima
donna drops dead, and her spirit visits her maid to tell her that she
may be reincarnated if only her former leading man pronounces his

love for her. When the maid sets out to find him, she inadvertently draws a pair of robbers to the actress's haunted house.

EXECUTIONERS (*aka* THE HEROIC TRIO II)
現代豪俠傳
Year: 1993
Director and Co-Producer: Johnny To
Co-Producer and Action Director: Ching Siu-tung
Stars: Michelle Yeoh, Maggie Cheung, Anita Mui, Damian Lau, Paul Chun, Anthony Wong, Takeshi Kaneshiro

After a nuclear explosion devastates the city, the three heroines from Part I must reunite to defeat an evil capitalist who controls all the fresh drinking water, and a mad general who wants to take over the government. A remarkably grim post-1997 allegory with a surprisingly high body count and a downbeat ending.

F

FALLEN ANGELS
墮落天使
Year: 1995
Director and Writer: Wong Kar-wai
Producer: Jeff Lau
Cinematographer: Christopher Doyle
Stars: Takeshi Kaneshiro, Leon Lai, Michelle Reis, Charlie Yeung, Karen Mok

Originally conceived as chapter three of the two-part *Chungking Express*, and stylistically similar to that earlier film, *Fallen Angels* depicts the lives of several of Hong Kong's demimonde. Among them are a hit man (Leon Lai) who is beginning to question both his career choice and his relationship to his cool-as-ice gun moll (Michelle Reis); and an enterprising ex-con (Takeshi Kaneshiro), who breaks into and runs other people's businesses at night. Charlie Yeung and Karen Mok round out the cast as women involved with the two leading men; Mok won Best Supporting Actress at the Hong Kong Film Awards.

FAREWELL CHINA
愛在別鄉的季節
Year: 1990
Director: Clara Law
Producer and Writer: Eddie Fong
Stars: Tony Leung (Ka-fai), Maggie Cheung

The wife-and-husband team of Clara Law and Eddie Fong, who recently bid farewell to Hong Kong to live in Melbourne, Australia, are responsible for this Dantesque view of New York City. A Chinese mainlander sends his wife to New York so that she can become an American citizen and help the rest of the family to emigrate, but after her letters stop coming, he journeys there to investigate. The wife, it turns out, has had to endure sexual assault and other depredations, and has lost her mind; she eventually stabs her husband in front of a miniature Statue of Liberty.

FATAL ENCOUNTER
奪命接觸
Year: 1994
Director: Ng Doi-yung
Stars: Ng Doi-yung, Lily Chung, Bobby Au Yeung

Hong Kong's first AIDS drama follows the lives of two people with the deadly virus. The first is a mainland teenage girl living in absolute poverty who turns to prostitution after being raped; the second is a Hong Kong truck driver who has a brief sexual encounter with her. When they discover they have AIDS, they are tormented by those around them – the girl by sadistic mainland police, and the truck driver by his unsympathetic family and friends. A surprisingly intelligent film, with an astute eye for class differences.

FATAL TERMINATION
赤色大風暴
Year: 1988
Director: Andrew Kam
Stars: Moon Lee, Simon Yam, Ray Lui, Phillip Ko, Robin Shou

An action film in the tradition of the "Angel" series, though with an unusual amount of character development, concerning a police investigation into a smuggling ring. The movie is best known for one explosive sequence, in which Moon Lee fights the bad guys from the hood of a speeding car, while her young daughter is dangled by her hair out the window.

FATHER AND SON
父子情
Year: 1981
Director: Allen Fong
Writers: Alfred Cheung, Chan Chiu, and Lilian Lee
Stars: Shek Lui, Chu Hung, Yung Wai-man

The directorial début of Allen Fong, Hong Kong's leading social-realist film-maker, from a screen story patterned somewhat on his own life. A young man from Hong Kong graduates from a United States college and learns that his father has died. He flies home for the funeral, and, in his mind, revisits his troubled relationship with his father – troubled because the father, a lowly office worker, had placed unreasonable demands on his only son to excel.

THE FINAL JUDGEMENT
紙盒藏屍之公審
Year: 1993
Director: Otto Chan
Stars: Simon Yam, Cecilia Yip, Bill Tung, Paul Chun

Drama based on the true story of a good-natured man who was falsely convicted of the sex murder of a young woman, purely on faulty scientific evidence. As the man's wife struggles to prove her husband's innocence, the murder is replayed in flashback – and in sufficiently graphic detail to earn this film a Category III rating.

THE FINAL OPTION
飛虎雄心
Year: 1994
Director: Gordon Chan
Stars: Michael Wong, Carman Lee, Peter Yung, Chan Kwok-bong,
Vindy Chan

Well-crafted film about new police recruits for Hong Kong's
version of a SWAT team, and their rigorous training at the hands
of unit leader Stone Wong (Michael Wong). The team hunts down
some cop killers, but the action is largely incidental; the film
lavishes its attention on how the young men relate to one another,
and to their wives and girlfriends, who tend to disapprove of their
high-risk profession. Nominated for Best Picture at the Hong Kong
Film Awards.

FINAL VICTORY
最後勝利
Year: 1987
Director: Patrick Tam
Producer: John Sham
Executive Producer: Dickson Poon
Writer: Wong Kar-wai
Stars: Eric Tsang, Tsui Hark, Loletta Lee, Margaret Lee

After working a job in the rough Mongkok district of Hong Kong,
Wong Kar-wai drew on his experiences to write a gangland trilogy.
Part I became his own *As Tears Go By*, Part II was never made, and
Part III was reworked by director Patrick Tam into this black
comedy, which is also notable for its award-winning performance
by Tsui Hark, as a cold, menacing gang boss on his way to jail. Eric
Tsang plays the gangster's faithful but inept buddy, who is
instructed to look after the boss's two girlfriends without tipping
them off to each other's existence. The women, naturally, are big
trouble, and Tsang makes matters worse by falling for one of them.

FIRST MISSION (*see* HEART OF THE DRAGON)

FIRST STRIKE (*aka* POLICE STORY IV)
警察故事 IV：簡單任務
Year: 1996
Director: Stanley Tong
Stars: Jackie Chan, Lau Hok-yin, Annie Wu, Bill Tung

Jackie Chan, who has played a comic Indiana Jones (*Armour of God*), now gives us a comic James Bond, in an espionage film that has little connection to the *Police Story* series of which it is ostensibly the fourth installment. In both the original Chinese print, and the dubbed and re-edited United States release, Inspector Chan jets from Hong Kong to Russia to Australia, to prevent a blackmailed CIA operative from selling a nuclear bomb to the Russian mafiya. En route, he makes an escape down a snow-covered mountain on a snowboard, fights off a group of adversaries with a stepladder, and tries out his kung-fu in a shark tank.

A FISHY STORY
不脫襪的人
Year: 1989
Director: Anthony Chan
Co-Writer: Eddie Fong
Stars: Kenny Bee, Maggie Cheung, Anthony Chan

A Fishy Story is one of the rare films to break the Hong Kong cinema's taboo against politics, by depicting the infamous Hong Kong riots of 1967. The riots, however, are mainly the backdrop to an unlikely romance between an upper-class aspiring actress and a taxi driver. The film plays as a bittersweet romance in the vein of *Breakfast at Tiffany's*.

FIST OF LEGEND
精武英雄
Year: 1994
Director: Gordon Chan
Action Director: Yuen Woo-ping
Stars: Jet Li, Chin Siu-ho, Ada Choi, Nakayama Shinobu, Yasuaki Kurata, Billy Chow, Paul Chun

In this remake of Bruce Lee's *Fist of Fury*, Jet Li plays a Chinese martial artist studying in Japan during the Japanese occupation of his homeland. When news reaches him that his master has died mysteriously, he bids his Japanese girlfriend goodbye and returns to China, where he uncovers the truth – his master was murdered. So begins a series of hand-to-hand duels, in which Jet Li is permitted to display his powerful martial-arts skills without the usual enhancement with wires. Unlike in the Bruce Lee original, the Japanese are not all bad.

FLASH FUTURE KUNG FU (*see* HEALTH WARNING)

FLIRTING SCHOLAR
唐伯虎點秋香
Year: 1993
Director: Lee Lik-chi
Stars: Stephen Chiau, Gong Li, Cheng Pei-pei, James Wong, Chan Bak-cheung, Leung Ka-yan, Gordon Liu

This pairing of Hong Kong's most popular comic actor and mainland China's number one movie goddess resulted in one of the biggest grossing films domestically in the colony's history. Chiau plays a prominent poet and scholar in Ming Dynasty China who grows bored with his eight wives, and, disguised as a peasant, sells himself to a family in order to win the love of its maiden daughter. Unfortunately, the family matriarch (Cheng Pei-pei, who starred in King Hu's 1967 classic *Dragon Gate Inn*) turns out to be a sworn enemy of Chiau's family. Many of the film's comedic highlights, including a poetry duel, are untranslatable.

FLYING DAGGER

神經刀與飛天貓

Year: 1993

Director: Chu Yin-ping

Producer: Wong Jing

Action Director: Ching Siu-tung

Stars: Tony Leung (Ka-fai), Jimmy Lin, Jacky Cheung, Maggie Cheung, Cheung Man, Gloria Yip, Ng Man-tat, Dicky Cheung

Wacky martial-arts comedy, similar in style to Wong Jing's *Holy Weapon*. In return for reward money, two male bounty hunters and two women are out to apprehend a forest bandit called Fox With Nine Tails (he grows foxtails to bind his enemies) and his flying catwoman wife. After numerous bouts of swordfighting and kung fu, the four hunters discover that the man who posted the reward is the real villain.

FONG SAI YUK

方世玉

Year: 1993

Director: Corey Yuen

Writer: Jeff Lau (uncredited)

Associate Producer: Ann Hui

Stars: Jet Li, Josephine Siao, Chu Kong, Michelle Reis, Sibelle Hu, Adam Cheng, Zhao Wen-zhou

The former child star Josephine Siao steals the show as Jet Li's kung-fu-fighting mother in this hit film. Li plays the legendary Shaolin patriot Fong Sai-yuk as a carefree young man who deliberately throws a martial-arts competition because he mistakenly believes the prize is a rich man's ugly daughter. Furious that he has lost, Fong's mother, disguised as a boy, wins the competition, and inadvertently becomes the love object of the rich man's wife. The comic tone of the film turns somber, however, when the emperor's emissary (Zhao Wen-zhou) arrests Fong's father and demands the membership list of the rebellious Red Lotus Society. Now, Fong must battle for his father's life, and the fate of China.

FONG SAI YUK II

方世玉 II：萬夫莫敵（功夫皇帝）
Year: 1993
Director: Corey Yuen
Stars: Jet Li, Josephine Siao, Michelle Reis, Corey Yuen, Adam Cheng

In this hastily made sequel, Fong is now a full-fledged member of the Red Lotus Society, in open rebellion against the Qing Dynasty. His pride and immaturity often get him into trouble, but his real problems begin when his mother comes to visit. In the well-choreographed finale, Fong must fight off a squadron of enemies while juggling a column of chairs that prop up his mother, whose neck is in a hangman's noose.

FORBIDDEN CITY COP

大內密探靈靈發
Year: 1996
Directors: Stephen Chiau and Vincent Kok
Stars: Stephen Chiau, Carina Lau, Carman Lee, Law Kar-ying

Something of a loose companion piece to *From Beijing with Love*, which finds Chiau an unlikely secret-service agent for the emperor. After being ejected from the palace because of his laziness, he redeems himself by foiling a supernatural villain's plot to kill the emperor and overthrow the government. Having been reinstated, Chiau procures a famous prostitute for the emperor, only to find himself drawn to her, to the dismay of Chiau's loving wife.

FROM BEIJING WITH LOVE

國產凌凌漆
Year: 1995
Directors: Stephen Chiau and Lee Lik-chi
Stars: Stephen Chiau, Anita Yuen, Law Kar-ying, Pauline Chan, Wong Kam-kong, Yu Rong-guang (cameo)

In this James Bond parody, Stephen Chiau is Ling Ling Chi – agent 007 – a pork vendor turned superspy for the Beijing government. With the help of a female agent (Anita Yuen), who is actually working undercover for the bad buys, Chiau is recruited to go on to Hong Kong and recover a stolen dinosaur skeleton. The comedy features a surprising amount of gore and violence – including a scene, played for laughs, in which Yuen removes a bullet from Chiau's leg – and a sendup of art-house director Wong Kar-wai's stop-motion editing style.

FROM RICHES TO RAGS
錢作怪
Year: 1979
Director and Writer: John Woo
Stars: Ricky Hui, Johnny Koo, John Woo (cameo), Richard Ng (cameo)

In one of John Woo's best-loved comedies, deadpan Ricky Hui is a working stiff who wins big at the races, only to be told by a doctor that he is terminally ill. Unable to cope with his illness, he hires an assassin to kill him, and then finds out that the doctor was mistaken. With no way to call off the killer, Hui goes on a mad run for his life, culminating in a showdown with the assassin at a mental asylum. Like many of Woo's comedies, *From Riches to Rags* is dark and almost surreal; and, in a foreshadowing of Woo's *Bullet in the Head*, the movie appropriates the Russian roulette sequence from *The Deer Hunter*.

FULL CONTACT
俠盜高飛
Year: 1992
Director and Producer: Ringo Lam
Stars: Chow Yun-fat, Simon Yam, Anthony Wong, Bonnie Fu, Ann Bridgewater, Frankie Chin

Though it failed at the box office in Hong Kong, this outrageous action movie is enormously popular with American audiences. Chow Yun-fat is Jeff, a bouncer in a Bangkok nightclub, who rescues his friend Sam from a murderous loanshark. Desperate for money, the friends agree to take part in a daylight heist with Judge, a gay sociopath (played by Simon Yam, who steals the picture); his slutty accomplice Virgin; and her beefy boyfriend Deano. But the robbery is a doublecross – Judge has been hired by the loanshark to kill Jeff, and Sam betrays his friend out of cowardice. Left for dead, Jeff is nursed back to health by monks, and then embarks for Hong Kong to take his revenge.

FULL MOON IN NEW YORK
人在紐約
Year: 1990
Director: Stanley Kwan
Stars: Maggie Cheung, Sylvia Chang, Siqin Gowa, Josephine Koo

The three faces of China meet in this drama set in New York. Maggie Cheung plays a lesbian from Hong Kong, Sylvia Chang is a Taiwanese performance artist, and Siqin Gowa is a mainland woman married to an American-born Chinese man. Though very different, the women become friends, and look to one another for help with a wide variety of problems. The movie caused a minor controversy by winning the Golden Horse for Best Picture, beating out Taiwanese director Hou Hsiao-hsien's politically charged *The Puppetmaster,* which was considered a superior film.

FULL THROTTLE
烈火戰車
Year: 1995
Director: Derek Yee
Stars: Andy Lau, Gigi Leung, David Wu, Paul Chun, Tsui Kam-kong, Chin Kar-lok

Derek Yee's follow-up to *C'est la Vie, Mon Cherie* proved to be another box-office smash. Andy Lau is a young motorcycle racer who, for a variety of reasons, is unable to compete in legitimate competition, and becomes the king of illegal road-racing in Hong Kong. Highlighted by dynamic race scenes, the film has a strong story that explores the racer's complicated relationship to his father, girlfriend, and chief rival.

GAMES GAMBLERS PLAY
鬼馬雙星
Year: 1974
Director: Michael Hui
Production Manager: John Woo
Stars: Michael Hui, Sam Hui, Roy Chiao

In the first of many successful comedies starring Michael and Sam Hui, the brothers play a pair of con men who strike up a friendship in jail. Upon their release, they embark on a series of gambling scams, ultimately inviting the wrath of an angry bookie, who sends his henchmen after Michael Hui in the film's climactic chase sequence.

GANGS
童黨
Year: 1987
Director: Larry Lau (Lawrence Ah Mon)
Stars: Ho Pui-tung, Wong Chung-cheun, Ma Hin-ting, Eleven Leung

Lawrence Ah Mon's documentary-style drama about youth gangs is considered one of the standouts of the Hong Kong new wave. Using a cast of unknowns, many with gang backgrounds, Ah Mon tells the story of gang kids on the run in the wake of a rumble that has left several dead. While dodging the police, the boys fight among themselves, as their girlfriends turn tricks to bring in money. The kidnap and rape of one of the girlfriends by another gang leads to the revenge-filled conclusion.

GOD OF GAMBLERS
賭神
Year: 1989
Director and Writer: Wong Jing
Producers: Charles Heung and Jimmy Heung
Stars: Chow Yun-fat, Andy Lau, Joey Wong, Charles Heung, Cheung Man, Shing Fui-on

In this action-comedy classic, Chow Yun-fat plays a clairvoyant gambler who never loses at cards, dice, or mahjong. After a head injury leaves him with the personality of a child, he is taken in by con man Andy Lau, who soon discovers and tries to exploit Chow's gambling abilities, which have remained intact. As an innocent boy in a man's body, Chow gets to show off the full range of his acting skills.

GOD OF GAMBLERS II
賭俠
Year: 1990
Director: Wong Jing
Producers: Charles Heung and Jimmy Heung
Stars: Andy Lau, Stephen Chiau, Cheung Man, Ng Man-tat, Charles Heung, Shing Fui-on

Having starred in *All for the Winner*, a parody of *God of Gamblers*, the comedian Stephen Chiau replaces Chow Yun-fat in this sequel. Villains from Part I are out for vengeance, and Andy Lau teams up with Chiau, the Saint of Gamblers, to fend them off. More of a screwball comedy than the original.

GOD OF GAMBLERS III: BACK TO SHANGHAI
賭俠 II 之上海灘賭聖
Year: 1991
Director: Wong Jing
Action Director: Yuen Woo-ping
Stars: Stephen Chiau, Ng Man-tat, Gong Li, Ray Lui, Sandra Ng, Charles Heung, Cheung Man (cameo), Wong Jing (cameo)

Supernatural villains transport Stephen Chiau to the Shanghai of the 1930s, where he helps a gang boss defeat his rivals, and meanwhile falls in love with the identical twin sister of the boss's girlfriend. (Both sisters are played by mainland movie goddess Gong Li.) Though Chow Yun-fat and Andy Lau are absent from this sequel, movie executive Charles Heung reprises his role, from Parts I and II, of a faithful bodyguard; here he helps out Chiau from present-day Hong Kong, via cellular phone.

GOD OF GAMBLERS' RETURN
賭神續集
Year: 1994
Director: Wong Jing
Stars: Chow Yun-fat, Tony Leung (Ka-fai), Chingmy Yau, Wu Xing-guo, Xie Miao, Cheung Man, Wu Chien-lien, Charles Heung, Blackie Ko, Tsui Kam-kong

In one of his final Hong Kong films before his move to Los Angeles, Chow Yun-fat returns as the God of Gamblers. Though a box-office smash in Asia, this film is a mix of genres – from splatter to madcap farce – that is certain to baffle the uninitiated American viewer. In the opening sequence, a mad Taiwanese gambler and his henchmen disembowel Chow's pregnant wife, whose dying wish is that Chow not reveal his identity as the God of Gamblers for a year. Chow travels through China, where he meets an odd assortment of characters, and ultimately ends up at a casino in Taiwan for a showdown with his wife's murderer.

THE GOLDEN GIRLS
山水有相逢
Year: 1995
Director: Joe Ma
Stars: Anita Yuen, Lau Ching-wan, Ada Choi, Pauline Suen, Allen Fong (cameo), Francis Ng (cameo), Vincent Kok (cameo), Lee Lik-chi (cameo)

Hong Kong's favorite romantic couple, Anita Yuen and Lau Ching-wan, pair up in this lightweight comedy, set in the 1960s. Yuen is a flat-chested movie actress who leaves town a failure, while her fuller-figured but less talented friend becomes a star. Lau, a smitten writer whom Yuen has left behind, takes up with the friend in her absence. Yuen then makes a triumphant return to the screen dressed as a man, and wins back Lau's heart.

GREEN SNAKE
青蛇
Year: 1993
Director: Tsui Hark
Stars: Maggie Cheung, Joey Wong, Wu Xing-guo, Zhao Wen-zhou

One of Tsui Hark's most expensive films, and one of his biggest flops, *Green Snake* has acquired a cult following in the West. The thousand-year-old White Snake (Joey Wong), and the five-hundred-year-old Green Snake (Maggie Cheung) try to evolve spiritually and physically to become women. Wong falls in love with an uptight scholar, while Cheung courts disaster by enraging a self-righteous priest bent on keeping humans and nonhumans separate. Based on a famous Chinese fable.

GUNMEN
天羅地網
Year: 1988
Director: Kirk Wong
Producer: Tsui Hark
Stars: Tony Leung (Ka-fai), Waise Lee, Carrie Ng, Elizabeth Lee, David Wu, Adam Cheng

In this spinoff of Brian DePalma's *The Untouchables*, set in 1930s Shanghai, Tony Leung plays a young war veteran turned policeman. Appalled to discover that the police force is turning a blind eye to opium smugglers, he recruits several war buddies and wages a violent campaign against the drug dealers. Carrie Ng plays Leung's loving but jealous wife, who mistakenly believes that her husband is having an affair with a prostitute informant.

GUN-N-ROSE
龍騰四海
Year: 1992
Director: Clarence Fok
Stars: Alan Tang, Andy Lau, Simon Yam, Leon Lai, Carrie Ng

When a Taiwanese gangster turns over the reins of his criminal enterprise to his adopted son, played by veteran actor Alan Tang, his two biological sons are enraged to have been passed over, and the family is torn apart. The father is killed, and Tang flees for his life, to Hong Kong, where he befriends a small-time hood and his sister, before returning home for a final confrontation with one of his step-brothers. A film that anticipates some of the more outrageous elements of Fok's follow-up feature, the cult classic *Naked Killer*.

H

HANDSOME SIBLINGS
絕代雙驕
Year: 1992
Director: Eric Tsang
Stars: Andy Lau, Brigitte Lin, Cheung Man, Ng Man-tat, Deannie Yip, Anita Yuen, Francis Ng

Period comedy-action film set in Tang Dynasty China. A swords-man is nearly killed when his wife tries to imprison eight of the Ten Untouchable Villains for a crime they did not commit. The eight escape, and raise up the warlord's son; eighteen years later, the son (Andy Lau) enters a martial-arts competition, and teams up with his step-sister (Brigitte Lin), in an attempt to clear the names of his eight guardians. Based on a novel by the prolific Gu Lung.

HARD-BOILED
辣手神探
Year: 1992
Director: John Woo
Producers: Terence Chang and Lynda Kuk
Writer: Barry Wong
Stars: Chow Yun-fat, Tony Leung (Chiu-wai), Teresa Mo, Anthony
Wong, Philip Kwok, Philip Chan, Kwan Hoi-shan, Bowie Lam,
John Woo (cameo)

Chow Yun-fat is Tequila, a renegade cop in the Dirty Harry mold,
itching to get revenge after his partner is killed in a shootout.
Meanwhile, his police chief has placed an undercover agent (Tony
Leung) inside the organization of Tequila's hated enemy, a triad
boss in the arms-smuggling business. Tension heats up as Tequila
moves in on his target, and he and Leung team up for a high-body-
count showdown at a local hospital, where a cache of weapons has
been secreted. John Woo has a small role as a sage bartender.

HARD-BOILED II (see THE LAST BLOOD)

HAUNTED COP SHOP II
猛鬼學堂
Year: 1988
Director: Jeff Lau
Stars: Jacky Cheung, Ricky Hui, Sandy Lam, Wong Kar-wai
(cameo)

One of the better-known examples of a Hong Kong subgenre – the
ghost story-comedy – and no relation at all to Part I. Jacky Cheung
and Ricky Hui are members of an elite police force assigned to stop
some bloodthirsty vampires in a large apartment complex. They
resort to a variety of unorthodox tactics, including having sex with
the undead, and urinating to complete an electrical circuit. The art-
house director Wong Kar-wai, a close associate of Jeff Lau, makes a
cameo appearance as a cop.

HE AIN'T HEAVY, HE'S MY FATHER
新難兄難弟
Year: 1993
Directors: Peter Chan and Lee Chi-ngai
Stars: Tony Leung (Chiu-wai), Tony Leung (Ka-fai), Carina Lau,
Anita Yuen, Waise Lee, Chor Yuen, Lawrence Cheng, Michael
Chow, Anita Lee, Lawrence Ng

The production company UFO (United Filmmakers Organization),
then relatively new, scored a hit with this gentle nostalgia piece,
which seems to have been inspired by *Back to the Future*. After a
principled and generous father (Tony Leung Ka-fai) lapses into a
coma, his greedy and self-centered son (Tony Leung Chiu-wai)
plunges into a wishing well, and is transported thirty years back in
time. He encounters his father as a young man his own age, comes
to understand him better, and finds his selfish nature crumbling.

HEALTH WARNING (*aka* FLASH FUTURE KUNG FU)
打擂台
Year: 1983
Director: Kirk Wong
Stars: Ray Lui, Wang Lung-wei, Eddie Ko

Grim allegory set in the near future, in which noble kung-fu
warriors are the last bastion against the neo-Nazis, who are
attempting to kill or lobotomize all their opponents. After their
kung-fu school is destroyed through the treachery of two sex-
crazed Nazi women, Ray Lui and Wang Lung-wei storm the Nazi
fortress. Kirk Wong uses stark photography and low-tech hard-
ware to create his depressing vision of a world gone mad.

HEART OF THE DRAGON (*aka* FIRST MISSION)
龍的心
Year: 1985
Director: Sammo Hung
Producers: Chua Lam and Wu Ma
Stars: Sammo Hung, Jackie Chan, Mang Hoi, Wu Ma, Lam Ching-ying, Emily Chu, Dick Wei, Melvin Wong, James Tien, Yuen Wah

Jackie Chan is a policeman who forsakes his dream of sailing the world in order to care for his mentally handicapped brother, played by Sammo Hung. When the uncomprehending Hung accidentally acquires a case of stolen jewelry, he finds himself hunted by criminals and the police. A movie that veers closer to drama than the typical Chan and Hung collaboration.

HEAVEN CAN'T WAIT
救世神棍
Year: 1995
Director: Lee Chi-ngai
Stars: Tony Leung (Chiu-wai), Jordan Chan, Karen Mok, Bowie Lam

Tony Leung is Fung, a huckster who pulls off the ultimate coup when he convinces Hong Kong that a simpleton he has found performing in a passion play is a genuine faith healer. With the help of a greedy news reporter (Karen Mok), Fung bilks the gullible out of loads of money; but matters take a precarious turn when a gangster tries to muscle in on the con. Another morality play from UFO.

HER FATAL WAYS
表姐，妳好嘢！
Year: 1990
Director: Alfred Cheung
Stars: Carol Cheng, Alfred Cheung, Tony Leung (Ka-fai), Michael Chow

In this well-regarded comedy, with shades of *Ninotchka*, a mainland policewoman (Carol Cheng) has been assigned to escort a criminal to Hong Kong to face charges. Unfortunately, the criminal escapes, and Cheng must help Hong Kong cop Tony Leung recapture him. Plenty of fish-out-of-water jokes as Cheng tries to comprehend the Hong Kong lifestyle in terms of the Class Struggle. The film almost threatens to become political allegory, but plays it safe. Three sequels followed.

HEROES SHED NO TEARS
英雄無淚
Year: 1987
Director: John Woo
Stars: Eddie Ko, Lam Ching-ying, Chien Yuet-san

After the success of *A Better Tomorrow*, this John Woo actioner, which had gone unreleased for five years, was re-edited and reissued by Golden Harvest. A mercenary (Eddie Ko) and his comrades set out to capture a drug-dealing general in Northern Thailand, and bring him back to Hong Kong to face justice. Getting the general proves the easy part; Ko and his expedition (which, inexplicably, includes his young son and elderly grandfather) must now escape the general's forces, and the local tribes under military control.

THE HEROIC TRIO
東方三俠
Year: 1993
Director: Johnny To
Producer and Action Director: Ching Siu-tung
Stars: Michelle Yeoh, Maggie Cheung, Anita Mui, Damian Lau, James Pak, Anthony Wong, Paul Chun

Reunification allegory masquerading as an eye-popping comic book of a movie. Anita Mui is Wonder Woman, a superheroine in the Hong Kong of the future, who has been called upon to stop the wave of kidnappings of male infants from a local hospital. The perpetrator is the Invisible Woman (Michelle Yeoh), who has been coopted into working for an aging supernatural eunuch with a scheme for world domination. Maggie Cheung, meanwhile, is the Thief Catcher, a high-priced mercenary hired to recover the baby of the police chief. The three women ultimately join forces in a struggle for survival.

THE HEROIC TRIO II (*see* EXECUTIONERS)

HE'S A WOMAN, SHE'S A MAN
金枝玉葉
Year: 1994
Director: Peter Chan
Stars: Leslie Cheung, Anita Yuen, Carina Lau, Eric Tsang, Jordan Chan, Law Kar-ying

Anita Yuen copped her second Best Actress prize at the Hong Kong Film Awards in UFO's most popular film to date. Yuen is a working girl obsessed with a famous pop singer (Carina Lau). When the singer's husband and producer (Leslie Cheung) announces an open audition for a new male singer, Yuen disguises herself as a boy just to get a few moments with her idol, and, to her astonishment, she is selected as the winning vocalist. Cheung soon begins to question his sexual orientation, as he finds himself falling for his new protégé.

HIGH RISK
鼠膽龍威
Year: 1995
Director, Producer, and Writer: Wong Jing
Action Director: Corey Yuen
Stars: Jet Li, Jacky Cheung, Chingmy Yau, Charlie Yeung, Valerie Chow, Wu Ma

A merciless Jackie Chan sendup, with shades of *Die Hard*. Jet Li is Kit, a despondent ex-cop who finds work as the bodyguard – and uncredited stunt double – for Frankie, Asia's number one movie star, played by Jacky Cheung. Frankie, who is famous for supposedly doing all his own stunts, is not only a fraud, but a lush and womanizer to boot. When terrorists take control of a posh high-rise, it is up to Kit to storm the building and save the hostages – including Frankie, who must overcome his cowardice and live up to his image at last.

HOLY WEAPON

武俠七公主

Year: 1993

Directors: Dennis Chan (uncredited) and Wong Jing

Action Director: Ching Siu-tung

Stars: Michelle Yeoh, Maggie Cheung, Sandra Ng, Cheung Man, Carol Cheng, Ng Man-tat, Damian Lau, Simon Yam, Dicky Cheung

A mad martial-arts comedy that could have come only from Hong Kong, and that virtually defies description. In Ming Dynasty China, the swordsman Mo Kake takes an invisibility drug, which enables him to wound Japan's fiercest fighter, but which also causes him to lose his sanity. Three years later, the Japanese warrior is back, and it will take the combined forces of a group of women – performed by some of Hong Kong's top actresses – to defeat him once and for all.

HOMECOMING

似水流年

Year: 1984

Director: Yim Ho

Stars: Siqin Gowa, Josephine Koo

Poignant story about a harried Hong Kong woman who decides to take a break by returning to the mainland village where she grew up. She is reunited with her two former best friends, who are now married to each other, and comes to discover that there is much to cherish in small-town life. Underlying concerns about the reunification of Hong Kong and China are intelligently drawn out.

HONG KONG 1941
等待黎明
Year: 1984
Director: Leong Po-chih
Producer: John Sham
Writer: John Chan
Stars: Chow Yun-fat, Cecilia Yip, Alex Man, Leong Po-chih, Wu Ma

Chow Yun-fat copped the Golden Horse for Best Actor in this drama, as a drifter who befriends a young couple in Hong Kong during World War II. The Japanese occupation shatters their brief happiness, and, amid a climate of inhumanity and opportunism, they plot their escape to America, leading them to a fateful encounter at sea with a Japanese gunboat. Director Leong Po-chih tells the story as a flashback, in nostalgic gold hues, with an unusual attentiveness to character and plot.

HU-DU-MEN (*aka* STAGE DOOR)
虎渡門
Year: 1996
Director: Shu Kei
Producer: Raymond Chow
Executive Producer: Clifton Ko
Writer: Raymond To
Stars: Josephine Siao, Anita Yuen, David Wu, Waise Lee, Danny Chan

Based on a popular stage play, this acclaimed new film tells the story of a famous Cantonese opera performer (Josephine Siao) on the eve of her retirement. As she and her family prepare to emigrate to Australia, she has to come to terms with her daughter's lesbianism, and the surprise arrival of a son she gave up at birth to further her career. Siao, fresh from her award-winning role in *Summer Snow*, turns in another strong performance. The title is an opera term for the line which separates the stage from the real world.

HUNTING LIST

終極獵殺

Year: 1994

Director: Chu Yen-ping

Stars: Ray Lui, Paul Chun, Tan Lap-man

Unexpectedly grim crime story from the Taiwanese director Chu Yen-ping, concerning a criminal's return to Hong Kong after several years on the lam in Taiwan. Once back, he rekindles a friendship with a drug dealer and an old flame. When the drug dealer kills a rival gang member, the murder sets off an escalating chain of violence.

I

ICEMAN COMETH (*aka* TIME WARRIORS)

急凍奇俠

Year: 1989

Director: Clarence Fok

Writers: Stephen Shiu and Johnny Mak

Stars: Yuen Biao, Yuen Wah, Maggie Cheung

Two of Jackie Chan's former schoolmates, Yuen Biao and Yuen Wah, play good and evil ancient Chinese swordsmen, respectively, who are transported to the present day via a Buddhist "time wheel." They are frozen alive in a glacier until they are rescued by arctic scientists, at which point they carry on their duel across modern Hong Kong. Yuen Biao is aided by Maggie Cheung, whom he is too naïve to realize is a prostitute.

I LOVE MARIA (*aka* ROBOFORCE)
鐵甲無敵馬利亞
Year: 1988
Director: David Chung
Producers: Tsui Hark and John Sham
Action Director: Ching Siu-tung
Stars: Sally Yeh, Tsui Hark, John Sham, Tony Leung (Chiu-wai),
Lam Ching-ying

In this science-fiction comedy, Sally Yeh plays Maria, the villainous
leader of a robot force planning world domination. When one of
her robots, which happens to look just like her, falls into the hands
of a secret-service man and an ex-gang member – Tsui Hark and
John Shum, respectively – they reprogram her as a force for good,
leading to a showdown between the real Maria and her mechanical
double.

IN THE LINE OF DUTY (*see* YES, MADAM!)

IN THE LINE OF DUTY II (*see* ROYAL WARRIORS)

IRON ANGELS (*see* ANGEL)

IRON MONKEY
少年黃飛鴻之鐵馬騮
Year: 1993
Director: Yuen Woo-ping
Producer: Tsui Hark
Stars: Donnie Yen, Yu Rong-guang, Jean Wong

The Iron Monkey is an herbal doctor turned people's hero in
corrupt Qing Dynasty China, whose principal nemesis, an evil
Manchu official called the Monk, is bent on capturing him. When
all else fails, the Monk kidnaps the young Wong Fei-hung (the
future hero of Tsui Hark's *Once upon a Time in China* series), to
try to compel Wong's father, a martial-arts master, to catch his
elusive prey. Non-stop action and wire-enhanced acrobatics helped

make this film a cult favorite in the United States, despite a poor showing in Hong Kong.

ISLAND OF FIRE
火燒島
Year: 1991
Director: Chu Yen-ping
Producer: Jimmy Wang Yu
Stars: Jimmy Wang Yu, Jackie Chan, Sammo Hung, Andy Lau, Tony Leung (Ka-fai)

Jimmy Wang Yu, the Taiwanese star of the 1960s Shaw Brothers classic *The One-Armed Swordsman*, assembled a powerhouse cast – including Jackie Chan, in a rare ensemble role – for this gritty prison movie. Tony Leung is a cop who goes undercover as a prisoner to expose an assassination ring that sends convicts on suicide missions. The John Woo-style finale pits several of the prisoners against a small army.

IT'S A WONDERFUL LIFE
大富之家
Year: 1994
Director: Clifton Ko
Producer: Raymond Wong
Writer: Raymond To
Stars: Leslie Cheung, Teresa Mo, Tony Leung (Ka-fai), Anita Yuen, Raymond Wong, Fung Bo-bo, Carol Cheng, Kwan Tak-hing, Lau Ching-wan

Another New Year's comedy from Raymond Wong, with the familiar theme of siblings searching for love. Teresa Mo plays a young woman returning to Hong Kong from the States, with a platonic friend in tow, and with no patience for her family's plans to marry her off to a cousin; Tony Leung is her stuttering brother, a comic-book artist with a crush on a schoolteacher. Comic high-lights include a musical parody of *Jurassic Park*.

IT'S NOW OR NEVER
飛女正傳
Year: 1992
Director: Louis Chan
Stars: Cheung Man, Ng Man-tat, Cynthia Khan, Alfred Cheung

Campy 1960s drama about a girl gang led by Cheung Man. As her gang gets in and out of trouble, Cheung finds herself strategically romancing a timid policeman and trying to save her gigolo father from a violent loanshark. This film is less about plot than it is about catfights, big hair, and leather jackets.

I WANT TO GO ON LIVING
我要活下去
Year: 1995
Director: Raymond Lee
Producer: Raymond Wong
Stars: Sylvia Chang, Anita Yuen, Winston Chao

Sylvia Chang plays a woman who is married off to a Chinese restaurant owner in England. The marriage is a failure, however, and Chang takes off for Hong Kong with her estranged husband's paralyzed daughter (Anita Yuen), to call on her wealthy relatives. Because Chang has no records to prove her family ties, she marries a lawyer (Winston Chiao), and meanwhile seeks treatment for Yuen to help her walk again. Based on a popular novel by Leung Fung-yi.

J

JUST HEROES
義膽群英
Year: 1989
Directors: John Woo and Wu Ma
Producer: Tsui Hark
Executive Producer: Chang Cheh
Stars: Wu Ma, Danny Lee, Stephen Chiau, David Chiang, Shing Fui-on, Ti Lung (cameo)

As a benefit for the Hong Kong directors union, Woo and Wu

collaborated on this unremarkable heroic-bloodshed film about two triad families vying for power after a gang leader is murdered. While there is a surprising dearth of action until the end, the film is at least notable for an early serious performance by the superstar comic Stephen Chiau.

K

KAWASHIMA YOSHIKO (*aka* THE LAST PRINCESS OF MANCHURIA)

川島芳子
Year: 1990
Director: Eddie Fong
Writer: Lilian Lee
Stars: Anita Mui, Andy Lau

Lilian Lee, who adapted her novel *Farewell My Concubine* for the screen, does the same for this tale of a Manchurian princess sent to Japan as a young girl and renamed Kawashima Yoshiko. When Japan invades China in the 1930s, Yoshiko – now a grown woman, played by Anita Mui – returns to China as a military official, and is ultimately tried for treason by her native land. Andy Lau plays an actor who drifts in and out of Mui's life. The video and film prints have wildly divergent endings: in the former, Mui is executed, but in the latter, she ends up in her dotage living in the United States.

THE KILLER

喋血雙雄
Year: 1989
Director and Writer: John Woo
Producer: Tsui Hark
Action Director: Ching Siu-tung
Stars: Chow Yun-fat, Danny Lee, Shing Fui-on, Sally Yeh, Chu Kong

The most famous of all Cantonese-language movies concerns a hired assassin (Chow Yun-fat) who accidentally blinds a nightclub singer (Sally Yeh) during what was to have been his final job. Danny Lee plays the disgruntled cop who tries to track down the killer through the singer, whom Chow has befriended in order to right his wrong. When a power-crazed former client tries to kill Chow in order to silence him, the hit man and the cop find themselves on the same side. Along with *Bullet in the Head*, this is Woo's strongest statement on the bonds of brotherhood.

KILLER'S ROMANCE
自由人
Year: 1989
Director: Phillip Ko
Stars: Simon Yam, Joey Wong

Simon Yam is an ace assassin who lives in England with his foster father, a Japanese gang leader. When the father is murdered, Yam sets out for revenge, and meanwhile becomes romantically involved with college student Joey Wong, who witnessed one of his hits. Soon Yam and his girlfriend are targeted for death by his father's real killers, who are not the ones he suspected. Loosely based on the Japanese anime *Crying Freeman*, and shot on location in the United Kingdom, the movie features some gruesome swordfighting, along with plenty of gunplay and kung-fu.

KING OF BEGGARS
武狀元：蘇乞兒
Year: 1993
Director: Gordon Chan
Stars: Stephen Chiau, Ng Man-tat, Cheung Man, Tsui Siu-keung, Chan Bak-cheung, Yuen Woo-ping

Hong Kong comic Stephen Chiau plays a rich playboy in love with a female revolutionary who, to get rid of him, persuades him to vie for the title of Martial Arts Scholar in Peking. Chiau surprisingly wins the physical competition, but cheats on the written exam – he's illiterate – and, as a punishment, the Emperor strips him and his father of all their wealth. Chiau soon finds himself the King of Beggars, and, through the use of some new martial-arts techniques, returns to win back his title and the woman he loves.

KING OF CHESS
棋王
Year: 1991
Directors: Yim Ho and Tsui Hark
Producer: Tsui Hark
Associate Producer: Hou Hsiao-hsien
Writers: Yim Ho and Tony Leung (Ka-fai)
Stars: Tony Leung (Ka-fai), John Sham, Yong Lin, John Chan

Though Yim Ho has essentially disowned this film – he walked off the project because of discord with co-director Tsui Hark – it does not lack admirers. *King of Chess* tells two separate stories: the first concerns a child chess prodigy who becomes a television sensation in modern-day Taipei, and the second, told in flashback, deals with an adult chess grandmaster who is persecuted during the Cultural Revolution in the China of the 1960s. The political content of the latter tale is considered daring by Hong Kong standards.

KUNG FU CULT MASTER
倚天屠龍記
Year: 1993
Director: Wong Jing
Producer: Charles Heung
Action Director: Sammo Hung
Stars: Jet Li, Chingmy Yau, Cheung Man, Sammo Hung, Richard Ng, Ngai Sing

Clan leaders seeking possession of a magical sword inflict a delayed death wound on a boy named Mo-kai and slaughter his parents. He is adopted by a powerful master (Sammo Hung), who keeps the boy alive by imparting his own internal energy. The adult Mo-kai, played by Jet Li, finally heals his childhood wound when he tricks a martial artist into teaching him the mysterious "solar" fighting stance, leaving him well prepared to take revenge against the murderous clans. Despite impressive wire-enhanced fight choreography, the film did surprisingly poorly at the box office, and a sequel that might have tied up many of the loose ends was cancelled.

L

LADY IN BLACK
奪命佳人
Year: 1986
Director: Sun Chung
Producer: Dean Shek
Stars: Brigitte Lin, Tony Leung (Ka-fai), Philip Kwok

Tony Leung is Brigitte Lin's sleazy husband, who cons her into embezzling a large sum of money from her company, ostensibly for a sure-fire stock investment. When he loses the money gambling, the couple take a trip to Taiwan to beg for money from Leung's rich uncle. Leung turns desperate when he is refused, and throws his wife off of a boat on the return trip home. Lin doesn't die, however; she returns to Hong Kong mute and disfigured, and sets a violent revenge scheme in motion.

LAI SHI, CHINA'S LAST EUNUCH
中國最後一個太監
Year: 1988
Director: Jacob Cheung
Producer: Sammo Hung
Writer: Eddie Fong
Stars: Max Mok, Andy Lau, Lam Ching-ying, Irene Wan, Sammo Hung, Wu Ma

In this strange historical drama, a nine-year-old boy in the Shantung Province of China chooses to become a eunuch in hopes of serving the emperor and lifting his family out of poverty. Unfortunately, just as the deed is done, the Manchus are overthrown by the forces of Republicanism, and the emperor is exiled. As a young adult, the protagonist (Max Mok) labors as an opera singer, before finding his place with the emperor in the Forbidden City. He ultimately leaves to try his hand at romance, and finds himself competing with a suave rebel (Andy Lau) for the affections of a woman.

THE LAST BLOOD (*aka* HARD-BOILED II)
驚天十二小時
Year: 1990
Director: Wong Jing
Stars: Andy Lau, Alan Tam, Eric Tsang

An assassination attempt on the Dalai Lama leaves him and an innocent young woman in dire need of blood transfusions; by an odd coincidence, both victims share the same extremely rare blood type. The would-be assassins get a list of all the possible donors, and begin picking them off one by one, until only Eric Tsang is left. It is up to a gung-ho cop (Alan Tam) and the woman's gangster boyfriend (Andy Lau) to keep the last donor alive.

LAST HERO IN CHINA
鐵雞鬥蜈蚣
Year: 1993
Director: Wong Jing
Action Director: Yuen Woo-ping
Stars: Jet Li, Cheung Man, Gordon Liu, Chan Bak-cheung, Yuen King-tan (cameo)

Jet Li, who played the Cantonese folk hero Wong Fei-hung in the popular *Once upon a Time in China* series, plays him for laughs in this well-regarded, action-filled parody. Wong is experiencing financial troubles, and is forced to relocate his kung-fu academy next to a brothel. Soon he is drawn into a violent confrontation with the Boxer Society, which has been kidnapping young women and selling them into prostitution.

LAST HURRAH FOR CHIVALRY
豪俠
Year: 1977
Director and Writer: John Woo
Stars: Wei Pai, Lee Hoi-san, Damian Lau

Considered by many fans to be the best of John Woo's martial-arts films. On his wedding day, a man's family is slaughtered by an arch-villain, and he hires two mercenaries to exact justice. The two fighters storm the villain's fortress, and take on a variety of martial-arts masters before achieving their goal. Numerous betrayals and plot twists keep the story ever from becoming predictable.

THE LAST PRINCESS OF MANCHURIA (*see* KAWASHIMA YOSHIKO)

LEGEND OF THE MOUNTAIN
山中傳奇
Year: 1979
Director: King Hu
Stars: Sylvia Chang, Hsu Feng

Filmed back-to-back with *Raining in the Mountain*, with the same sumptuous cinematography and many of the same actors. A young scholar picks up a Buddhist scripture from a monastery in order to have it translated. Soon he discovers that the sutra, as rumored, may have the power to conjure spirits, as strange people appear and vanish during his journey. Matters turn worse after he arrives at a villa, where the spirit world lies in wait for him.

LONG ARM OF THE LAW
省港旗兵
Year: 1984
Director: Johnny Mak
Producers: Sammo Hung and Johnny Mak
Writer: Philip Chan
Stars: Lam Wai, Wong Kin, Kong Lung, Chan King

In this celebrated crime thriller, mainland gang members illegally cross the border to Hong Kong to pull off a jewelry heist. En route back to the border, they kill an undercover cop, setting the entire police force at their heels. In a further mishap, the buyer of their stolen jewels is a police informant who fingers them, leading to a bloody showdown. Mak cast unknowns, and consulted with mainland gangs, to create an air of realism unusual in the Hong Kong cinema.

LONG ARM OF THE LAW II
省港旗兵 II
Year: 1987
Director: Michael Mak
Producer: Johnny Mak
Stars: Tsui Kam-kong, Alex Man, Ben Lam

Johnny Mak's brother Michael took over the directing reins for the second installment, which is not a sequel. Hong Kong police detectives try to deal with the growing problem of mainland gangs by sending three convicts undercover. The convicts, unfortunately, have plans of their own; presently, the cop escorting them is hung upside-down, tortured with rats, and decapitated.

LONG ARM OF THE LAW III
省港旗兵 III
Year: 1989
Director: Michael Mak
Producer: Johnny Mak
Stars: Andy Lau, Max Mok, Elizabeth Lee, Tsui Kam-kong

Another crime film centered on illegal immigrants from south China. Andy Lau is a mainlander who escapes a death sentence for a crime he did not commit, and ends up in Hong Kong, with a Red Army captain on his tail. A fellow immigrant (Elizabeth Lee) is kidnapped and forced into prostitution, and Lau must try to rescue her while evading capture himself.

LORD OF EAST CHINA SEA
上海皇帝
Year: 1993
Director: Poon Man-kit
Producers: Raymond Chow, Johnny Mak, and Stephen Siu
Writers: Johnny Mak and Stephen Siu
Stars: Ray Lui, Kent Cheng, Carina Lau, Cecilia Yip, Tsui Kam-kong, Lam Wai, Ken Tong, Miu Kiu-wai, Ching Siu-lung, Ho Ka-kui, Wong Siu

Historical epic about a fruit vendor (Ray Lui) who manages to become a powerful triad during the early 1900s. Lui gains favor with the local Shanghai police chief (Kent Cheng), who asks him to help foil an opium shipment; instead, the fruit vendor corrupts the police officer, putting them both in the drug business. Cecilia Yip is a songstress, and Lui's sometimes girlfriend.

LOVE AMONG THE TRIAD
愛在黑社會的日子
Year: 1993
Director: Andy Chin
Stars: Rosamund Kwan, Cecilia Yip, Simon Yam, Veronica Yip, Wan Yuen-ming, Pauline Wong

Unusual combination of gangster film and woman's drama, in which triad kingpin Simon Yam romances Rosamund Kwan in order to effect a gangland merger. His real love interest is his brother's mistress, the glamorous singer Cecilia Yip. The brother's wife, meanwhile, is intent on ending her husband's affair. Amid the obligatory gang fights, most of emphasis lies on the troubled love lives of the protagonists.

LOVE AND THE CITY
都市情緣
Year: 1994
Director: Jeff Lau
Stars: Leon Lai, Wu Chien-lien, Ng Man-tat

Unexpected change of pace from king of comedy Jeff Lau. Leon Lai plays a young hood with a chip on his shoulder because of his troubled relationship with his weak father. When the father, a widower, plans to remarry, his prospective wife's daughter fakes being raped by Lai in order to scuttle the wedding. Lai, meanwhile, steals the girlfriend of a triad boss, setting off a chain of violence.

LOVE, GUNS AND GLASS
玻璃槍的愛
Year: 1995
Director: Ivan Lai
Stars: Simon Yam, Cecilia Yip, Roy Cheung, Farini Cheung

Drug-smuggler Simon Yam gets out of jail, and attempts to rebuild his life after he is rejected by both his wife and daughter. He finds romance with Cecilia Yip, who owes money to triads because her manufacturing business is failing. Against his wishes, Yam is drawn back into a life of violence, in order to protect Yip from the very gangster he once disfigured in a fight.

LOVE IN A FALLEN CITY
傾城之戀
Year: 1984
Director: Ann Hui
Art Director: Tony Au
Stars: Cora Miao, Chow Yun-fat

Art-house director Ann Hui traces her commercial decline from the financial failure of this adaptation of a novel by Eileen Chang (the Shanghai writer whose *Red Rose, White Rose* was brought to the screen by Hui's former assistant director Stanley Kwan). Amid the fall of Shanghai in the 1940s, fate brings Cora Miao into the life of rich playboy Chow Yun-fat. The war drives them both to Hong Kong, where they continue their romance.

LOVE IN THE TIME OF TWILIGHT
花月佳期
Year: 1995
Director: Tsui Hark
Stars: Nicky Wu, Charlie Yeung, Eric Kot, Law Kar-ying

An aspiring opera singer (Charlie Yeung) and a banker (Nicky Wu) loathe each other in life, but are drawn together after Wu is killed by a bank robber. In a quest to regain his earthly corpus, Wu's spirit persuades Yeung to travel back in time with him to the day he was killed. The couple succeed at last in getting the robber killed instead; but then the criminal's restless spirit begins to wreak havoc on their lives. A romantic comedy from the versatile Tsui Hark.

LOVE MASSACRE
愛殺
Year: 1981
Director: Patrick Tam
Writer: Joyce Chan
Music: Patrick Tam and Joyce Chan
Stars: Brigitte Lin, Charlie Chin, Zhang Gouzhu, Deannie Yip

An unlikely slasher film from art-house director Patrick Tam. In San Francisco, Brigitte Lin is carrying on a relationship with two men, one of whom goes berserk, and graphically murders the women who live in Lin's dorm building.

LOVE ON DELIVERY
破壞之王
Year: 1994
Director: Lee Lik-chi
Stars: Stephen Chiau, Christy Chung, Ng Man-tat, Jacky Cheung (cameo)

Stephen Chiau is a timid delivery boy in love with Christy Chung, who, he learns, abhors cowards. With the aid of con man Ng Man-tat, he learns how to be a superhero, and, clad in a Garfield mask, he saves Chung from a masher. Unfortunately, a Japanese karate expert takes the credit, and Chiau must challenge him to hand-to-hand combat in order to win back the girl.

THE LOVERS (*aka* BUTTERFLY LOVERS)
梁祝
Year: 1994
Director: Tsui Hark
Stars: Charlie Yeung, Nicky Wu, Carrie Ng

A young upper-class girl (Charlie Yeung) is sent off to school disguised as a boy, where she befriends a poor student (Nicky Wu), who is confused by his attraction to the "new guy." Soon the truth is revealed, and the two fall in love, but unfortunately, Yeung is to be married off to someone else for political reasons; so she and her lover conspire to join hands in death. Based on a famous Chinese story, previously adapted by King Hu in the 1960s drama *Love Eternal*.

LOVE UNTO WASTE
地下情
Year: 1986
Director: Stanley Kwan
Stars: Tony Leung (Chiu-wai), Chow Yun-fat, Elaine Kam

Downbeat movie about three friends whose lives are shattered when a fourth friend is murdered. Chow Yun-fat is the police officer who tails the friends, not because he suspects them, but because he is lonely and secretly very ill. The three friends eventually travel to Taiwan to visit the murdered woman's family. Chow and Leung, who years later acted opposite one another in John Woo's *Hard-Boiled*, turn in strong performances.

LOVING YOU
無味神探
Year: 1995
Director: Johnny To
Stars: Lau Ching-wan, Carman Lee

Johnny To, the director responsible for the comic-book fantasy *The Heroic Trio* and its sequel, shifts gears in this realistic crime drama. Lau Ching-wan is a hard-driving cop whose arrogance has alienated both his wife (Carman Lee) and his colleagues. Just after his wife informs him that she is pregnant by another man, he is ambushed by a criminal and shot in the head. He recovers slowly, and tries to reconcile with his wife and co-workers, before the criminal returns for the action-packed finale.

M

MACK THE KNIFE (*aka* DOCTOR MACK)

流氓醫生

Year: 1995

Director and Producer: Lee Chi-ngai

Stars: Tony Leung (Chiu-wai), Lau Ching-wan, Andy Hui, Alex To, Christy Chung, Gigi Leung

A loose adaptation of a Japanese manga (comic-book novel), in which Tony Leung plays the not-quite-certified Dr. Lau Man, who treats the prostitutes on Lantern Street. Despite a cool exterior, Leung turns out to have an abiding concern for his fellow human beings – not to mention a romantic interest in a woman psychiatrist (Christy Chung) whose surgeon boyfriend was Leung's chief rival in medical school, and the reason that Leung never formally graduated. Other romantic subplots – between Leung's assistant and a cancer patient, and an undercover cop and a brainy hooker – abound in this stylish production from UFO.

MAGIC COP

驅魔警察

Year: 1989

Director: Stephen Tung

Stars: Lam Ching-ying, Wilson Lam, Billy Chow, Michiko Nishiwaki, Frankie Chin, Wu Ma

An evil sorceress is using zombies to smuggle drugs. Strange problems require strange solutions, so Lam Ching-ying, a cop and Taoist priest, is called upon to do some ghostbusting. He is teamed up with two skeptical young police officers; but once they hunt down the witch, the real showdown begins. A supernatural romp in a modern urban setting.

THE MAGIC CRANE
仙鶴神針
Year: 1993
Director: Benny Chan
Producer: Tsui Hark
Stars: Anita Mui, Tony Leung (Chiu-wai), Rosamund Kwan,
Damian Lau, Lawrence Ng

During a meeting of all the martial-arts clans, Anita Mui (who
travels astride a giant crane) tries to keep the peace with the aid of a
novice fighter. Rosamund Kwan, however, seeks vengeance against
Mui for inadvertently destroying her family, and the entire world of
martial arts is thrown into chaos. A slick, all-star Tsui Hark
production in the manner of *Swordsman*; the film nevertheless
bombed in Hong Kong.

THE MAGNIFICENT BUTCHER
林世榮（仁者無敵）
Year: 1980
Director: Yuen Woo-ping
Stars: Sammo Hung, Kwan Tak-hing, Yuen Biao, Fong Hak-on,
Lam Ching-ying, Chung Fat, Wei Pei

The late Kwan Tak-hing, who played the Cantonese folk hero
Wong Fei-hung in around a hundred movies in the 1950s and
1960s, reprises the role for the last time in this and a companion
film, *Dreadnought*. Sammo Hung is Wong's top student, and
something of a renegade, who is put to the test when his brother's
wife is kidnapped by the Five Dragon sect.

MAGNIFICENT WARRIORS
中華戰士
Year: 1987
Director: David Chung
Action Director: Stanley Tong
Stars: Michelle Yeoh, Lowell Lo, Richard Ng, Matsui Tetsuya,
Derek Yee

Michelle Yeoh plays a whip-cracking motorcycle-riding heroine in the style of Indiana Jones. Here she battles the occupying Japanese forces in China during World War II, with the aid of local resistance fighters. Richard Ng provides the comic relief as an itinerant swindler who gets caught up in Yeoh's mission of liberation. One of Yeoh's last movies before her marriage to mogul Dickson Poon, and prolonged absence from the screen.

MIRACLES (*aka* THE CANTON GODFATHER; MR. CANTON AND LADY ROSE)

奇蹟

Year: 1989
Director: Jackie Chan
Producer: Leonard Ho
Stars: Jackie Chan, Anita Mui, Wu Ma, Richard Ng, Bill Tung

Chan's personal favorite of his own movies is a remake of Frank Capra's *Pocketful of Miracles*, with more emphasis on the acting, and the sumptuous production, than on the stunts and fight scenes. Here he plays a roustabout in 1930s Hong Kong who quite unexpectedly is made the boss of a powerful crime syndicate. Chan thinks he owes his change of fortune to an old woman who sells roses on the street, and he helps prepare her for the visit of her daughter's future husband and father-in-law, who believe she is a proper lady. Meanwhile, gangland rivals want him dead, leading to a final showdown in a dockside rope factory that Capra could not have imagined.

A MOMENT OF ROMANCE

天若有情

Year: 1990
Director: Benny Chan
Producers: Johnny To, Ringo Lam, and Wong Jing
Stars: Andy Lau, Wu Chien-lien, Ng Man-tat

Andy Lau plays a criminal whose skill as a getaway driver saves him and his partners in the wake of a robbery gone awry. The gang members have taken a female hostage while making their escape, however, and they want her killed. Lau, who is attracted to the innocent woman, flees with her, and soon realizes that he must eliminate his former crime partners if he and the woman hope to survive.

A MOMENT OF ROMANCE II
天若有情 II 之天長地久
Year: 1993
Director: Benny Chan
Producer: Johnny To
Stars: Aaron Kwok, Wu Chien-lien, Anthony Wong

Unrelated sequel finds Wu Chien-lien as a young mainland woman who becomes a prostitute in order to raise money to bribe Chinese officials who are holding her brother in jail. When she inadvertently witnesses a triad murder, she is framed for the killing, and hunted by vengeful triads and the police. Rebellious drag-racer Aaron Kwok comes to her aid.

A MOMENT OF ROMANCE III
天若有情 III 烽火佳人
Year: 1996
Director and Producer: Johnny To
Stars: Andy Lau, Wu Chien-lien, Alex Fong

The two stars of Part I reunite in this hyper-melodrama set during the Japanese occupation. Andy Lau is a young flyboy whose plane crash-lands near a small isolated village. He develops a crush on Wu Chien-lien who, unfortunately, is slated to marry the son of the village chief. After Lau is rescued, Wu runs off to find him, just as he is about to embark on what may be a suicide mission.

MONEY CRAZY
發錢寒
Year: 1977
Director and Writer: John Woo
Stars: Ricky Hui, Richard Ng

A decade before John Woo became the king of the gunplay movies with *A Better Tomorrow*, he made his name as a top comedy director with this box-office smash. Ricky Hui and Richard Ng play two hustlers who try to help a young woman and her aging uncle recover some diamonds that were swindled by a dirty businessman. In scene after scene, their attempts to steal the diamonds are foiled for one unlucky reason or another.

MOON WARRIORS
戰神傳說
Year: 1992
Director: Sammo Hung
Action Director: Ching Siu-tung
Stars: Andy Lau, Kenny Bee, Anita Mui, Maggie Cheung

Andy Lau plays a gentle fisherman with remarkable martial-arts skills, and with a killer whale for a sidekick. When the exiled emperor (Kenny Bee) is betrayed by his power-hungry brother, Lau's services are called upon, but complications ensue when Lau falls for the emperor's fiancée (Anita Mui). Meanwhile, the emperor's bodyguard (Maggie Cheung) reveals her love for him. As the foursome try to work out their romantic troubles, the evil brother closes in.

MR. BOO (*see* THE PRIVATE EYES)

MR. CANTON AND LADY ROSE (*see* MIRACLES)

MR. VAMPIRE
殭屍先生
Year: 1985
Director: Ricky Lau
Producer: Sammo Hung
Production Supervisor: Jacob Cheung
Stars: Lam Ching-ying, Ricky Hui, Pauline Wong, Moon Lee, Wu Ma (cameo)

The Hong Kong comedy thriller which launched a thousand sequels, and forever typecast Lam Ching-ying as a vampire-busting priest. In the early days of Republican China, a landowner hires priest Lam to disinter and move his father's corpse; but in the process, the corpse turns into a vampire with a powerful thirst for the living. The situation worsens as one of Lam's two disciples falls in love with a beautiful ghost (Pauline Wong), and the other is turned into a creature of the night himself by a vampire bite.

MURDER
黃蜂尾後針
Year: 1993
Director: Lawrence Cheng
Stars: Carol Cheng, Damian Lau, Deannie Yip

Thriller with shades of *Regarding Henry*, about an unscrupulous lawyer (Carol Cheng) who squabbles with her equally sleazy husband (Damian Lau) after she steals $10 million from him, and ends up with a bullet in her head. She lives, but loses her memory, and is cared for by a nurse she once wronged in a lawsuit. Rendered more kindly by her head trauma, Cheng settles into new-found marital bliss – that is, until the memory of what her husband did to her starts to come back.

MY AMERICAN GRANDSON
上海假期
Year: 1991
Director: Ann Hui
Stars: Wu Ma, Wong Kwan-yuen, Carina Lau, Wong Loi, Suen Pang

A gentle drama about culture clash from Ann Hui. With her ten-year-old son in tow, Carina Lau leaves her husband in the United States, and rejoins her aging father (Wu Ma) in mainland China. Not surprisingly, the boy has been spoiled by his American upbringing, and has no appreciation for his own heritage, or patience for the mainland's primitive standard of living.

MY FATHER IS A HERO
給爸爸的信
Year: 1995
Director: Corey Yuen
Stars: Jet Li, Anita Mui, Xie Miao, Yu Rong-guang, Blackie Ko

Something of a low-tech *True Lies*. Jet Li, unbeknownst to his adoring family, is a secret agent for the Chinese government, and is sent to Hong Kong to infiltrate a violent gang. Anita Mui is the tough Hong Kong cop who has a run-in with Li, and travels to the mainland to investigate his background. When Li's wife dies of an illness, Mui takes her young son – a budding martial-arts champion – back to Hong Kong to search for his father. One of Jet Li's more successful modern-day ventures, with a fine balance of gunplay and kung-fu.

MY HEART IS THAT ETERNAL ROSE
殺手蝴蝶夢
Year: 1989
Director: Patrick Tam
Cinematographers: David Chung and Christopher Doyle
Stars: Joey Wong, Kenny Bee, Gordon Liu, Ng Man-tat, Tony Leung (Chiu-wai)

When Joey Wong's boyfriend and father bungle an attempt to help a gangster's son illegally enter Hong Kong, she is forced to marry another powerful gangster to save her father's life. Years later, after her father's death, she wants out of the marriage, and runs off with her old boyfriend. The gangster, who is none too pleased, sends a vicious enforcer to bring her back.

N

NAKED KILLER
赤裸羔羊
Year: 1992
Director: Clarence Fok
Producer and Writer: Wong Jing
Stars: Chingmy Yau, Simon Yam, Carrie Ng, Svenwara Madoka

For many fans, this is the quintessential Hong Kong film – a giddy mixture of sex and violence not to be seen anywhere else. A young woman named Kitty kills her father's murderer, making a favorable impression on Sister Cindy, a professional hitwoman, who adopts her as a pupil. Kitty finds herself the object of desire of a traumatized cop who throws up at the sight of a gun, and Sister Cindy's ex-pupil, a lesbian assassin with a contract on her former mentor.

NEW LEGEND OF SHAOLIN
洪熙官之少林五祖
Year: 1994
Director: Wong Jing
Action Directors: Corey Yuen and Yuen Tak
Stars: Jet Li, Chingmy Yau, Xie Miao, Deannie Yip, Damian Lau,
Wang Lung-wei, Corey Yuen, Wong Jing (cameo)

Jet Li portrays another folk hero, this time the legendary Hung Shi-
kwan. The massacre of Shaolin wipes out Hung's entire family,
though he manages to save his young son (kung-fu prodigy Xie
Miao, who also plays Li's son in *My Father is a Hero*), and together
they fight the evil Manchus. Presently, Hung sets out on a
dangerous mission – to save five Shaolin children on whose backs
an abbot has tattooed equal parts of a treasure map.

NEW TENANT
新房客
Year: 1995
Director: Anthony Wong
Stars: Anthony Wong, Dolphin Chan, Lawrence Ng, Lau Ching-
wan (cameo)

Anthony Wong is released from a mental hospital, unable to recall
why he had been admitted in the first place, and moves into a
condemned apartment building. There he discovers he has the
ability to travel ten years back in time. The previous tenants go
about their lives unaware of Wong's presence – all except for
Dolphin, a teenage girl, who gradually is able to see him. When
Dolphin's sister disappears, the sister's creepy boyfriend is held to
blame; but as Dolphin and Wong search for the truth, it begins to
appear that Wong might himself be implicated.

NIGHT CALLER
平安夜
Year: 1985
Director and Writer: Philip Chan
Stars: Melvin Wong, Philip Chan, Pauline Wong, Pat Ha

A cop looking into the carving-knife murder of a model is kidnapped in the course of his investigation. He is tortured by his captors, while his partner desperately tries to solve the case before it is too late. Philip Chan, a former Hong Kong police detective who always seems to play police officials (other examples include *Hard-Boiled* and *Supercop*) crafts a sleek horror film in the tradition of Italian director Dario Argento.

NOMAD
烈火青春
Year: 1982
Director: Patrick Tam
Producer: Dennis Yu
Assistant Director: Stanley Kwan
Co-Writer: Eddie Fong
Stars: Leslie Cheung, Cecilia Yip, Pat Ha, Ken Tong, Chan Bak-cheung

A young Leslie Cheung stars in this coming-of-age story, directed by one of the pacesetters of the Hong Kong new wave. During a humid Hong Kong summer, Cheung befriends three other teens; but trouble ensues when the friends harbor a Japanese man who turns out to be an AWOL Red Army soldier. As the group prepares for a trip aboard Cheung's father's boat (the Nomad), a Red Army official shows up, and the carnage begins. Though tame by today's standards, the film's violence and nudity were considered shocking at the time.

NOW YOU SEE LOVE . . . NOW YOU DON'T
我愛扭紋柴（流氓遇到兵）
Year: 1992
Director: Alex Law
Producer: Terence Chang
Stars: Chow Yun-fat, Carol Cheng, Anthony Wong, Teresa Mo, Terence Chang (cameo)

Chow Yun-fat, who grew up in the stix of Hong Kong, gets to play one of his favorite character types – a bumpkin – in this hit romantic comedy. Carol Cheng returns to mainland China from a sojourn in London, where she has acquired airs and become too sophisticated for boyfriend Chow. The hapless man follows her to Hong Kong, and tries to class himself up in order to win her back.

O

OH! MY THREE GUYS
三個相愛的少年
Year: 1994
Director: Chiu Sung-kee
Writer: Raymond To
Stars: Lau Ching-wan, Eric Kot, Dayo Wong, Wu Chien-lien, Chan Ka-ling, Chik King-man, Lui Yu-yeung, Joseph Cheng, Anthony Wong (cameo)

One of several recent Hong Kong films concerning homosexuality (other examples include *How Deep Is Your Love* and *I Wanna Be Your Man*), reflecting changing attitudes in the city – up to a point. *Oh! My Three Guys* depicts, with a certain ambivalence toward its protagonists, the trying times of three gay male roommates. Kot, a sometime film extra, has AIDS (and is hiding the fact from his friends); Wong, a frustrated screenwriter, is being dumped by his boyfriend; and Lau, a successful advertising executive, has had to keep his homosexuality a secret at work, though now one of his co-workers is on to him.

ONCE A COP (*see* PROJECT S)

ONCE A THIEF
縱橫四海
Year: 1991
Director and Writer: John Woo
Producer: Terence Chang
Stars: Chow Yun-fat, Leslie Cheung, Cherie Chung

An action-comedy from John Woo, about three adopted siblings –
two men and a woman – who have been raised by a triad boss as
expert art thieves. The heist of a rare painting goes terribly wrong
when the thieves are betrayed by their adoptive father, and one of
the siblings, Chow Yun-fat, ends up in a wheelchair. To get revenge,
the threesome plot an even more daring heist, of the same painting,
now in the triad boss's possession. Woo's trademark violence is
evident, but so is his skill for physical comedy and visual humor; in
one memorable scene at a ball, Chow dances in his wheelchair.

ONCE IN A LIFETIME
終生大事
Year: 1995
Director: Wellson Chin
Stars: Lau Ching-wan, Dayo Wong, Yuen King-tan

In this breezy romantic comedy, Lau Ching-wan plans a fake
marriage to assuage the dying mother of his supposed bride.
Unfortunately, Lau's own mother dies, and her funeral is set for the
same day as his mock wedding; now, he must disprove the adage
that one cannot be in two places at one time.

ONCE UPON A TIME IN CHINA
黃飛鴻
Year: 1991
Director and Producer: Tsui Hark
Executive Producer: Raymond Chow
Stars: Jet Li, Rosamund Kwan, Yuen Biao, Kent Cheng, Jacky
Cheung

Jet Li plays Wong Fei-hong, a character based on a real Cantonese
folk hero, and on the protagonist of a movie serial spanning about
a hundred Hong Kong films from the 1940s through the 1970s.
Here the martial-arts master takes control of the local militia in
1870s Canton, to help fight off invading British powers and a
group of Chinese bandits. This film singlehandedly revitalized the
declining martial-arts genre, and made Li a superstar.

ONCE UPON A TIME IN CHINA II
黃飛鴻之二：男兒當自強
Year: 1992
Director: Tsui Hark
Action Director: Yuen Woo-ping
Stars: Jet Li, Donnie Yen, Rosamund Kwan, Max Mok, David
Chiang

In this worthy sequel, Wong Fei-hong, who is a physician as well as
a martial artist, attends an international medical conference, and
introduces the British to acupuncture. Presently, Wong and his
followers find themselves in mortal danger at the hands of the
virulently anti-foreign White Lotus cult, and they take refuge at the
British embassy. Wong teams up with Dr. Sun Yat-sen to fight back
the cultists, and keep a name list of revolutionaries from falling into
the wrong hands.

ONCE UPON A TIME IN CHINA III
黃飛鴻之三：獅王爭霸
Year: 1992
Director: Tsui Hark
Stars: Jet Li, Rosamund Kwan, Max Mok, Xiao Xin-xin

In Part III, Wong Fei-hung and his two faithful sidekicks, Aunt Yee (Rosamund Kwan) and Fu (Max Mok), travel to Peking to visit Wong's father. There Aunt Yee meets an old Russian flame who is involved in a plot to overthrow the Chinese government. Considered lacking in the inspiration of the first two installments, the film is perhaps best known for its climactic lion-dance competition.

ONCE UPON A TIME IN CHINA IV
黃飛鴻之四：王者之風
Year: 1993
Director: Yuen Bun
Producers: Tsui Hark, Raymond Chow, and Ng See-yuen
Stars: Zhao Wen-zhou, Jean Wong, Max Mok, Lau Shun, Xiao Xin-xin

Zhao Wen-zhou (who plays the principal villain opposite Jet Li in *Fong Sai Yuk*) replaces Li in Part IV of this popular series. This time, Wong Fei-hung teams up with Aunt Yee's sister (Jean Wong), and together they try to stop a violent, all-female sect. Meanwhile, villainous foreigners restage the lion-dance competition from Part III, as part of a plot to undermine the Chinese government.

ONCE UPON A TIME IN CHINA V
黃飛鴻之五：龍城殲霸
Year: 1994
Director: Tsui Hark
Stars: Zhao Wen-zhou, Rosamund Kwan, Jean Wong, Max Mok, Kent Cheng, Elaine Lui

Pirates on the South China Sea are terrorizing a Cantonese town, and the local officials have fled. Master Wong, who has been reunited with his father, and Aunt Yee, his love interest from the first three installments, stick around to take on the bad guys. Director Tsui Hark tries to revitalize the series by mixing in some new elements, including romantic comedy and gunplay.

ONE AND A HALF
跟我走一回
Year: 1995
Director: Lawrence Ah Mon
Stars: Zhang Feng-yi, Carrie Ng, Siu Chun-kwan, Paul Chun

Drama about a man (Zhang Feng-yi) sentenced to prison, and forced to divorce his pregnant wife. When he is released seven years later, the ex-wife is remarried, and, in an effort to keep Zhang away, claims her son was fathered by another man. After a variety of humiliations, Zhang kidnaps the boy and takes him on a trip through China.

ONE OF THE LUCKY ONES
伴我同行
Year: 1994
Director: Clifton Ko
Writer: Raymond To
Stars: Alice Lau, Hui Fan, Law Koon-lam, So Yuk-wah, Fung Wai-hung, David Wu

This film recounts the true story of Lucy Ching, a blind Hong Kong woman who would eventually study in the United States and return home to set up China's first school for the blind. The movie's central relationship is that of Ching and her selfless maid, played by Hui Fan (Best Actress nominee, Hong Kong Film Awards), who is convinced that the blind girl is capable of making her own way in the world, despite the prevailing prejudice that the blind are mainly useful as street performers.

ON THE RUN
亡命鴛鴦
Year: 1988
Director: Alfred Cheung
Producer: Raymond Chow
Action Directors: Corey Yuen and Yuen Tak
Stars: Yuen Biao, Pat Ha, Lo Lieh, Charlie Chin, Philip Ko, Yuen Wah

In this tough-minded cop story, police officer Yuen Biao's wife is gunned down by a professional hitwoman from the Golden Triangle. When the assassin is betrayed by her bosses, she is forced to team up with Biao to take them on. A departure for director Alfred Cheung, who usually makes comedies, and action star Biao (one of Jackie Chan's classmates from childhood), in a rare dramatic role.

OPERATION CONDOR (*aka* ARMOUR OF GOD II)
飛鷹計劃
Year: 1991
Director: Jackie Chan
Stars: Jackie Chan, Carol Cheng, Eva Cobo de Garcia

Asian Hawk, Jackie Chan's Indiana Jones-style adventurer, is back; and this time, he is hired to find a cache of gold hidden by the Nazis at the end of World War II. Accompanied by two women – an historian, and the granddaughter of the man who hid the gold – Chan treks through the desert, and ends up in a subterraneous research complex built by the Germans. The last reel contains a fight scene in a wind tunnel that took Chan four months to film.

ORGANIZED CRIME AND TRIAD BUREAU
重案實錄 O 記
Year: 1993
Director: Kirk Wong
Stars: Anthony Wong, Danny Lee, Cecilia Yip, Fan Siu-wong

Part II of Kirk Wong's police trilogy (in-between *Crime Story*, with Jackie Chan, and *Rock 'n Roll Cop*), this film concerns a detective

(Danny Lee) who will go to any lengths to catch a criminal, including the torturing of suspects. Anthony Wong is one such suspect, and though he turns out to be a gang leader, Lee's brutal methods leave the viewer uncertain of whom to root for.

OUT OF THE DARK
回魂夜
Year: 1995
Director: Jeff Lau
Stars: Stephen Chiau, Karen Mok, Wong Yat-fei

Stephen Chiau plays a mental patient who, knowing no fear, finds employment as a ghostbuster. After an old lady is murdered by her son and daughter-in-law at a housing project, Chiau comes in to eradicate her spirit, but only makes matters worse when he accidentally offs the killers during a mad chase. The dead couple vow a rampage, and Chiau has to use every trick of his trade to finish the job once and for all.

THE OWL VS. BUMBO
貓頭鷹與小飛象
Year: 1984
Director: Sammo Hung
Producer: Dickson Poon
Stars: Sammo Hung, George Lam, Michelle Yeoh, Deannie Yip, Season Ma

Two retired thieves – George Lam as the Owl, and Sammo Hung as Bumbo (evidently a misspelling of Dumbo) – are tricked by a police chief into helping him get revenge on an unscrupulous land developer. A slight film, notable primarily for marking Michelle Yeoh's screen début (in a non-action role), and for demonstrating, in an homage to Gene Kelly, that the portly Hung can tap-dance.

P

PAINTED FACES
七小福
Year: 1988
Director: Alex Law
Producers: Leonard Ho and Mona Fong
Writers: Mabel Cheung and Alex Law
Stars: Sammo Hung, Lam Ching-ying, Cheng Pei-pei, Wu Ma

Biopic of Hong Kong's famous movie triumvirate – Jackie Chan, Sammo Hung, and Yuen Biao – during their early years at a Peking Opera school. Hung plays Master Yu, the despotic *sifu* (master) who molds his students into acrobatic performers through harsh, sometimes torturous, training. As Hong Kong becomes more modern and Westernized, the Peking Opera declines in popularity, and Master Yu is forced to make some hard decisions. Though Jackie Chan has derided the film for soft-pedaling the violent treatment he and his fellow students received, *Painted Faces* has been praised for its depiction of the changing face of Hong Kong, and Chinese cultural traditions, during the 1960s.

PASSION 1995
冒險遊戲
Year: 1995
Director: Clarence Fok
Stars: Simon Yam, Christy Chung, Teresa Mak, David Wu, Yuen King-tan, Melvin Wong

Three intersecting stories, from the director of *Naked Killer*. Christy Chung is a young woman blindly in love with a man who has become the boy-toy of a violent, gay druglord; Simon Yam is an émigré from San Francisco, searching for his missing girlfriend; and Teresa Mak is a young woman addicted to phone-dating services. Director Clarence Fok mixes action with pathos in a film that seems to have taken inspiration from the disjointed storytelling style of Wong Kar-wai.

PASSION UNBOUNDED
四級殺人狂
Year: 1995
Director: John Hau
Stars: Carrie Ng, David Wu, Kam Wai-ying

A Category III thriller, in which a police detective searches for a sexually kinky serial murderer (Carrie Ng) who preys on men and women. Ng, it turns out, is suffering from ennui, but finds happiness with a new neighbor, who shares her nasty, murderous proclivities. Their criminal life gets complicated when Ng's younger sister and another neighbor stumble on the truth. Surreal plotting makes this stylish movie unpredictable from first to last.

PEACE HOTEL
和平飯店
Year: 1995
Director: Wai Ka-fai
Producer: John Woo
Stars: Chow Yun-fat, Cecilia Yip, Wu Chien-lien (cameo)

A quasi-Western, circa 1920, which casts Chow Yun-fat as a desperado known only as the Killer. After taking part in a massacre, Chow decides to lay down his gun and open up the Peace Hotel, a safe haven from frontier violence. All goes well until the arrival of a mysterious, conniving woman, who is wanted by a gang for murdering its boss; now Chow must choose between her expulsion and an all-out war. This was Chow's final film before departing for Hollywood, and his character in the movie seems to be a winking reference to his world-famous role in John Woo's *The Killer*.

PEDICAB DRIVER
群龍戲鳳
Year: 1989
Director: Sammo Hung
Stars: Sammo Hung, Nina Li Chi, Sun Yueh, Max Mok, Fennie Yuen, John Sham, Lam Ching-ying, Lau Kar-leung, Mang Hoi, Billy Chow

Considered by many Hong Kong film fans to be one of Sammo Hung's best films, *Pedicab Driver* is set in postwar Macao. Hung is the leader of a quartet of working men who drive pedal-powered rickshaws, and are searching for love. One of the drivers falls for a young woman, whom he discovers is a prostitute; when he tries to buy her freedom and marry her, the brothel owner sends his goons to have the couple killed. Now it is up to Hung to take revenge.

PEKING OPERA BLUES
刀馬旦
Year: 1986
Director and Producer: Tsui Hark
Action Director: Ching Siu-tung
Writer: Raymond To
Stars: Brigitte Lin, Sally Yeh, Cherie Chung, Mark Cheng, Wu Ma, Cheung Kwok-keung, Leong Po-chih, Kenneth Tsang

An undisputed classic, *Peking Opera Blues* tells the story of three strong-willed women in China's capital city amid the political chaos two years after the revolution of 1911. Brigitte Lin is the mannish daughter of a general, willing to betray her father to further the cause of revolution. She finds two unlikely accomplices in Sally Yeh, an acrobat who yearns to break the all-male sex barrier and perform Peking Opera at her father's theater; and Cherie Chung, the servant of a deposed warlord, who wants to get her hands on the jewels stolen from his palace. The action moves back and forth between palace and theater at a furious pace, and director Tsui Hark has been praised for his ability to combine farce, pageantry, drama, and stuntwork.

PEOPLE'S HERO
人民英雄
Year: 1987
Director: Derek Yee
Producer: John Sham
Stars: Ti Lung, Tony Leung (Chiu-wai), Tony Leung (Ka-fai), Paul Chun, Elaine Kam, Wong Pan

A bank is taken over by two inexperienced robbers (including a young Tony Leung Chiu-wai), who find themselves trapped and surrounded by police. Also in the bank is Ti Lung, a cool-headed gangster and wanted cop-killer, who quickly takes charge of the hostage negotiations. What might easily have been a Hong Kong rip-off of *Dog Day Afternoon* takes a far more imaginative turn, as director Derek Yee draws out the characters of the hostages, and provides Ti Lung with possibly his greatest star vehicle.

PLAIN JANE TO THE RESCUE
八彩林亞珍
Year: 1982
Director: John Woo
Stars: Josephine Siao, Ricky Hui, Roman Tam, John Woo (cameo)

John Woo's only film to feature a woman in the lead role is this almost surreal comedy, starring Josephine Siao, who recreates the character of Lam Ah-chun, a tomboyish working-class woman she had played in a TV series and two prior films. This time, she is hired as an assistant to the elderly owner of the Zanda Corporation, a monstrous conglomerate that is taking over Hong Kong. When the owner's greedy son kidnaps his father as part of a plan for world domination, it is up to Siao, and her sidekick Ricky Hui, to take heroic action, à la James Bond.

POLICE CONFIDENTIAL
震撼性醜聞
Year: 1995
Director: Raymond Lee
Producer: Kirk Wong
Stars: Simon Yam, Carrie Ng, Zhang Feng-yi, Linda Wong

Hyper-stylized film follows Simon Yam as a cop who moonlights as a peeping tom. After witnessing a top government official having kinky sex with a prostitute, Yam finds himself caught in a deadly coverup that could end both the prostitute's life and his own. He teams up with a woman lawyer to expose the corruption, but when the matter comes to trial, it appears that the fix is in.

POLICE STORY
警察故事
Year: 1985
Director: Jackie Chan
Stars: Jackie Chan, Brigitte Lin, Maggie Cheung, Bill Tung

Ground-breaking Jackie Chan film which casts him as a policeman determined to collar a gang boss at all costs. After the frenetic opening – a car chase that levels an entire shantytown – Chan takes custody of the gangster's moll (Brigitte Lin), a potential star witness, and has to protect her from thugs while convincing his jealous girlfriend (Maggie Cheung) he is not having an affair. The gang boss turns the tables on Chan, framing him for a murder, leading up to one of Chan's most celebrated set pieces – a fifteen-minute demolition match against the bad guys at a shopping mall.

POLICE STORY II
警察故事續集
Year: 1988
Director: Jackie Chan
Stars: Jackie Chan, Maggie Cheung, Benny Lai, Bill Tung

Jackie Chan returns as the maverick police officer, and the paper-thin plot has him chasing a group of terrorists who have blown up the very mall he almost destroyed at the conclusion of Part I.

Maggie Cheung, meanwhile, reprises her role as Chan's long-suffering girlfriend, who manages to get in the middle of all the action when she is kidnapped.

POLICE STORY III (*see* SUPERCOP)

POLICE STORY IV (*see* FIRST STRIKE)

POM POM AND HOT HOT
神槍手與咖喱雞
Year: 1992
Director: Joe Cheung
Stars: Jacky Cheung, Lam Ching-ying, Loletta Lee, Bonnie Fu, Stephen Tung, Alfred Cheung, Austin Wai, Cheung Kwok-leung

This film about two cops who share an apartment with two mainland Chinese relatives starts out as a routine actioner, but the final reel contains a series of gun battles which, in sheer intensity – and bullets expended – rivals those of director John Woo. Lam Ching-ying co-stars as the gun-crazy policeman who is called in to help the two eponymous heroes after they get in over their heads.

PRINCESS FRAGRANCE (*aka* ROMANCE OF BOOK AND
    SWORD II)
香香公主
Year: 1987
Director: Ann Hui
Stars: Cheung Doh-fuk, Ngai Nok

The conclusion to Hui's epic martial-arts drama – about two brothers, a Manchu emperor, and an anti-Manchu rebel – picks up where the first film left off. The brothers are reconciled, and the rebel helps a Muslim tribe defeat a powerful general, ostensibly with the emperor's blessing. The victory is shortlived, however; the emperor sends another army to wipe out the Muslims, pitting him once more against his sibling.

PRISON ON FIRE
監獄風雲
Year: 1987
Director: Ringo Lam
Producer: Karl Maka
Stars: Chow Yun-fat, Tony Leung (Ka-fai), Roy Cheung, Hon Kwan

In one of Ringo Lam's best-known films, Tony Leung plays a newly arrived convict at a prison on Lantau Island, guilty of an accidental manslaughter, and too timid for prison life. Chow Yun-fat is Mad Dog, a tough but good-hearted inmate who takes Leung under his wing, earning him the enmity of other convicts, and giving a sadistic prison guard the opportunity to put him in harm's way.

PRISON ON FIRE II
逃犯（監獄風雲續集）
Year: 1991
Director and Producer: Ringo Lam
Stars: Chow Yun-fat, Tsui Kam-kong, Chan Chung-yung, Tommy Wong, Roy Cheung (cameo)

Chow Yun-fat is still incarcerated on Lantau Island, and this time he befriends a mainland Chinese prisoner named Dragon (Chan Chung-yung). Unfortunately, there is growing tension between the mainland prisoners and those from Hong Kong, and Chow finds himself again at the center of a struggle. Meanwhile, a sadistic new superintendent is fomenting the conflict among prisoners for his own ends, ultimately leaving Chow and Dragon no choice but to attempt a jailbreak.

PRIVATE EYE BLUES
非常偵探
Year: 1994
Director and Writer: Eddie Fong
Producer: Teddy Robin Kwan
Stars: Jacky Cheung, Kathy Chow, Mavis Fan

A beer-guzzling, stonefaced private detective (Jacky Cheung) is hired to find a mainland girl with supernatural powers, and return her to Chinese officials. Before long, the Hong Kong triads and the British government also want to get their hands on the girl, and she and the detective take refuge at his soon-to-be-ex-wife's apartment. An offbeat and entertaining black comedy from one of Hong Kong's growing corps of expatriate directors, Eddie Fong, who has acknowledged that the film is an allegory for 1997 anxieties.

THE PRIVATE EYES
半斤八兩
Year: 1976
Director: Michael Hui
Production Designer: John Woo
Stars: Michael Hui, Sam Hui, Ricky Hui

The first feature film starring all three Hui brothers was a smash hit comedy that helped bring about the resurgence of Cantonese as the principal dialect of the Hong Kong cinema. Michael Hui plays a penny-pinching private eye; Ricky Hui is his dejected sidekick; and Sam Hui is a kung-fu expert looking for a job. The film is mostly a succession of skits – it isn't hard to detect the Hui brothers' roots in television – with the emphasis on working-class humor. The grand finale pits the Huis against a group of robbers who are attempting to hold up an entire movie audience.

PRODIGAL SON
敗家仔
Year: 1981
Director: Sammo Hung
Stars: Yuen Biao, Sammo Hung, Lam Ching-ying, Frankie Chan

Yuen Biao plays a wealthy young man who is convinced that he is a martial-arts champ. After a humiliating defeat by a Peking Opera performer (Lam Ching-ying), Yuen finds out that his prevous fights had all been rigged by his father, and he enlists Lam's help in order to become the expert he always thought he was. The final martial-arts match, pitting Yuen Biao against Frankie Chan, is generally considered one of the best fight scenes ever committed to film.

PROJECT A

A 計劃

Year: 1983

Director: Jackie Chan

Stars: Jackie Chan, Sammo Hung, Yuen Biao, Dick Wei

Project A was not merely a breakthrough for Jackie Chan – it marked his transition from a kung-fu artist to a comedy-action star who did his own stunts – but, along with its sequel, it is arguably one of the pinnacles of the modern Hong Kong cinema. Chan plays a coast guard officer in turn-of-the-century Hong Kong doing battle with the pirates who infest the South China sea. Coming to his aid are Yuen Biao, as a police official, and Sammo Hung, as a good-hearted scoundrel. Most of the action takes place on land; the set pieces include a mad bicycle chase through narrow streets, and Chan's famous tribute to Harold Lloyd, in which he dangles from a giant clock, and plummets through two awnings.

PROJECT A II

A 計劃續集

Year: 1987

Director: Jackie Chan

Stars: Jackie Chan, Maggie Cheung, Rosamund Kwan, Carina Lau, Bill Tung

In the exhilarating sequel, Jackie Chan is once again a coast guard officer in turn-of-the-century Hong Kong, pitted this time against a corrupt police force, anti-Manchu revolutionaries, and revenge-seeking pirates left over from Part I. The second half of the film moves from one frenetic set piece to another, including a sequence in which Chan, manacled to a police superintendent who wants him dead, tries to escape from a group of pirates more than willing to kill them both. In the stunt-filled finale, Chan runs down the wall of a collapsing building, and, in a tribute to Buster Keaton's *Steamboat Bill, Jr.*, avoids being crushed under a second wall by passing through the window.

PROJECT S (*aka* ONCE A COP)
超級計劃
Year: 1993
Director: Stanley Tong
Stars: Michelle Yeoh, Yu Rong-guang, Fan Siu-wong, Bill Tung, Yukari Oshima (cameo), Jackie Chan (cameo), Eric Tsang (cameo)

In this worthy sequel to *Supercop*, Michelle Yeoh is back as mainland Chinese police superintendent Hua. (Jackie Chan appears only briefly, as an undercover cop in drag.) This time, she is sent to Hong Kong to help catch a group of mainland criminals who knocked off a bank. Little does she know that the gang is led by her former boyfriend (Yu Rong-guang). Yeoh proves once again that she is Chan's equal when it comes to doing her own dangerous stunts.

Q

QUEEN OF TEMPLE STREET
廟街皇后
Year: 1990
Director: Lawrence Ah Mon
Cast: Sylvia Chang, Rain Lau, Alice Lau, Lo Lieh, Ha Ping

Sylvia Chang stars in this award-winning drama as a seasoned prostitute who works in the sleazy red-light district of Temple Street, in Hong Kong. Conflict arises as Chang's teenaged daughter (Rain Lau) becomes a hostess at a Temple Street bar, and the mother tries to prevent the daughter's own slide into degradation. Lau has little use for her mother, however, apart from needing her services to repossess some nude photographs, and to help locate her father, whom she has never met.

R

RAINING IN THE MOUNTAIN
空山靈雨
Year: 1979
Director: King Hu
Stars: Paul Chun, Hsu Feng, Tien Feng

Later work by auteur film-maker King Hu, centered around a Buddhist monastery at a turbulent time, when the head abbot is searching for a replacement, causing rivalry among the monks. Matters are complicated further by thieves who are trying to steal a valuable scroll from the monastery's archive. The film has much less sword action than the average King Hu production; it focuses more on suspense, enhanced by exquisite cinematography. Shot back to back with *Legend of the Mountain*, featuring many of the same actors.

RED DUST
滾滾紅塵
Year: 1990
Director: Yim Ho
Stars: Brigitte Lin, Chin Han, Maggie Cheung

Epic melodrama set during the Japanese occupation, and based on the life of Eileen Chang, a well-known Shanghainese novelist. Brigitte Lin plays the novelist, who finds herself a social outcast because of her husband (Chin Han), who supposedly collaborated with the Japanese. New-wave director Yim Ho, who shot the film on location in China not long after the Tiananmen Square Massacre, stirred up trouble with Communist officials for his sympathetic portrayal of the husband.

RED ROSE, WHITE ROSE
紅玫瑰白玫瑰
Year: 1994
Director: Stanley Kwan
Cinematographer: Christopher Doyle
Stars: Winston Chao, Joan Chen, Veronica Yip

Based on a novel by Eileen Chang, *Red Rose, White Rose* is set in
Shanghai before and during World War II, and concerns a
controlling man (Winston Chao), and the two very different
women in his life. In the first half of the film, Chao is drawn into a
passonate affair with a friend's wife, a headstrong woman he dubs
his Red Rose (played by Joan Chen, who won a Golden Horse
award for Best Actress). When Chen announces plans to divorce
her husband, however, Chao makes a hasty retreat. In the film's
second half, Chao tries to begin life anew by courting and marrying
his White Rose – a shy, virginal Shanghai woman (demurely played
by Category III star Veronica Yip, in a bit of reverse typecasting);
but that relationship is doomed as well.

RED TO KILL
弱殺
Year: 1994
Director: Billy Tang
Stars: Lily Chung, Ben Ng, Money Lo

From the demented creator of *Run and Kill* comes an even sicker
Category III exploitation film, set in an apartment building in
which one floor is a school for the mentally handicapped. A serial
rapist-murderer, who also happens to be a necrophiliac, is at large,
and has his eye on one of the retarded girls. When the law fails to
exact justice on him, it is up to one of the women teachers to take
revenge.

REINCARNATION OF GOLDEN LOTUS
潘金蓮之前世今生
Year: 1989
Director: Clara Law
Writer: Eddie Fong
Stars: Joey Wong, Wilson Lam, Eric Tsang

One of Clara Law's most accessible films is a modern retelling of the old Chinese erotic novel *Story of Golden Lotus*. Joey Wong is the title character, a promiscuous, murdered woman whose spirit is in hell, and who is asked to drink the "tea of forgetfulness" so she can be reincarnated and begin anew. She refuses the drink – she wants revenge against those who killed her – and instead is reborn in China just before the Cultural Revolution. As she grows up, events in her new life mirror those of her remembered past.

REMAINS OF A WOMAN
郎心如鐵
Year: 1993
Director: Clarence Fok
Writer: Dennis Chan
Stars: Carrie Ng, James Pak, Loletta Lee, Melvin Wong

Carrie Ng caused an upset by winning Best Actress at the Golden Horse Awards for her role in this Category III shocker – an unprecedented feat for an actor in an exploitation film. A year after Ng and James Pak have been convicted of the murder and dismemberment of a young woman, a detective begins interviewing Ng to find out what actually happened. She recounts how Pak strung her and the murder victim along, gradually getting them hooked on drugs and increasingly violent sex.

RETRIBUTION SIGHT UNSEEN
盲女 72 小時
Year: 1992
Director: Chang Wing-chin
Producer: Alfred Cheung
Stars: Veronica Yip, Anthony Wong

In this slick Hong Kong adaptation of *Wait Until Dark*, Veronica Yip is a happily married woman whose husband is a well-to-do lawyer. Left alone in the house with a medical condition that has rendered her temporarily blind, Yip becomes the prey of one of her husband's disgruntled clients (Anthony Wong), who torments her until her husband returns for a violent confrontation.

THE RETURNING
等著你回來
Year: 1994
Director: Jacob Cheung
Writer: Raymond To
Stars: Tony Leung (Chiu-wai), Wu Chien-lien, Sandra Ng

Ghostly thriller from the UFO production company. Tony Leung plays an editor at a publishing house working on a book about a woman writer who committed suicide. Leung and his wife (Wu Chien-lien) move into the writer's house, and gradually Wu begins to be possessed by the writer's spirit. An above-average script and a strong performance from Wu – not to mention a rare dramatic performance from Sandra Ng – add to the chilling atmosphere.

RETURN TO A BETTER TOMORROW
新英雄本色
Year: 1994
Director: Wong Jing
Stars: Chingmy Yau, Lau Ching-wan, Dior Cheng, Michael Wong

Not a sequel to the John Woo/Tsui Hark series, though perhaps something of an homage. Dior Cheng plays a rising triad who is betrayed by his boss and ambushed in the mainland. He survives, and returns to Hong Kong, where he enlists the help of another triad and an undercover cop to bring down his enemy. Chingmy Yau plays Cheng's bad-girl love interest, who is disfigured and turned into a heroin addict.

ROBOFORCE (*see* I LOVE MARIA)

ROBOTRIX
女機械人
Year: 1991
Director: Jamie Luk
Stars: Amy Yip, Billy Chow, David Wu, Hui Hiu-tan, Aoyama Chikako, Ken Goodman

A mad Japanese scientist commits seppuku, transfers his mind into the body of a robot, and embarks on a spree of kidnapping, rape, and murder. The police turn for help to a woman scientist and her two androids – one of them the busty soft-porn star Amy Yip – to bring him down. A cult favorite.

ROCK 'N ROLL COP
省港一號通緝犯
Year: 1994
Director: Kirk Wong
Stars: Anthony Wong, Carrie Ng, Yu Rong-guang, Wu Xing-guo

Anthony Wong plays a hard-boiled Hong Kong cop sent to the mainland to help stop a gang of arms smugglers. Wong's reckless ways infuriate the methodical mainland Chinese police inspector, who is further horrified to learn that his ex-girlfriend is mixed up with the gang, and who tries to solve the case while keeping her out of trouble. The third film in Kirk Wong's police trilogy – the others are *Crime Story* and *Organized Crime and Triad Bureau* – all supposedly based on actual cases.

ROMANCE OF BOOK AND SWORD
書劍恩仇錄
Year: 1987
Director: Ann Hui
Stars: Cheung Doh-fuk, Chang Da-shi, Ai Nuo, Liu Jia-len

Ann Hui's artful swordplay film, based on a novel by Louis Cha, follows the lives of two Han Dynasty brothers who were separated at childhood. One brother was raised a Manchu, and groomed to be emperor; the other became a member of the anti-Manchu Red Flower Society. The sequel, *Princess Fragrance*, picks up the story where Part I leaves off.

ROMANCE OF BOOK AND SWORD II (*see* PRINCESS FRAGRANCE)

ROOF WITH A VIEW
天台的月光
Year: 1993
Director: Tony Au
Stars: Tony Leung (Ka-fai), Veronica Yip, Kent Cheng (cameo)

What starts out as a police drama turns into a sweet-natured romantic comedy. After the death of his partner, police officer Tony Leung takes some time off to get himself together. Romantic sparks fly when he meets his new neighbor, a single mother, and the two share a series of adventures. Tony Au, a former art director and set designer, directs with a distinct visual flair.

ROSE, ROSE I LOVE YOU
玫瑰玫瑰我愛你
Year: 1993
Director: Jacky Pang
Stars: Tony Leung (Ka-fai), Kenny Bee, Veronica Yip, Carina Lau, Simon Yam

Loose sequel to 92 *Legendary La Rose Noire*, with musical numbers, and comparable goofiness, but a heavier emphasis on action. Detective Tony Leung is hot on the trail of an escaped criminal whom he had helped put away. Leung and another cop conduct surveillance on the criminal's old girlfriend, unaware that she and her neighbor are actually the notorious White Rose and Black Rose, two feuding superheroines.

ROUGE
胭脂扣
Year: 1987
Director: Stanley Kwan
Producer: Jackie Chan
Writers: Lilian Lee and Yau Tai On-ping
Stars: Anita Mui, Leslie Cheung, Alex Man, Emily Chu

Winner of five Hong Kong Film Awards, including Best Picture, Best Director and Best Actress, *Rouge* belongs to a popular Hong Kong genre, the ghost story, and also to a more select category, the Cantonese art film. Anita Mui is Fleur, a courtesan in a Hong Kong brothel in the 1930s, who falls for Chan (Leslie Cheung), the opium-smoking son of a rich family. When their marriage is thwarted, Fleur and Chan form a suicide pact, but Chan loses his nerve, and Fleur's spirit returns to modern-day Hong Kong to search for him. Made almost entirely without special effects, the film relies on Mui's exceptional performance, and Kwan's sure-footed direction, to work its magic.

ROYAL TRAMP
鹿鼎記
Year: 1992
Director: Wong Jing and Gordon Chan (uncredited)
Action Director: Ching Siu-tung
Stars: Stephen Chiau, Cheung Man, Damian Lau, Chingmy Yau, Sandra Ng, Ng Man-tat, Tsui Kam-kong

An all-star cast mercilessly parodies the Tsui Hark period sword-play movies (especially *Swordsman*). Stephen Chiau plays Wilson Bond, a fast-talking con artist who finds himself allied with the powerful leader of the Heaven and Earth Society, which is intent on overthrowing the Ming Dynasty. Chiau is sent undercover to the Forbidden City, where he becomes friends with the young emperor, and, in the process, becomes involved with a woman he thinks is the empress dowager (Cheung Man), but who is actually a sorceress.

ROYAL TRAMP II
鹿鼎記 II 之神龍教
Year: 1992
Director: Wong Jing and Gordon Chan (uncredited)
Action Director: Ching Siu-tung
Stars: Stephen Chiau, Brigitte Lin, Chingmy Yau, Sandra Ng, Michelle Reis, Yang Yee-kwan

The direct continuation of Part I ups the stakes as the imposter empress changes form (becoming Brigitte Lin, who played Asia the Invincible in *Swordsman II*). In the meantime, Wilson Bond continues to play undercover operative, while acquiring fortune and status (not to mention wives). He sleeps with Lin, absorbs much of her kung-fu power, and allies with her to take on the duplicitous Ming Dynasty leader Master Wong.

ROYAL WARRIORS (*aka* IN THE LINE OF DUTY II)
皇家戰士
Year: 1986
Director: David Chung
Stars: Michelle Yeoh, Michael Wong, Henry Sanada

Michelle Yeoh reprises her role as the policewoman from *Yes, Madam!* in the film that established her as the queen of Hong Kong action. Returning from vacation aboard a plane, Yeoh, along with a Japanese secret agent and a Hong Kong security officer, foil a daring attempt by a gang to rescue a brother member from his police escort. Once in Hong Kong, a surviving brother tracks down the threesome for a game of revenge. A nonstop showcase for Yeoh's high-kicking martial-arts skills.

RUMBLE IN THE BRONX
紅番區
Year: 1995
Director: Stanley Tong
Stars: Jackie Chan, Anita Mui, Bill Tung, Françoise Yip

Jackie Chan achieved his dream of American success when New Line released a dubbed and recut version of this action comedy, shot almost entirely in Vancouver. He plays a Hong Kong cop who comes to the Bronx to help his uncle sell his grocery store to businesswoman Anita Mui, and then sticks around to help Mui protect the establishment from a nasty group of bikers. When the bikers steal diamonds from some mafiosi, however, they find they need to ally themselves with Chan to save their own skins.

RUN AND KILL
烏鼠
Year: 1993
Director: Billy Tang
Producer: Danny Lee
Stars: Simon Yam, Kent Cheng, Danny Lee, Melvin Wong, Wang Lung-wei

Kent Cheng plays a relatively nice guy who gets drunk at a karaoke club, and, without realizing what he is doing, hires a triad to kill his cheating wife. After the wife is brutally murdered in Cheng's presence, he is presented with the bill, which is more than he can pay. He takes refuge in his hometown in China, where a Vietcong renegade tries to help him, only to lose his life. As a result, the Vietcong's mad brother (Simon Yam) vows to kill Cheng and his entire family. *Run and Kill* ultimately plays like a black comedy, with a Category III rating, for violence, that is well deserved.

S

SAVIOUR OF THE SOUL

九一神雕俠侶

Year: 1991

Director: Corey Yuen and David Lai

Uncredited Co-Director: Jeff Lau

Producer: Andy Lau

Writer: Wong Kar-wai (uncredited)

Stars: Anita Mui, Andy Lau, Kenny Bee, Gloria Yip, Aaron Kwok, Carina Lau

A paradigm of the comic-strip-style of Hong Kong film-making, *Saviour of the Soul* is loosely based on the Japanese anime *City Hunter*. Anita Mui is cast as twin sisters, one of them a suave hit woman, and the other a mad inventor of high-tech weapons, including a yo-yo that transforms into a sword. When hit woman Mui blinds a master criminal and sends him to jail, his apprentice, Silver Fox, vows revenge, and it is up to city mercenary Andy Lau to help save her.

SCHOOL ON FIRE

學校風雲

Year: 1988

Director and Producer: Ringo Lam

Stars: Fennie Yuen, Lam Ching-ying, Damian Lau, Roy Cheung

A nihilistic film that suffered the censor's knife, *School on Fire* concerns the hard times of Fennie Yuen, a girl who makes enemies with the wrong triads at school. A new teacher and a local cop try to help, but the students are much too violence-prone, or else they're pill-popping, abused prostitutes. After turning into one of the latter, Yuen tries unsuccessfully to burn down the school, and then hunts down her main nemesis for a twenty-minute orgy of violence.

THE SECRET
瘋劫
Year: 1979
Director: Ann Hui
Writer: Joyce Chan
Stars: Sylvia Chang, Teresa Chiu, Tsui Siu-keung, Li Hai-suk, Alex
Man, George Lam

Ann Hui's first theatrical feature is an eerie murder mystery that
seems to have been inspired by Nicholas Roeg's *Don't Look Now*,
and the films of Roman Polanski. When the bodies of a man and a
woman are found strung from a tree in a forest, the police are quick
to pin the murders on a mentally retarded local. A family friend
(Sylvia Chang) conducts her own investigation, however, and soon
is caught in a web of terror.

SECURITY UNLIMITED
摩登保鑣
Year: 1981
Director: Michael Hui
Producer: Raymond Chow
Writers: Michael Hui and Sam Hui
Music: Sam Hui
Stars: Michael Hui, Sam Hui, Ricky Hui, Wong Tso-sze

The most popular of the Hui brothers' films finds the comic
threesome in a series of misadventures while working at a security
agency. Very similar in style to their earlier comedy *The Private
Eyes*, this film is essentially a series of skits.

SEMI-GODS AND SEMI-DEVILS
新天龍八部之天山童姥
Year: 1994
Director: Andy Chin
Stars: Brigitte Lin, Gong Li, Cheung Man, Tsui Kam-kong, Frankie
Lam, Tsui Siu-keung, James Pak, Liu Kai-chi

Though it boasts two movie goddesses – Taiwan's Brigitte Lin, and
mainland China's Gong Li – this sword-and-sorcery film is

regarded as something of a glorious mess. A kung-fu master is fatally poisoned, but refuses to die until he finds the man fated to receive his supernatural powers, throwing the martial-arts world into disarray. Brigitte Lin plays good and evil twin sisters, both of them disciples of the master; Gong Li has her hands full battling the evil twin, while pining for the good one, who was once her lover.

SEX AND ZEN
肉蒲團之偷情寶鑒
Year: 1991
Director: Michael Mak
Stars: Lawrence Ng, Amy Yip, Kent Cheng, Lo Lieh, Carrie Ng, Yuen King-tan

Outrageous sex comedy based on the seventeenth-century novel *The Carnal Prayer Mat* by Li Yu, concerning an arrogant scholar (Lawrence Ng) who shuns Zen Buddhist enlightenment in order to experience the sensual pleasures of the world. Though married to the voluptuous Amy Yip (who claims that triads forced her to appear in this movie totally nude), Ng is unsatisfied, and tries to improve his sex life by getting a penis transplant from a horse. The film's utter absurdity has helped make it a cult classic in the West.

SEXY AND DANGEROUS
古惑女之決戰江湖
Year: 1996
Director: Billy Tang
Producer: Wong Jing
Stars: Loletta Lee, Karen Mok, Francis Ng

A tribute to Hong Kong efficiency, *Sexy and Dangerous* was made from start to finish in about three weeks, to capitalize on the success of *Young and Dangerous*, which was similarly based on a popular Cantonese comic book. This movie centers around a tough girl gang led by Bo Ji (Loletta Lee), whose ex-boyfriend, Brother One, has not gotten over her. When another of Brother One's girlfriends is released from prison, she sets in motion a violent revenge scheme against Bo Ji and her gang.

SHANGHAI BLUES
上海之夜
Year: 1984
Director and Producer: Tsui Hark
Stars: Sylvia Chang, Kenny Bee, Sally Yeh

One of Tsui Hark's most admired films, this is a romantic comedy, set in Shanghai during and after World War II. In 1937, Kenny Bee and Sylvia Chang meet under a bridge, where they are taking shelter from a Japanese air-raid; though it is dark, and they cannot see one another, they vow to meet again after the war. Ten years later, Bee settles into a Shanghai apartment building, unaware that Chang, for whom he is searching, is his neighbor.

SLAVE OF THE SWORD
劍奴
Year: 1993
Director: Chu Yen-ping
Stars: Pauline Chan, Max Mok, Joyce Ngai

Category III remake of the 1972 film *Intimate Confessions of a Chinese Courtesan*, about a woman in Ming Dynasty China who is forced to work at a brothel after her father is killed. The proprietress of the brothel, along with her beefy boyfriend, is an assassin, at the beck and call of an evil eunuch. Part erotic thriller, and part martial-arts film, *Slave of the Sword* is replete with surprising plot twists.

SOMEBODY UP THERE LIKES ME
浪漫風暴
Year: 1996
Director: Patrick Leung
Producer: John Woo
Stars: Aaron Kwok, Carman Lee, Sammo Hung, Michael Tong, Hilary Tsui, Law Koon-lan

Patrick Leung, a former assistant to John Woo, makes his directorial début with this boxing melodrama, which Woo produced. Aaron Kwok is a drifter who falls for Carman Lee, and takes up boxing – to impress her, and defend himself against her quarrelsome brother, the reigning Hong Kong champion. When a professional bout between Kwok and the brother goes horribly wrong, Kwok turns to a dangerous life of high-stakes underground boxing, until he is given a second chance.

SONG OF THE EXILE
客途秋恨
Year: 1990
Director: Ann Hui
Stars: Maggie Cheung, Waise Lee, Luk Siu-fan

Song of the Exile is Ann Hui's most personal film, with a storyline drawn somewhat from her own life. Maggie Cheung has left Hong Kong to study broadcast reporting in London, but returns home for a wedding, where she is reunited with her Japanese-born mother – unhappily, because the two are constantly arguing. When the mother decides to move back with her estranged family in Japan, Cheung tags along, and gradually discovers the strong similarities between her mother and herself, both of whom have lived as exiles.

SOUL
老娘狗騷
Year: 1986
Director: Shu Kei
Stars: Deannie Yip, Elaine Kam, Dennis Chan, Hou Hsiou-hsien, Jackie Cheung

A very different sort of gangster film, in the spirit of John Cassavetes' *Gloria*, from Shu Kei, a noted Hong Kong film critic. Deannie Yip plays a woman married to a police officer with secret ties to triads, and who one day mysteriously leaps to his death. That same day, three inept gangsters try to kill Yip and her neighbor (Elaine Kam), but succeed only in killing Kam. Yip takes custody of Kam's son – fathered illegitimately, it turns out, by Yip's late husband – and hits the road, with the gangsters in pursuit. The noted Taiwanese art-house director Hou Hsiou-hsien (*A City of Sadness*), in a rare acting role, plays Yip's ex-boyfriend.

THE SPOOKY BUNCH

撞到正

Year: 1980
Director: Ann Hui
Assistant Director: Stanley Kwan
Producer: Josephine Siao
Writer: Joyce Chan
Stars: Josephine Siao, Kenny Bee, Tina Lui, Kwan Chung

In Ann Hui's classic ghostly comedy, a second-rate opera troupe is hired by a rich man who wants to marry off his nephew (Kenny Bee) to the troupe's leading lady (Josephine Siao), in the hopes that the marriage will remove a family curse. Instead, the troupe is bedeviled by a female spirit named Cat Shit, a harbinger of even worse to come – it turns out that the grandfathers of both Bee and Siao had fatally poisoned an entire army battalion with bad medicine, and the day of reckoning is at hand. Unlike Sammo Hung's *Encounters of Spooky Kind*, made the same year – and its innumerable knockoffs – Hui's film features virtually no martial arts or special effects.

SPOOKY ENCOUNTERS (*see* ENCOUNTERS OF THE SPOOKY KIND II)

STAGE DOOR (*see* HU-DU-MEN)

STARRY IS THE NIGHT

今夜星光燦爛

Year: 1988
Director: Ann Hui
Stars: Brigitte Lin, George Lam, David Wu, Derek Yee, John Woo

In this politically tinged melodrama, filmed against the Hong Kong riots of 1967, Brigitte Lin is a student having an affair with her married English literature professor. The doomed romance thwarts Lin from forming lasting relationships with men for two decades, but in the 1980s she takes up happily with a younger man, only to discover that he is the professor's son.

STONE AGE WARRIORS
魔域飛龍
Year: 1990
Director: Stanley Tong
Stars: Elaine Lui, Nina Li Chi, Fan Siu-wong

When a rich man disappears in the rain forest of New Guinea, his daughter and a female insurance investigator attempt to find him. Once in the jungle, they team up with a missionary skilled in martial arts, and fight off cannibals, komodo dragons, insects, and, ultimately, the drug dealers who kidnapped the rich man. The film that put Stanley Tong on the map as a director, paving the way for a number of successful collaborations with Jackie Chan.

STORY OF RICKY
力王
Year: 1991
Director: Lan Nai-kai
Stars: Fan Siu-wong, Yukari Oshima, Gloria Yip, Frankie Chin

Adapted from *Riki-Oh*, a Japanese anime, this film is set in a bleak future in which prisons are run by private corporations. Ricky is a new inmate who soon finds himself pitted against other convicts, and a corrupt warden. The film is unstinting in its comic-book gore – in one scene, a man strangles an opponent with his own intestines. Japanese action icon Yukari Oshima appears in a trouser role, as one of the warden's henchmen.

THE STORY OF WOO VIET
胡越的故事
Year: 1981
Director: Ann Hui
Assistant Director: Stanley Kwan
Producer: Teddy Robin Kwan
Writer: Alfred Cheung
Art Director: Tony Au
Stars: Chow Yun-fat, Cherie Chung, Cora Miao, Lo Lieh

Chow Yun-fat was still a soap-opera hunk on television when he proved his mettle as an actor in this bleak drama by Ann Hui. He plays a Vietnamese boat person who lands in a refugee camp in Hong Kong, where he is targeted for death after he learns about a murder committed by an undercover agent. He and a Vietnamese girlfriend acquire fake passports and set out for the United States, but the woman gets waylaid en route, in the Philippines, and forced into prostitution. Desperate to rescue his girlfriend, Chow becomes the unwilling assistant to the crime boss who now controls her.

STREET ANGELS
紅燈區
Year: 1996
Director: Billy Tang
Stars: Chingmy Yau, Simon Yam, Valerie Chow, Michael Tao, Tsui Kam-kong

Chingmy Yau is a young woman who takes the rap for a crime she didn't commit, while sleazy boyfriend Simon Yam flees to Holland. After her release from jail, she ends up as a madam at a high-priced karaoke club, incurring a bitter rivalry with another such club across the street. Soon the rivalry turns deadly, and Yam returns – to help out the wrong side.

SUMMER SNOW
女人四十
Year: 1995
Director: Ann Hui
Stars: Josephine Siao, Roy Chiao, Law Kar-ying, Ha Ping

Ann Hui's comeback picture swept the Hong Kong Film Awards, and garnered the Best Actress prize at the Berlin Film Festival for Josephine Siao. Siao plays a forty-year-old professional woman whose life is turned upside down when her husband's father (Roy Chiao) is diagnosed with Alzheimer's Disease, and she is the only person who can communicate with him. A simple, surprisingly uplifting film.

SUNLESS DAYS
沒有太陽的日子
Year: 1990
Director: Shu Kei
Stars: Hou Hsiao-hsien, Yang Wong, Francis Yum, Manfred Wong

In 1989, a Japanese television station hired film critic and director
Shu Kei to produce a documentary about a Taiwanese composer.
Then the Tiananmen Square Massacre took place, and Shu Kei
instead made *Sunless Days*, a series of interviews among the
Chinese diaspora in Hong Kong and around the world –
everywhere but the mainland itself – recording the effect of the
crackdown on the Chinese psyche. After a theatrical version of the
film took a prize at the Berlin Film Festival, the censorship board
in Hong Kong unexpectedly cleared the film for release at home.

SUPERCOP (*aka* POLICE STORY III)
警察故事 III：超級警察
Year: 1992
Director: Stanley Tong
Stars: Jackie Chan, Michelle Yeoh, Maggie Cheung, Yuen Wah,
Ken Lo, Bill Tung

Jackie Chan's Hong Kong cop is teamed up with Michelle Yeoh's
straitlaced police inspector from mainland China for an undercover
assignment that lands them both inside a drug-smuggling gang,
posing as brother and sister. They win the confidence of Panther, a
high-ranking gang member, who brings them to Hong Kong to
meet the boss; but their cover is blown in Malaysia by Chan's
jealous girlfriend. For the climactic chase sequence, which involves
a train and a helicopter, Chan and Yeoh both do their own life-
threatening stunts. In the slightly cut American version, they also
do their own English dubbing.

SUPER MISCHIEVES
無敵反斗星
Year: 1995
Director: Chu Yen-ping
Stars: Ng Man-tat, Eric Kot, Carol Cheng, Sik Siu-lung, Kok Siu-man

Another in the series of children's action-comedies from Chu Yen-ping (*China Dragon*), which finds his stock characters, the Shaolin Popeys – two kid monks – teaming up with an unruly older monk to regain a sacred scroll purloined by a witch. En route, they pick up a strange man who claims to be the original Forrest Gump. Like other films in the series, this one features plenty of surreal comedy and martial-arts mayhem.

THE SWORD
劍
Year: 1980
Director: Patrick Tam
Action Director: Ching Siu-tung
Stars: Tsui Siu-keung, Adam Cheng

Considered a classic of the Hong Kong new wave, this film tells the story of a cursed sword which brings doom on its owner. An old man gives the sword to a former lover, who turns it over to a wandering swordsman looking to duel the old man. The bad luck of the sword takes a backseat, however, to the villainy of Tsui Siu-keung, who masterminds a revenge scheme against nearly every character in the film.

SWORD OF MANY LOVES
飛狐外傳
Year: 1992
Director: Poon Man-kit
Stars: Leon Lai, Michelle Reis, Cheung Man, Tsui Kam-kong

Loosely based on a novel by Louis Cha (*Romance of Book and Sword*), this is the story of a wandering young swordsman who befriends a female monk conceived when her mother was brutally raped by a villainous martial artist. Along the way, the couple teams up with an expert in potent poisons, one of which causes a person to grow until his bones crack. The film is chock full of fight sequences, some of which are exceedingly strange.

SWORDSMAN
笑傲江湖
Year: 1990
Credited Director: King Hu
Acting Directors: Tsui Hark, Raymond Lee, and Ching Siu-tung
Producer: Tsui Hark
Cinematographer: Peter Pau
Stars: Sam Hui, Cecilia Yip, Yuen Wah, Jacky Cheung, Cheung Man, Lam Ching-ying, Wu Ma, Fennie Yuen

Yet another sword epic adapted from a Louis Cha novel. In Ming Dynasty China, a swordsman named Fox (Sam Hui), and his female sidekick Kiddo (Cecilia Yip), are inadvertently caught up in a power struggle among several martial-arts clans, all trying to obtain a sacred scroll that imbues supernatural powers. Superb cinematography and fighting effects redefined the swordplay genre, and paved the way for the even more successful sequel. *Swordsman* was to be directed by the legendary King Hu, but he and producer Tsui Hark clashed, and he walked off the set. Tsui took over, along with Raymond Lee and Ching Siu-tung. (A fourth uncredited director, Ann Hui, says her role in the film was "negligible.")

SWORDSMAN II
笑傲江湖之東方不敗
Year: 1991
Director and Action Director: Ching Siu-tung
Producer: Tsui Hark
Stars: Jet Li, Brigitte Lin, Rosamund Kwan, Michelle Reis, Fennie Yuen, Waise Lee

Virtually the entire cast of Part I was replaced for the sequel, one of the biggest successes ever for Tsui Hark's Film Workshop. The story picks up a year later as Fox (Jet Li) and Kiddo (Michelle Reis) learn that the sacred book from Part I has fallen into the hands of Asia the Invincible (Brigitte Lin), a man who has changed his sex in the process of acquiring unthinkable power. As part of her plan of conquest, Asia the Invincible has imprisoned the father of a woman to whom Fox is beholden, drawing Fox into an inevitable showdown with Asia. Considered the archetypal new-wave swordplay film, with wire-enhanced fight choreography that has seldom been surpassed.

SWORDSMAN III (*see* EAST IS RED)

T

TAI CHI MASTER
太極張三丰
Year: 1993
Director: Yuen Woo-ping
Stars: Jet Li, Michelle Yeoh, Fennie Yuen, Chin Siu-ho

Jet Li and Chin Siu-ho are two young Shaolin monks unjustly kicked out of the monastery and forced to adapt to life in the secular world. The power-hungry Chin becomes a soldier for an evil eunuch, a betrayal of Buddhist principals that literally causes Li to lose his mind. With the help of some local rebels, including Michelle Yeoh, Li regains his stability, and meanwhile invents the Tai-Chi style of fighting, which he uses to defeat his former friend.

TAXI HUNTER
的士判官
Year: 1993
Director: Herman Yau
Stars: Anthony Wong, Yu Rong-guang, Ng Man-tat

Anthony Wong gives a memorable performance as a meek architect whose life is destroyed when his pregnant wife dies because of a taxi driver's negligence. He turns vigilante, taking cab rides at night, and killing any driver who is so much as discourteous. By a coincidence, the cop assigned to investigate the string of murders is Wong's best friend. Despite a Category III rating, the violence is restrained; the film plays mainly as a character study of a man pushed over the edge.

TEMPTATION OF A MONK
誘僧
Year: 1993
Director: Clara Law
Producer: Teddy Robin Kwan
Writers: Eddie Fong and Lilian Lee
Stars: Joan Chen, Wu Xing-guo, Zhang Feng-yi

Slow-moving epic set during the Tang Dynasty over a thousand years ago. A general is disgraced – and his mother commits suicide – when royal travelers under his protection are massacred in battle. To win his redemption, he becomes a monk, and so do the remnants of his men; but within the walls of the monastery, the soldiers cannot resist plotting their revenge. International star Joan Chen plays two roles, including a bald-headed assassin.

TEPPANYAKI
鐵板燒
Year: 1983
Director and Writer: Michael Hui
Producer: Raymond Chow
Stars: Michael Hui, Sally Yeh, Frances Yip, Lo Hoi-pang

Michael Hui plays a knife-wielding teppanyaki chef at a Japanese restaurant, unhappily married to an obese wife with an overbearing father. He leads a double life, however, with stewardess Sally Yeh, who invites him to join her on an island in the Philippines. Unfortunately, Hui's wife and father-in-law decide to tag along on his ostensible business trip, causing a series of mishaps and close calls. Gradually, Hui learns to be a man and take responsibility for his life. Stronger on plot than many of the earlier comedies featuring Hui with brothers Sam and Ricky.

THE TERRACOTTA WARRIOR

古今大戰秦俑情

Year: 1989
Director: Ching Siu-tung
Producer: Tsui Hark
Cinematographer: Peter Pau
Stars: Zhang Yimou, Gong Li, Yu Rong-guang

In a triumph of memorable casting, art-house director Zhang Yimou (*Raise the Red Lantern*) stars opposite his then-favorite leading lady, Gong Li, who was also his mistress at the time, in this most unusual love story. Zhang plays a guardsman in ancient China who has a forbidden affair with Li, one of the emperor's concubines; she is burned to death, and he is encased in a clay statue. In the twentieth century, Li, now playing the girlfriend of gangster Yu Rong-guang, stumbles on the statue; it cracks apart, and Zhang is set free, alive. Yu wants Zhang to lead him to the treasures of the emperor's lost lair, while Zhang wants only to rekindle his relationship with the woman he believes is his lover.

THUNDERBOLT

霹靂火

Year: 1995
Director: Gordon Chan
Uncredited Co-Directors: Corey Yuen, Sammo Hung, and Frankie Chan
Stars: Jackie Chan, Anita Yuen, Michael Wong, Ken Lo

Thunderbolt began as a small film about auto racing, but after the success of Jackie Chan's *Rumble in the Bronx*, it ballooned into the most expensive Hong Kong movie up to that time; along the way, it acquired at least four directors, but not much of a plot. Chan plays an auto mechanic who helps the Hong Kong police catch a murderous Caucasian race-car driver. When the villain gets out of jail, he terrorizes Chan and his family – in one big-budget scene, a house and its occupants are hoisted off the ground by a crane – and will not relent until Chan agrees to challenge him in a car race in Japan.

TIGER CAGE
特警屠龍
Year: 1988
Director: Yuen Woo-ping
Producer: Stephen Shin
Stars: Jacky Cheung, Carol Cheng, Simon Yam, Ng Man-tat, Donnie Yen, Leung Ka-yan

Martial-arts director Yuen Woo-ping took the helm of this modern-day cop movie, about three police officers who bring down a drug gang, to the dismay of some of their superiors, who have had illegal dealings with the gang. As the cops begin to uncover the truth about corruption in the force, they find their own lives in peril.

TIGER CAGE II
洗黑錢
Year: 1990
Director: Yuen Woo-ping
Stars: Donnie Yen, Rosamund Kwan, Cynthia Khan, David Wu, Robin Shou, Michael Woods, Carol Cheng (cameo)

Unrelated sequel finds Donnie Yen (who got bumped off playing a different character in Part I) as a headstrong former cop who, along with attorney Rosamund Kwan, witnesses a botched robbery that ends in murder. Yen and Kwan immediately find themselves suspects, and they flee the police handcuffed to one another. Worse yet, the unsuccessful robbers believe the couple got away with the money, and they, too, give chase.

TIGER ON BEAT
老虎出更
Year: 1988
Director: Lau Kar-leung
Producer: Karl Maka
Stars: Chow Yun-fat, Ti Lung, Conan Lee, Nina Li Chi, Tsui Sui-keung, Gordon Liu

A smash hit in Hong Kong, *Tiger on Beat* is a buddy film which finds Chow Yun-fat as a clownish cop mismatched with the humorless, muscle-bound Conan Lee. The two men attempt to use Nina Li Chi to get to her brother, who is involved in a drug syndicate, but matters get complicated when Chow becomes interested in her romantically. The film mixes comedy with some hair-raising action sequences, including a climactic duel with chainsaws.

TIME WARRIORS (*see* ICEMAN COMETH)

TO BE NUMBER ONE
跛豪
Year: 1991
Director: Poon Man-kit
Producer: Johnny Mak
Stars: Ray Lui, Kent Cheng, Cecilia Yip, Waise Lee, Amy Yip, Lawrence Ng, Lo Lieh, Ng Man-tat, Tsui Kam-kong

This ambitious though uneven gangster film – Hong Kong's attempt at a *Godfather* epic, without the corresponding production values – surprisingly beat out Tsui Hark's *Once upon a Time in China* for Best Picture at the 1991 Hong Kong Film Awards. It traces the rise and fall of Limpy Ho (Ray Lui), a Shantou mobster who overthrows the head of a crime syndicate and takes his place. Ho's arrogance ultimately brings him down, at the hands of his own former friends.

TO LIV(E)
浮世戀曲
Year: 1990
Director: Evans Chan
Stars: Lindsay Chan, Josephine Koo, Anthony Wong (Yiu-ming), Fung Kin-chung, Elsie Tu, Ha Ping, Suen Ming-chui

Critical success and winner of two Golden Horse awards (Lindsay Chan, Best Actress, and Josephine Koo, Best Supporting Actress). Chan is a young intellectual who becomes incensed when the Swedish actress Liv Ulmann condemns Hong Kong for deporting Vietnamese refugees. Chan begins composing a letter of rebuke, and carries on a discussion about Hong Kong identity with a variety of friends. Meanwhile the movie explores Chan's troubled relationship with her family members, including a younger brother engaged to a much older woman. A film unlike any other to come out of Hong Kong.

TO LIVE AND DIE IN TSIMSHATSUI
新邊緣人
Year: 1994
Director: Andrew Lau
Stars: Jacky Cheung, Tony Leung (Ka-fai), Wu Chien-lien, Roy Cheung, Shing Fui-on

Slick production featuring Jacky Cheung as a cop who goes undercover as a triad in order to achieve a quick promotion. He undergoes an identity crisis, however, when he is treated better by the triads than by his police superiors. Meanwhile, he falls for the mentally unstable sister of the one of the triads (Wu Chien-lien, in a departure from her usual good-girl role).

TOM, DICK AND HAIRY
風塵三俠
Year: 1993
Directors: Peter Chan and Lee Chi-ngai
Cast: Tony Leung (Chiu-wai), Tony Leung (Ka-fai), Lawrence Cheng, Ann Bridgewater, Anita Yuen, Athena Chu, Michael Chow (cameo)

The movie that put the United Filmmakers Organization on the map is a comedy featuring the two Tony Leungs (Chui-wai as Tom, and Ka-fai as Dick) and Lawrence Cheng (Hairy), three roommates in present-day Hong Kong. The plot mainly concerns their sexual and romantic escapades. Tom's plans for upward mobility via a loveless marriage gets a jolt when he meets Cat, a woman from an escort service; Dick is a promiscuous tour guide for Japanese visitors; while Hairy (whose real name is Giorgio) careers from one disastrous relationship to another.

TOP BANANA CLUB
金裝香蕉俱樂部
Year: 1996
Director: Anthony Wong
Stars: Anthony Wong, Dayo Wong, Vivian Chow

Anthony Wong's second outing as a director is a sendup of an insipid – not to mention overbearingly sexist – Michael Chow comedy called *Banana Club*. Using the same plot device as the film it satirizes, the three hosts of a radio talk show listen to callers describe their romantic travails, and then visualize themselves acting out the callers' stories. In one scenario, a would-be suitor tries to curry favor with a woman's father by capturing some killers; in another, a man tries to persuade his wife to get breast implants; and in a third, Anthony Wong tries to seduce three lesbians.

A TOUCH OF LOVE (*see* WITCH FROM NEPAL)

TREASURE HUNT
花旗少林
Year: 1994
Director: Jeff Lau
Stars: Chow Yun-fat, Wu Chien-lien, Gordon Liu, Philip Kwok, Michael Wong (cameo)

A blend of genres – from gangster film to romance to supernatural comedy – that has "made in Hong Kong" written all over it. Chow Yun-fat plays a CIA agent sent to a Buddhist temple in China on a mission to protect a national treasure. The "treasure" turns out to be Wu Chien-lien, a girl gifted with supernatural powers. While most of the film deals with Chow's humorous attempts to westernize the monks, and his budding romance with Wu, the calm is disrupted by Chinese gangsters, providing Chow an opportunity to play the heroic gunfighter that his fans expect.

TRICKY BRAINS
整蠱專家
Year: 1991
Director: Wong Jing
Stars: Stephen Chiau, Andy Lau, Ng Man-tat, Rosamund Kwan, Chingmy Yau, Wong Jing, Waise Lee, Shing Fui-on (cameo)

Stephen Chiau stars as the "Handsome Trick Expert," a man hired to pull elaborate pranks on people. He experiences remorse, however, after a business executive uses him to thwart the romance of office manager Andy Lau and clerk Rosamund Kwan, because he wants Kwan for himself. Chiau demonstrates once again why his style of comedy is called *mo lai to*, or "makes no sense" – one scene, for instance, is carried off in the style of Peking Opera, with no explanation given.

TWENTY SOMETHING
晚 9 朝 5
Year: 1994
Director: Teddy Chan
Producer: Peter Chan
Stars: Valerie Chow, Jordan Chan, Moses Chan, Farini Cheung, Yau Chau-yuet

Another box-office success from UFO, a relatively new film-makers' collective that takes inspiration from American movies and television. *Twenty Something* reworks the basic premise of *St. Elmo's Fire*, following the lives of several people in their twenties who occupy themselves with drinking, dancing, and sex, and who lack the ability to commit emotionally. The film won praise for its strong ensemble cast, largely of newcomers, including Jordan Chan, who snagged the Best Supporting Actor statue at the Hong Kong Film Awards; the sex and nudity, meanwhile, earned the film a Category III rating.

TWIN DRAGONS
雙龍會
Year: 1992
Directors: Tsui Hark and Ringo Lam
Producer: Teddy Robin Kwan
Stars: Jackie Chan, Teddy Robin Kwan, Maggie Cheung, Nina Li
Chi

In a conceit borrowed from Jean-Claude Van Damme's *Double
Impact*, Jackie Chan plays twins separated at birth and unaware of
each others' existence. One has grown up to become a Hong Kong
garage attendant and streetfighter, while the other is a renowned
concert pianist and conductor raised in the West. When the musical
twin arrives in Hong Kong to give a concert, he and his brother
inadvertently swap places, befuddling their respective girlfriends,
and presenting each of them with challenges he is ill-equipped to
handle. Chan, as usual, does some life-threatening stunts; in one
scene, he is nearly crushed by a car dropped from a hydraulic lift.

TWINKLE, TWINKLE LUCKY STARS
夏日福星
Year: 1985
Director: Sammo Hung
Stars: Sammo Hung, Jackie Chan, Yuen Biao, Eric Tsang, Andy
Lau, Richard Ng, Sibelle Hu, John Sham, Fung Shui-fan, Richard
Norton, Rosamund Kwan, Yasuaki Kurata, Michelle Yeoh (cameo)

Like *My Lucky Stars*, its predecessor, this is an action comedy
directed by Sammo Hung, featuring himself and his two childhood
friends, Jackie Chan and Yuen Biao. The Lucky Stars are a group of
clownish crimebusters who, this time around, try to spare a Hong
Kong drug lord from assassination by Thailand rivals. Hung's
action choreography helps redeem the lightweight plot; in one
memorable sequence, he trounces a villain with a pair of tennis
racquets.

U

UMBRELLA STORY
人間有情
Year: 1995
Director and Producer: Clifton Ko
Writer: Raymond To
Stars: Alice Lau, Law Koon-lan, So Yuk-wah, Fung Wai-hung

Though not a true story, this warmly nostalgic film is centered around a real umbrella shop which stood the test of time by lasting a century. Over three generations, the family that owns the shop experiences the fall of the Qing Dynasty, the Japanese occupation, and the 1967 riots. The film also takes a page from *Forrest Gump* by integrating contemporary actors with historical figures, both real and cinematic.

UNDERGROUND BANKER
香港奇案之吸血貴利王
Year: 1993
Director: Bosco Lam
Producer: Wong Jing
Stars: Anthony Wong, Lawrence Ng, Wong Chi-yeung

Anthony Wong stars in this black comedy, which satirizes the very Category III films of which he is a staple. He plays a timid truck driver whose wife borrows a large sum of money from loansharks, and, unable to pay her debt, is forced into prostitution. Still dissatisfied, the loansharks turn violent; but luckily, Wong's new neighbor and ally is the psychotic Dr. Lamb, the main character from another exploitation film.

WEB OF DECEPTION (*see* DECEPTION)

WE'RE GOING TO EAT YOU
地獄無門
Year: 1980
Director: Tsui Hark
Stars: Tsui Siu-keung, Eddie Ko, Melvin Wong

Tsui Hark's second film is one of his strangest – a horror-comedy about a secluded island community whose inhabitants are cannibals. Tsui Siu-keung is the secret agent sent to the island to hunt a dangerous criminal, only to discover that all strangers to the community are classified as food. Tsui throws elaborate kung-fu and graphic gore into the mix, making this film a cult favorite in the West.

WHAT A WONDERFUL WORLD
奇異旅程之真心愛生命
Year: 1995
Director and Writer: Samson Chiu
Stars: Andy Lau, Kenny Bee, Theresa Lee, Kent Cheng, Paul Fonoroff

Andy Lau is a reporter who finds out he is terminally ill, and decides to go out with a bang. In order to cover the story of a daring heist, he volunteers himself as a hostage, but matters take an unexpected turn when the robber (Kenny Bee) is killed while making his getaway. It is now up to Lau to carry a vital message to Bee's prostitute girlfriend.

WHAT PRICE SURVIVAL
94 獨臂刀之情
Year: 1994
Director: Lee Yan-kong
Stars: David Chiang, Tsui Siu-keung, Charlie Yeung, Wu Xing-guo, Damian Lau, Ko Kin

An Oedipal swordplay film from first-time director Lee Yan-kong.

When Tsui Siu-keung wins a duel by cheating, he asks not for his opponent's life, but rather the man's newborn son. Tsui raises the boy as his stepson, and ultimately sends him out to kill his real father. After the patricide is done, the son discovers the truth, and swears vengeance against Tsui. The movie has a strong visual flair, which was to be expected from Lee, who previously directed music videos.

WHEELS ON MEALS
快餐車
Year: 1984
Director: Sammo Hung
Stars: Jackie Chan, Yuen Biao, Sammo Hung, Lola Forner, Benny "The Jet" Urquidez, Richard Ng (cameo), John Sham (cameo), Wu Ma (cameo)

One of the most popular films featuring the threesome of Jackie Chan, Yuen Biao, and Sammo Hung. In Barcelona (where the movie was shot), Chan and Yuen run a fast-food Chinese restaurant out of a high-tech van. They both find themselves attracted to a mysterious Spanish woman, who unknowingly is an heiress to a vast fortune. When some heavies, sent by a greedy stepbrother, attempt to kidnap the woman, it is up to Chan and Biao, and bumbling detective Sammo Hung, to rescue her.

THE WICKED CITY
妖獸都市
Year: 1992
Director: Peter Mak
Producer: Tsui Hark
Stars: Jacky Cheung, Leon Lai, Michelle Reis, Carman Lee, Roy Cheung

For all its emphasis on special effects, the Hong Kong cinema is not big on science fiction; this film, based on a Japanese anime of the same name, is a notable exception. In the Hong Kong of the future, two policemen (Jacky Cheung and Leon Lai) are assigned to the anti-raptor squad. Raptors are ferociously predatory aliens able to take human form. As of late, some raptors have been dealing a drug called Happiness, which has the unfortunate side-effect of killing the user. Matters become more complicated when it is revealed that Cheung is actually half a raptor, while Lai is in love with one (Michelle Reis).

WILD SEARCH
伴我闖天涯
Year: 1989
Director and Producer: Ringo Lam
Stars: Chow Yun-fat, Cherie Chung, Roy Cheung, Paul Chun

Drama similar in story line to Peter Weir's *Witness*. Chow Yun-fat plays a tough cop assigned to protect a little girl who has witnessed the triad murder of her mother. The girl now lives in the countryside, in the custody of her aunt (Cherie Chung), for whom Chow, a widower, soon develops a romantic interest. Such distractions need to be set aside, however, when a Vietnamese hit man shows up, determined to do whatever is necessary to kill the girl.

WING CHUN
詠春
Year: 1993
Director: Yuen Woo-ping
Stars: Michelle Yeoh, Donnie Yen, Waise Lee, Yuen King-tan, Cheng Pei-pei, Tsui Siu-keung

Michelle Yeoh plays the title character, a real Ming Dynasty woman who invented the fighting style that bears her name; but director Yuen Woo-ping is less interested in historical accuracy than in fashioning a feminist action-comedy. When she isn't driving off the local bandits, Wing Chun helps run the town's local bean-curd shop, where the men customers find her intimidating. One bad guy, however, is so bold as to kidnap a young widow under Wing's care, leading to a series of showdowns.

WINNERS AND SINNERS
奇謀妙計五福星
Year: 1983
Director: Sammo Hung
Writers: Sammo Hung and Barry Wong
Stars: Sammo Hung, Jackie Chan, Richard Ng, John Sham, James Tien, Yuen Biao (cameo)

Action comedy about five criminals who set up a legitimate cleaning service after being released from jail. Unfortunately, one of their customers is a counterfeiter; while cleaning his home, the ex-cons inadvertently take possession of a printing plate, and find themselves hunted by triads. A precursor to Sammo Hung's *Lucky Stars* series, this film is largely a series of comedy skits, peppered with dynamic martial arts, and stunt sequences, including one in which Jackie Chan roller-skates under a fast-moving truck.

WITCH FROM NEPAL (*aka* A TOUCH OF LOVE)
奇緣
Year: 1986
Director: Ching Siu-tung
Stars: Chow Yun-fat, Cherie Chung, Dick Wei, Emily Chu, Yammie Nam

In Nepal, a religious master is fatally wounded by an evil warlock seeking a medallion that grants telekinetic power. Before the master dies, he sends good witch Cherie Chung to Hong Kong to bestow the coveted pendant on an unsuspecting Chow Yun-fat. Chow soon finds himself locked in battle with the warlock, in a showdown heavy on special effects, including a simulated zombie attack. Though uneven, *Witch from Nepal* foreshadows the fantasy films, including *A Chinese Ghost Story*, that brought fame to director Ching Siu-tung.

WONDER SEVEN
七金剛
Year: 1994
Director: Ching Siu-tung
Stars: Michelle Yeoh, Li Ning, Kent Cheng, Hilary Tsui, Xiong Xin-xin, Andy Hui, Tsui Kam-kong, Kam Wai-ying

The Wonder Seven are a mainland special-forces team working undercover in Hong Kong on cases that cross border lines. While tracking some stolen bank cards, the septet runs head on into Michelle Yeoh, the accomplice of bad guy Kam Wai-ying, who is trying to recover the cards for himself. Kam's treachery causes Yeoh to switch sides and join forces with the special-forces team, and the finale finds them, along with the Chinese army and a passel of villains, battling it out in a high rise.

Y

YES, MADAM! (*aka* IN THE LINE OF DUTY)
皇家師姐
Year: 1985
Director: Corey Yuen
Producer: Sammo Hung
Stars: Michelle Yeoh, Cynthia Rothrock, Tsui Hark, John Sham, Mang Hoi, Wu Ma (cameo)

The action-heroine film, a thriving Hong Kong subgenre, began with this groundbreaking movie, which made an overnight star of Michelle Yeoh. She and American martial artist Cynthia Rothrock play mismatched cops who are tracking down microfilm that incriminates some top gangsters, while Tsui Hark and John Sham provide the comic relief.

YOUNG AND DANGEROUS

古惑仔之人在江湖

Year: 1996
Director: Andrew Lau
Producer: Wong Jing
Stars: Dior Cheng, Jordan Chan, Gigi Lai, Simon Yam, Francis Ng, Jerry Lam, Michael Tse, Jason Chu, Shing Fui-on (cameo)

This film, based on the Chinese comic book *Teddy Boy*, was so popular that it spawned two sequels the same year – not to mention the semi-sequel *Sexy and Dangerous*. Two honorable young gangsters (Dior Cheng and Jordan Chan) rise through the ranks, ultimately coming into the employ of Simon Yam, the head of the notorious Hung Hing Society. Unfortunately, a rival triad named Ugly Kwan wants Cheng and Chan dead in order to settle an old score.

YOUNG AND DANGEROUS II

古惑仔 II 之猛龍過江

Year: 1996
Director: Andrew Lau
Stars: Jordan Chan, Dior Cheng, Anthony Wong, Chingmy Yau, Gigi Lai, Simon Yam, Lui Chun, Halina Tam, Jerry Lam

The triad boys are back, this time conducting business in Taipei, where Jordan Chan encounters femme fatale Chingmy Yau, the head of a rival Taiwanese crime syndicate. More sophisticated than Part I, this film also makes a mockery of the corrupt Kuomintang legislature – a sign of the times, since Taiwan, historically the biggest export market for Hong Kong films, was long held sacrosanct.

YOUNG AND DANGEROUS III
古惑仔 III 之隻手遮天
Year: 1996
Director: Andrew Lau
Stars: Dior Cheng, Jordan Chan, Karen Mok, Simon Yam, Anthony Wong, Gigi Lai, Roy Cheung, Jerry Lam

In Part III, Jordan Chan returns from Taiwan to rejoin his old triad society, and becomes involved with a preacher's daughter (Karen Mok) who is anything but straitlaced. Dior Cheng, meanwhile, is trying to help his wounded girlfriend recover from a bout of amnesia. Presently, the Hung Hing gang ventures to Amsterdam, where its ranks are depleted in an ambush, for which Cheng is wrongly held accountable.

Z

ZODIAC KILLERS
極道追蹤
Year: 1991
Director: Ann Hui
Stars: Andy Lau, Cherie Chung, Yasuaki Kurata

A dark crime drama from art-house director Ann Hui, set in Japan, where Hong Kong student Andy Lau takes a shine to fellow student Cherie Chung. She already has a boyfriend, however – a former Yakuza – though presently he is murdered by his ex-colleagues. Chung turns to Lau to help her leave the country, and to deliver evidence that incriminates the murderers into the proper hands.

ZU: WARRIORS FROM THE MAGIC MOUNTAIN
蜀山
Year: 1983
Director: Tsui Hark
Producer: Raymond Chow
Stars: Yuen Biao, Sammo Hung, Adam Cheng, Brigitte Lin, Mang Hoi, Moon Lee, Damian Lau

Director Tsui Hark recruited a number of the special-effects people who worked with George Lucas on *Star Wars* to create this groundbreaking Chinese fantasy film. Yuen Biao is a disillusioned soldier who finds himself lost in the Magic Mountain, an evil place inhabited by ghosts and demons. He meets several righteous masters and their disciples, and joins in the battle to prevent the Blood Monster from destroying the world. As with Tsui's three earlier features, the style is relatively cold and detached; but the all-star cast and dazzling effects helped make this film a cult classic.

4 Recommended Viewing

Twelve Critics Choose Their Favorite Hong Kong Films

Peggy Chiao, Howard Hampton, Dave Kehr, Andy Klein, Law Kar, Barry Long, Ric Meyers, Jimmy Ngai, John Powers, Tony Rayns, Barbara Scharres, and Chuck Stephens

Introduction
Fredric Dannen

American viewers are drawn to the Hong Kong cinema for a variety of reasons, but my own interest in the genre was piqued in a rather unusual way. In November, 1992, I published an article in *The New Yorker* about a Chinese youth gang in New York, and became fascinated with Chinese organized crime. A journalist friend, Frank DiGiacomo at *The New York Observer*, urged me to take a look at *The Killer*, by John Woo, a film and a director I'd frankly never heard of. As it turned out, the movie did not realistically depict the workings of triad societies, but no matter – I was hooked on Woo, and on his charismatic leading man, Chow Yun-fat.

In the interim, another journalist friend, Jeff Ressner, at *Time* magazine in Los Angeles – an authentic Hong Kong movie buff, which Frank was not – had been urging me for some time to rent Hong Kong films from Kim's Video on St. Mark's Place, in New York. During one of his visits, we dropped by Kim's, and he handed me a copy of Jackie Chan's *Project A II*. Once assured that it was not necessary to have seen the first installment in the series, I rented it, but the subtitles were unreadable, and I gave up after five minutes. (I have since seen *Project A II* several times on the screen, and it is one of my very favorite Hong Kong movies – if not movies, period.) Jeff also persuaded me to go to a midnight screening of *A Chinese Ghost Story* – another excellent choice. And it was Jeff who ultimately suggested that I write about the Hong Kong movie business for *The New Yorker*. Once I got the assignment, my real education in the genre began.

I went back to Kim's, and struck up a friendship with Barry Long, the store's assistant manager, who was not so much a Hong Kong film buff as an addict. On the backs of video boxes that contained Hong Kong movies, he had written plot summaries, many of which have been adapted for use in this book. Under Barry's guidance, I began to rent laser disks from stores in Chinatown, and probably saw at least a hundred movies at his suggestion; and while our taste in films differs considerably, Barry introduced me to many of my all-time favorites, including *Fong Sai Yuk*, *Peking Opera Blues*, *Rouge*, and the films of Ann Hui.

Since I am a journalist and not a critic – I consider the two roles almost antithetical – I shall refrain from singling out any other specific titles. Instead, I have had the good fortune to assemble for this book a round table of twelve diverse and exceptional critics, from the United States, Hong Kong, Taiwan, and Great Britain. I asked each critic to look over the list of the more than three hundred titles for which this book has provided a plot summary, and assign grades to them: three stars for "most highly recommended"; two stars for "highly recommended"; and one star for "recommended." Several critics have provided commentary to accompany their selections. The absence of a grade may mean that the critic has simply not seen the film in question, but a few critics have also supplied a list of movies they emphatically do not recommend. Nowhere is the diversity of opinion better demonstrated: Barbara Scharres, for instance, recommends three movies that Tony Rayns says to avoid; and while Scharres rates Clarence Fok's *Naked Killer* as "horrible," Howard Hampton gives it three stars.

I shall formally introduce each of the reviewers, and present their individual grades and comments; but first, I have prepared a tally of their combined grades. To keep it simple, I counted each star as one point. (While no film achieves a perfect score of 36 – three stars apiece from twelve critics – the top-ranking movie, John Woo's *Bullet in the Head*, does manage a rather impressive 31.) I expect that every critic in the survey will take exception with the relative rankings of some films; it's also fair to say that the composite list makes a reliable guide to some of the best that the modern Hong Kong cinema has to offer.

The Highest-Rated Hong Kong Films
Rank/Title
Director/Year
Score

1. *Bullet in the Head*
John Woo, 1990
31

2. *Center Stage*
Stanley Kwan, 1991
30

3. *Chungking Express*
Wong Kar-wai, 1994
29

4. *Peking Opera Blues*
Tsui Hark, 1986
28

5. *A Better Tomorrow*
John Woo, 1986
27

5. *Days of Being Wild*
Wong Kar-wai, 1991
27

5. *The Killer*
John Woo, 1989
27

5. *Rouge*
Stanley Kwan, 1987
27

6. *Hard-Boiled*
John Woo, 1992
24

7. *A Chinese Ghost Story*
Ching Siu-tung, 1987
22

8. *Swordsman II*
Ching Siu-tung, 1991
21

9. *Ashes of Time*
Wong Kar-wai, 1994
20

9. *Project A*
Jackie Chan, 1983
20

10. *Drunken Master II*
Lau Kar-leung,[1] 1993
19

10. *Police Story*
Jackie Chan, 1985
19

11. *The Spooky Bunch*
Ann Hui, 1980
18

12. *Boat People*
Ann Hui, 1982
17

12. *Once upon a Time in China*
Tsui Hark, 1991
17

13. *A Better Tomorrow II*
John Woo, 1987
16

---

1 Uncredited co-director: Jackie Chan

13. *Fong Sai Yuk*
Corey Yuen, 1993
16

13. *Painted Faces*
Alex Law, 1988
16

13. *People's Hero*
Derek Yee, 1987
16

13. *Project A II*
Jackie Chan, 1987
16

13. *Zu: Warriors from the Magic Mountain*
Tsui Hark, 1983
16

14. *Ah Ying*
Allen Fong, 1982
15

14. *Autumn Moon*
Clara Law, 1992
15

14. *Drunken Master*
Yuen Woo-ping, 1978
15

14. *Fallen Angels*
Wong Kar-wai, 1995
15

14. *The Heroic Trio*
Johnny To, 1992
15

14. *Once a Thief*
John Woo, 1991
15

14. *Once upon a Time in China II*
Tsui Hark, 1991
15

14. *Police Story II*
Jackie Chan, 1988
15

15. *A Better Tomorrow III: Love and Death in Saigon*
Tsui Hark, 1989
14

15. *Shanghai Blues*
Tsui Hark, 1984
14

16. *As Tears Go By*
Wong Kar-wai, 1988
13

16. *The Bride with White Hair*
Ronny Yu, 1993
13

16. *Butterfly Murders*
Tsui Hark, 1979
13

16. *Dangerous Encounter of the First Kind*
Tsui Hark, 1980
13

16. *The Day the Sun Turned Cold*
Yim Ho, 1994
13

16. *Dragons Forever*
Sammo Hung, 1988
13

16. *Full Contact*
Ringo Lam, 1992
13

16. *Song of the Exile*
Ann Hui, 1989
13

17. *The Blade*
Tsui Hark, 1995
12

17. *Dragon Inn*
Raymond Lee, 1992
12

18. *92 Legendary La Rose Noire*
Jeff Lau, 1992
11

18. *Eastern Condors*
Sammo Hung, 1986
11

18. *East is Red*
Ching Siu-tung and Raymond Lee, 1993
11

18. *Miracles*
Jackie Chan, 1989
11

18. *Naked Killer*
Clarence Fok, 1992
11

18. *Red Rose, White Rose*
Stanley Kwan, 1994
11

18. *Romance of Book and Sword*
Ann Hui, 1987
11

18. *Saviour of the Soul*
Corey Yuen and David Lai,[1] 1991
11

18. *Summer Snow*
Ann Hui, 1995
11

18. *Supercop*
Stanley Tong, 1992
11

18. *Swordsman*
Tsui Hark, Raymond Lee, and Ching Siu-tung,[2] 1990
11

19. *Chicken and Duck Talk*
Clifton Ko, 1988
10

19. *City on Fire*
Ringo Lam, 1987
10

19. *Dream Lovers*
Tony Au, 1986
10

19. *The Private Eyes*
Michael Hui, 1976
10

19. *Red Dust*
Yim Ho, 1990
10

20. *A Chinese Ghost Story II*
Ching Siu-tung, 1990
9

1 Uncredited co-director: Jeff Lau
2 King Hu is credited

20. *A Chinese Odyssey II: Cinderella*
Jeff Lau, 1995
9

20. *The Dead and the Deadly*
Wu Ma, 1982
9

20. *The Eagle Shooting Heroes*
Jeff Lau, 1993
9

20. *Full Moon in New York*
Stanley Kwan, 1990
9

20. *God of Gamblers*
Wong Jing, 1989
9

20. *Iron Monkey*
Yuen Woo-ping, 1993
9

20. *Long Arm of the Law*
Johnny Mak, 1984
9

20. *Prison on Fire*
Ringo Lam, 1987
9

20. *The Secret*
Ann Hui, 1979
9

20. *The Story of Woo Viet*
Ann Hui, 1981
9

20. *The Sword*
Patrick Tam, 1980
9

The Critics

PEGGY CHIAO (Chiao Hsiung-ping)

The Taiwanese film critic and historian Peggy Chiao has a résumé so extensive that it would take several pages to reproduce in full. Chiao was born and educated in Taipei, though she got her master's in film at the University of Texas, in Austin (where Tsui Hark had earlier studied cinematography); her 1981 thesis was on the evolution of the Hong Kong kung-fu and swordplay genre. She writes two weekly columns of film commentary for the *China Times Express*, and is the author of more than a dozen books, including *Hong Kong Films, 1975–1986* (1987); *Peggy Chiao on Films: Hollywood* (1985); and *Taiwan New Cinema* (1988). She is the editor and translator of two dozen additional volumes.

Chiao is currently producing three feature-length documentaries, to be directed by Stanley Kwan, Ann Hui, and Hsu Hsiao-ming. In 1995, she founded and became director of the Taiwan Film Center, to promote Taiwanese films and make them available to festivals around the world – including the Venice Film Festival, for which she is a representative; she is also a juror at nine other festivals, in Canada, Switzerland, Spain, and elsewhere. Meanwhile, Chiao is an associate professor of film studies at the National Institute of the Arts and the National Chengchi University, in Taipei. Chiao co-authored the screenplay for *Center Stage,* Stanley Kwan's 1992 biopic about the Chinese silent movie actress Ruan Ling-yu; and while she found the finished film "a little stagey for me," she has nevertheless awarded it three stars. Here follows her list of recommendations:

Most Highly Recommended

Ah Ying

Center Stage

Chungking Express

Days of Being Wild

Father and Son
   "Autobiographical material, delicately portraying the love between father and son in a typical Chinese patriarchal family."

The Spooky Bunch

Highly Recommended

Boat People

Love Massacre
   "Patrick Tam's modernist work, revealing his status as one of the best formalist directors in Hong Kong."

People's Hero

Police Story II

The Private Eyes
   "One of the best comedies from Hong Kong, with a strong colloquial sense, and acid humor."

Romance of Book and Sword

Rouge

The Secret

Swordsman II

Zu: Warriors from the Magic Mountain

Recommended

A Chinese Ghost Story

Dirty Ho
   "A prototype kung-fu film – all generic irony."

Encounters of the Spooky Kind

Once upon a Time in China

Summer Snow

The Sword
   "A romantic swordplay film with a tinge of modernism."

Winners and Sinners

HOWARD HAMPTON

Born in the Virgin Islands, and currently living in a section of the Mojave Desert, Howard Hampton III has what he calls a "genetic predisposition" for the stunt-driven Hong Kong cinema. His late father, Howard II, was a Hollywood stunt man who, among other accomplishments, doubled for Errol Flynn in Flynn's last movie, *Cuban Rebel Girls*, which was shot in Havana in the late 1950s, just as Castro came to power. Hampton started out as a rock critic for the Boston *Phoenix* and *The Village Voice* over a decade ago, then went on to write about movies and pop culture for publications such as *Art Forum* and the *L.A. Weekly*. His essay on the intersection of Hollywood and rock music, "Everybody Knows This Is Nowhere," was published in *The Last Great American Picture Show* (Vienna: Wespennest, 1995), and he is now completing a book for Harvard University Press on pop culture in the Reagan era.

Hampton is currently a regular contributor to *Film Comment*, for which he recently wrote a cover story on Brigitte Lin. His film criticism has won him many admirers, including the former *New Yorker* movie reviewer Pauline Kael, to whom he periodically sends tapes of Hong Kong films. "She likes *A Better Tomorrow III*, but just gave up on *Ashes of Time*," Hampton says. Hampton's own recommendations follow:

Most Highly Recommended

Ashes of Time

"An action film about inaction, *Ashes of Time* makes exile and loss seem impossibly seductive. Stunningly photographed, with the performers looking like so many beautifully dishevelled refugees, the result suggests a mutant combination of Resnais and Kurosawa – The Seven Samurai at Marienbad."

A Better Tomorrow III: Love and Death in Saigon

"Heretical as it is suggest, this is the best of the series. One could cite Tsui Hark's richer emotional palette, extending the romance beyond guys and guns locked in a death-waltz of guilt and expiation. But in the end, it all comes down to Anita Mui, who gives a wondrously iconic performance that's Bogart and Jeanne Moreau rolled into a single trenchcoated figure."

Bullet in the Head

"Woo seems determined to compress every piece of film history that's ever mattered to him into this movie. Evoking the chaos of the 60s in order to revel in it, at the same time mourning the illusions which perished in the flames, this is a supremely ambivalent film – part grinning-skull ode to annihilation, and part cry of disgust."

Burning Paradise

"Ringo Lam – master of claustrophobic male ordeals and the violence that erupts out of confined spaces – would seem like the last person to direct a swordplay epic. But this apocalyptic blowout is his most accomplished film, mainly because he smuggles the form into a heart-of-darkness labyrinth."

Center Stage

East Is Red

"A hallucinatory tapestry – the closest it comes to realism is when goddess/antichrist Brigitte Lin says 'Give me your hearts,' and they obliging explode out of the chests of several men. Uneven, to be sure; but Ching Siu-tung demands to be ranked with the most idiosyncratic visionaries in film history."

Executioners

"Suffused with bitter echoes of the Tiananmen Square Massacre ('Imprison those alive as rioters, burn the corpses,' commands an army officer), the movie plays out as a mixture of political allegory and comic-book poetry."

The Heroic Trio

"Pop-art enchantment, a fairytale with live ammunition. The movie has a delightful sense of childhood wonder, as well as childhood dread – a playful nightmare vision of a world overrun by demon-fathers and saved by magical superheroines."

The Killer

"Woo's signature picture spiritualizes pulp with so much cinema-as-religion zeal it's virtually an homage to itself."

Naked Killer

"A trash-surrealist girl-gangster classic – its violence is so swift and flamboyantly savage, it's practically an aria of subliminal images. (When sensuous hitwoman Carrie Ng finishes off her tough-guy prey with a bullet to the groin, the exploding squib is like an exclamation point.) Director Clarence Fok has an omnivorous audacity."

Peace Hotel

"An elegiac farewell to the Hong Kong cinema, and the Chow Yun-fat/John Woo synergy that helped put it on the map. When the dust settles, all that remains is the uncertainty of tomorrow – and no better one in sight."

Peking Opera Blues

"Still unsurpassed. Tsui Hark recapitulates nearly the whole history of cinema – from slapstick farce to tragic heroism – in one gleeful, manic burst of inspiration. The last twenty minutes are so exhilarating, it's as though your entire moviegoing life flashed before your eyes."

Swordsman II

"A gender-bending, gravity-defying, mystical-surreal fantasy beyond your wildest dreams. One could spend a lifetime, or at least a master's thesis, just trying to untangle the layers of sexual ambiguity here – and love every minute of it."

Highly Recommended

A Better Tomorrow

Autumn Moon

The Big Heat

"From the vicious élan of the opening shot, it's as though the film-makers set out to make the most violent film in history. Leaving no corpse unturned, or unburned, the film investigates the applied physics of death; there's a sense of clinical wonder at how many ingenious ways can be found for bodies in motion to come to a sudden, terrible end – often in sections."

The Blade
"A film that reinvents the sword-opera as a pageant of grim, crazed hunger for sex and revenge – not necessarily in that order."

A Chinese Ghost Story

Chungking Express
"This carnival of lost (well, misplaced) souls is a cheerful comedy of melancholia. A lovely but intensely superficial film."

City on Fire

Days of Being Wild

Dragon Inn
"A wonderfully satisfying midsummer night's dream of swords, intrigue, and droll romance."

Dream Lovers

Drunken Master II
"The martial-arts movie equivalent of Elvis's '68 comeback special."

Hard-Boiled
"Woo's most expansive film, very assured, but also mechanical at times, as though he were a prisoner of his own technique."

Moon Warriors
"Fatalistic romance and startling violence for the whole family."

Operation Condor
"Unlike in *Armour of God*, the screen doesn't just go dead when the action lets up."

Red Dust

Red Rose, White Rose

Run and Kill
"You have to marvel at the movie's desire to give a horrifically new, charred-remains meaning to the term 'black comedy.'"

School on Fire
"Welcome to the blackboard jungle: a breathtakingly trashy

milieu of student gangsters and babyfaced schoolgirl prostitutes, helpless teachers and corrupt administrators. Even with some especially sordid material cut, what remains is pretty remarkable: a kamikaze teen hooker who drives her bike headlong into a truck, her good-girl pal who flips out and burns down the school library, and an ending where a classroom rape is averted when the perpetrator is knifed, shot, and pushed out a window onto the spikes of the school fence below. As one bemused spectator says amid the carnage, 'This is such chaos, you should clap your hands.'"

Wild Search

Zodiac Killers

Recommended

All the Wrong Clues . . . For the Right Solution
"If this good-natured nutball farce originated in France or Spain, it might be hailed as a neo-Dadaist coup; if it were American, it might be trashed as juvenile idiocy."

Armour of God

A Better Tomorrow II
"A footnote, written in blood."

Black Cat

The Black Panther Warriors

The Bride with White Hair

Butterfly and Sword
"Pleasant, adroit, completely generic."

Dragon from Russia

Drunken Master

Dr. Wai in "The Scripture with No Words"
"An engaging introduction to Hong Kong fantasy. Still, I can't escape the feeling that the material could have been taken much further, perhaps into the realm of a Cantopop Dennis Potter (Jet Li is 'The I-Chinging Detective'?)."

Eastern Condors

Full Contact

Green Snake
  "Knowingly flirts with camp, but this cockeyed fable has a core of real passion – and Maggie Cheung, who blissfully slithers away with the picture."

Handsome Siblings

He's a Woman, She's a Man

Iron Monkey

New Legend of Shaolin

Nomad

Once a Thief
  "It feels like nothing so much as a Hope-Crosby-Lamour version of *Beat the Devil*, in which the gunfire is just a form of snappy patter. And has anyone ever been more debonair in a wheelchair than Chow Yun-fat?"

Once upon a Time in China

Organized Crime and Triad Bureau

Police Story II

Prison on Fire II

Project A

Rock 'n Roll Cop

Rouge

Rumble in the Bronx

Shanghai Blues

Song of the Exile
  "A decent but rather drab film: its air of stifling respectability explains why it received more international attention than many better, more irreverent Hong Kong films."

The Sword

Swordsman

Temptation of a Monk

The Terracotta Warrior

What Price Survival?
"An almost geometrically abstract cross between *Ashes of Time* and *The Killer*."

The Wicked City
"If the film had stayed faithful to the twisted sexuality of its source, it could have been a kinky classic instead of a beautiful misstep."

Wonder Seven

Not Recommended

92 Legendary La Rose Noire

As Tears Go By
"A promising but ultimately attenuated film. Call it anorexic Scorsese – 'Lean Streets.'"

Bride with White Hair II
"Intensely disappointing – one anticlimax after another."

Deception
"Constantly in danger of becoming an interesting movie, but never makes good on the threat."

The Eagle Shooting Heroes
"The *Ashes of Time* gang cavorting in Pee Wee Herman's playhouse. Fun for a while, then the eyes start to glaze over."

Fallen Angels
"Isn't it a little early for Wong Kar-wai to be recycling his mannerisms?"

Final Victory
"Under the brutal direction of Patrick Tam, one sees more clearly

the element of cruel caricature often present in Wong Kar-wai's view of women."

First Strike

Fist of Legend
"Jet Li is an enigma. The camera loves him – he's like a lithe, compact Schwarzenegger – yet he withholds himself so much he might as well be wearing a hairshirt and a cowl."

God of Gamblers
"The dumb movie that unforgivably launched a thousand even dumber ones. How come Jim Carrey hasn't bought the rights to remake it yet?"

Lady in Black
"Anyone who remembers the classic Carol Burnett parody *Mildred Fierce* will feel a pang of regret that she never did a takeoff on this movie."

Love, Guns and Glass
"An atrocious, masochistic wallow, though if the art-house crowd ever lays eyes on it, it may well be acclaimed as some sort of neo-Douglas Sirk classic. I can't recommend it – but everyone should see it."

Magic Cop

Magic Crane

Reincarnation of Golden Lotus
"Compared to Clara Law's later work, this has an aura of repression to it – perhaps censorship (self- or otherwise)."

Robotrix
"Barbarella lives – well-photographed pin-ups valiantly struggle against the awesome forces of inanity. Would perk up the Playboy Channel, though."

Semi-Gods and Semi-Devils
"The pairing of the century – Brigitte Lin and Gong Li – is largely wasted in this crummy sorcery epic."

DAVE KEHR

Since 1993, Dave Kehr has been a movie critic for the New York *Daily News*. He grew up in surburban Chicago, and became interested in movies as a child – particularly the silent comedies, an affinity that later attracted him to the films of Jackie Chan. He was an English major at the University of Chicago – "I never took a film course in my life," he says – and began writing movie criticism for the college newspaper, *The Maroon*, in 1973. After graduating, he went on to write for *The Chicago Reader*, and, in 1986, became a film critic for the *Chicago Tribune*, his most recent post before moving to New York.

Kehr was singularly responsible for a milestone in Jackie Chan's long struggle for acceptance in the United States. In the mid-1980s, Kehr was appointed to the selection committee of the New York Film Festival, and, at his urging, Chan's *Police Story*, which he'd seen in the market at Cannes, was put on the program for 1987. The movie was one of the standout hits of the festival, though Vincent Canby, then the chief film critic for *The New York Times*, sarcastically dismissed it as worthier of a screening on 42nd Street, and described Chan as "a scaled-down, Oriental Sylvester Stallone." It seems fair to say that *Police Story* has aged better than Canby's review; not surprisingly, the movie is among Kehr's three-star selections.

Most Highly Recommended

A Better Tomorrow
   "The *Citizen Kane* of Hong Kong cinema."

Bullet in the Head
   "The *Magnificent Ambersons* of Hong Kong cinema."

Chicken and Duck Talk
   "Michael Hui's masterpiece – social satire on par with W.C. Fields."

A Chinese Ghost Story

Chungking Express

Drunken Master

Fong Sai Yuk

Hard-Boiled
"Relatively shallow, but tremendous formal invention."

The Killer
"Magnificent, noble, ironic, sublime."

Miracles

Once upon a Time in China
"Tsui Hark's take on 1997 – a creative rebirth."

Peking Opera Blues

People's Hero

Police Story
"Jackie Chan at his richest, funniest, and most daring."

Project A

Project A II

Rouge
"Stanley Kwan's best and least pretentious work."

Shanghai Blues

Highly Recommended

Armour of God

A Better Tomorrow II

Boat People

Butterfly Murders

Center Stage

The Day the Sun Turned Cold

Dragon Inn

Drunken Master II

Eastern Condors
    "Great action direction by Sammo Hung – what happened later?"

First Strike

Fong Sai Yuk II

Full Moon in New York

King of Chess

Once a Thief

Painted Faces

Peace Hotel
    "The distilled essence of Chow Yun-fat."

Police Story II

The Spooky Bunch

The Story of Woo Viet

Summer Snow

Swordsman

Zu: Warriors from the Magic Mountain

Recommended

Aces Go Places

As Tears Go By

Ashes of Time

Autumn Moon

The Bride with White Hair

A Chinese Ghost Story II

City Hunter

City on Fire

Crime Story

Days of Being Wild

Dragons Forever

Dream Lovers

Full Contact

God of Gamblers

Gunmen

The Heroic Trio

Mr. Vampire

Naked Killer

New Legend of Shaolin

Once upon a Time in China II

Once upon a Time in China III

Operation Condor

Red Rose, White Rose

Romance of Book and Sword

Royal Tramp

Rumble in the Bronx

Sex and Zen

Song of the Exile

Supercop

Swordsman II

Temptation of a Monk

Tiger on Beat

Twinkle, Twinkle Lucky Stars

Wheels on Meals

Winners and Sinners

ANDY KLEIN

Andy Klein grew up in surburban Philadelphia, graduated from Harvard with an English degree in 1972, moved to Los Angeles with vague notions of landing a job in the movie or music business, and ended up, as he puts it, "living a *Day of the Locust* existence in a rented room in Hollywood." He enrolled in the master's program in critical studies at UCLA film school, dropped out just shy of earning his degree, and, after a brief stint as a screenplay doctor, moved into full-time movie criticism. He is currently film critic for *Los Angeles New Times*, which absorbed his longtime employer, the *Los Angeles Reader*, in August 1996.

Klein first began to learn about Hong Kong films under the tutelage of David Chute, one of the earliest American critics to discover the genre; after Klein caught *A Better Tomorrow*, *A Chinese Ghost Story*, and *Peking Opera Blues* in one heady week at the Nuart Theater, he went from disciple to apostle. In the past several years, he has played a significant role in promoting Hong Kong films in Los Angeles. In June 1996, as part of the Show Biz Expo trade show, he organized and moderated a panel on the melding of the Asian and American film industries; the speakers included Kirk Wong, Terence Chang, and Lee Stollman, the William Morris agent who represents Chow Yun-fat.

Most Highly Recommended

A Better Tomorrow
"Even though Woo has since refined and expanded his trademark style, there is no replacing the sheer joy of a director discovering his true voice."

The Blade
"After reviving the period martial-arts film with the *Once upon a Time in China* series, Tsui Hark turned around and reinvented it yet again with this tale of gritty realism."

The Bride with White Hair

"One of the few films that seem to span the gap between Hong Kong's mainstream commercial fare and its rarer art-house pictures. A good choice to show to a mixed crowd of aesthetes and action fans."

Bullet in the Head

"I think it's Woo's greatest accomplishment, even though I'd be hard pressed to call it my favorite – it's just too unsettling."

Center Stage

"Stanley Kwan is the best of Hong Kong's artsier directors; and this is all the proof anyone should need that no other actress in Hong Kong can surpass Maggie Cheung in range."

The Chinese Feast

"All the worst and best aspects of Hong Kong cinema – the plot appears to have been made up as it goes along, but there are wonderful star performances, hilarious low slapstick bits, and an eagerness to please that American films can't match."

A Chinese Ghost Story

Chungking Express

"Wong Kar-wai is so full of artistic pretension that his work generally gives me a headache. But the one time he relaxed, he knocked off this gentle art-house masterpiece."

Dragons Forever

Drunken Master II

"The last great Jackie Chan movie to date. The final fight sequence is extraordinary, though it's also Chan's most masochistic – and the film's dreadful last shot is one of his few major lapses of taste."

Fong Sai Yuk

"The lightest of all Jet Li films – a mix of ridiculous 'wire-fu,' farce, and romance. As Mother Fong, Josephine Siao displays a remarkable ability to be imperious and goofy at the same time."

Full Contact

Hard-Boiled
"John Woo's last Hong Kong film is almost a distillation of his post-1986 work. Even if the plot is full of holes, and the emotional tug isn't quite as strong as in *The Killer*, the action sequences (nearly the whole movie) are among the greatest ever filmed."

Iron Monkey
"Another dazzling Yuen Woo-ping action movie."

Mack the Knife
"This oddball slice-of-life story reminds me of a 1930s Warner Bros. film, probably with Cagney and Pat O'Brien, directed by Raoul Walsh or Roy Del Ruth. Lovable, archetypal characters, ridiculous displays of nobility, heartbreak, comedy – all the basics."

Once upon a Time in China

Painted Faces
"Jackie and Sammo say that this is a greatly softened portrait of their upbringing, but seen as a Hong Kong version of *Goodbye, Mr. Chips*, it's irresistible."

Peking Opera Blues
"Hong Kong cinema is too wide-ranging for there to be a 'best' picture . . . but if you put a gun to my back, Tsui Hark's masterpiece would be my choice. I've seen it at least twenty times, and counting."

Police Story

Project A
"It's hard to overstate the leap Jackie Chan took as a writer/ director when he followed the barely so-so *Dragon Lord* with this turn-of-the-century masterpiece. This would be his best film, had he not surpassed it with the sequel."

Project A II
"Jackie Chan's greatest movie. Period. Sustained inspiration, alternating brilliant farce sequences with equally brilliant action."

Project S
   "Probably the best sampler of Michelle Yeoh's action skills, *Project S* also proves that Stanley Tong is a first-rate director and not simply Jackie Chan's gofer."

Rouge

Supercop

Swordsman II
   "The apotheosis of Brigitte Lin's gender ambiguity."

Twin Dragons
   "Absolute disorganized silliness, with two Jackies and at least three directors."

Wing Chun
   "Because Cantonese is not her first language, Michelle Yeoh generally plays serious, uncommunicative characters. This time, she manages to show off her comedy skills along with her action chops."

Highly Recommended

Aces Go Places

Au Revoir, Mon Amour

A Better Tomorrow II

Bodyguard from Beijing

Cageman

C'est la Vie, Mon Cherie
   "I'm at a loss to explain why this mawkish *Love Story* knockoff is so much more effective than its model – it must be the charisma gap between Ali McGraw and Anita Yuen."

A Chinese Ghost Story II

A Chinese Ghost Story III

Comrades, Almost a Love Story

Crime Story

Dragon Inn

Drunken Master

The Eagle Shooting Heroes
"Silly, silly, silly . . . but irresistible to anyone who's just about had their fill of Hong Kong period adventures. Not recommended for novices."

Eastern Condors

East Is Red

Farewell China
"Absolutely depressing realism."

Flirting Scholar

Fong Sai Yuk II

From Beijing with Love
"For the American viewer, the best introduction to the comedy of Stephen Chiau."

God of Gamblers' Return

The Heroic Trio

High Risk

Hu-Du-Men

The Killer

King of Beggars

Lady in Black

The Lovers
"After a series of hyper action films, Tsui Hark made this romance, of which the first half is a gentle *Yentl* clone, and the second half is wrenchingly tragic."

Miracles

My Father Is a Hero

Naked Killer

New Legend of Shaolin

Now You See Love . . . Now You Don't

Once a Thief

Once upon a Time in China II

Once upon a Time in China III

Operation Condor

Organized Crime and Triad Bureau

Police Story II

Raining in the Mountain

Red Dust

Royal Tramp II

Rumble in the Bronx
"The Cantonese version serves Jackie Chan better than the cut down, dubbed American release. It's no masterpiece, but the fun parts make up for any problems."

Saviour of the Soul

Shanghai Blues

Song of the Exile

Tai Chi Master

The Terracotta Warrior

Tom, Dick and Hairy

Treasure Hunt

Wheels on Meals

The Wicked City
"The perfect midnight movie, with more interesting concepts than a dozen *Judge Dredds*."

Zu: Warriors from the Magic Mountain

Recommended

92 Legendary La Rose Noire
  "Hysterical parody of 1960s TV shows in Hong Kong."

Aces Go Places III: Our Man from Bond Street

All's Well, Ends Well

Armour of God

As Tears Go By

A Better Tomorrow III: Love and Death in Saigon

Burning Paradise

Butterfly Murders

A Chinese Odyssey I

A Chinese Odyssey II

City Hunter

City on Fire
  "Ringo Lam's cop thriller has dated a lot, partly because Tarantino lifted enough – and did it better – in *Reservoir Dogs*."

The Day the Sun Turned Cold

Duel to the Death

First Strike

God of Gamblers

Green Snake
  "The final special effects are horrendous, but up until then, this is a very clever and sexy film. Maggie Cheung turns in another great performance, including a strange Indian-flavored production number."

Handsome Siblings

Heart of the Dragon

Hong Kong 1941

I Love Maria

King of Chess

Last Hurrah for Chivalry

Once upon a Time in China V

Prison on Fire

Prison on Fire II

Reincarnation of Golden Lotus

Robotrix

Sex and Zen
   "Moderately sexy, occasionally very funny. But the American success of this film was a sheer triumph of marketing."

The Sword

Swordsman

Temptation of a Monk

To Live and Die in Tsimshatsui

Not Recommended

Ashes of Time
   "The most egregiously overrated film of recent years. Straining for capital-A art with every shot, *Ashes of Time* remains (after three viewings) an incoherent hodgepodge."

Bride with White Hair II
   "If it weren't for the unwatchable *Iron Monkey II*, this would be the worst sequel to a great Hong Kong movie that I've ever seen."

LAW KAR (Lau Yiu-kuen)

Law Kar is the program coordinator for the Hong Kong International Film Festival, founded in 1977, and approaching its twentieth anniversary with an average yearly attendance of more than 100,000. He is also one of forty members of the Hong Kong Film Critics Society, established in Hong Kong in 1995 to publish criticism and present awards (the society's Internet address is http://zero.com.hk/filmcritics/).

Law was born in Macao, and moved to Hong Kong at seventeen; he studied mathematics in college, and feeling "quite bored" with the subject, took refuge by going every day to the movies. After graduating, he wrote an influential movie column for the *Chinese Student Weekly*, made experimental films, and, in 1971, went to Rome for two years to study cinematography. On his return to Hong Kong, he joined the television station TVB as a director and screenwriter; he was one of the three original directors of the police drama *C.I.D.*, along with Patrick Tam and Ann Hui. After eleven years at the station, Law left to concentrate on writing criticism. His books include *Journey into Film* (1983), an anthology of two decades of criticism; and a 1985 volume of interviews with filmmakers such as Lau Kar-leung and Tsui Hark. He is now at work on a comparative history of the movie industries of Shanghai and Hollywood from the 1920s through the 1940s.

Most Highly Recommended

Ah Ying

A Better Tomorrow

Boat People

Center Stage

Chungking Express

City on Fire

Days of Being Wild

Father and Son

Homecoming

Raining in the Mountain

Rouge

Highly Recommended

92 Legendary La Rose Noire

An Amorous Woman of the Tang Dynasty

Autumn Moon

An Autumn's Tale

Bullet in the Head

Butterfly Murders

Cageman

C'est la Vie, Mon Cherie

A Chinese Ghost Story

A Chinese Odyssey II: Cinderella

Comrades, Almost a Love Story

Dangerous Encounter of the First Kind

The Day the Sun Turned Cold

Dragon Inn

Drunken Master II

Eight-Diagram Pole Fighter

Fallen Angel

First Strike

Fong Sai Yuk

Full Contact

Full Throttle

Hard-Boiled

Her Fatal Ways

He's a Woman, She's a Man

The Killer

Long Arm of the Law

Love unto Waste

Mr. Vampire

Nomad

Once upon a Time in China II

Painted Faces

Pedicab Driver

Peking Opera Blues

People's Hero

Police Story

Prison on Fire

The Private Eyes

Project A

Project A II

Red Dust

Rumble in the Bronx

Song of the Exile

The Spooky Bunch

The Story of Woo Viet

Summer Snow

The Sword

Swordsman II

Wild Search

Recommended

Aces Go Places

Aces Go Places II

Aces Go Places III: Our Man from Bond Street

All for the Winner

All Night Long

Ashes of Time

As Tears Go By

A Better Tomorrow II

A Better Tomorrow III: Love and Death in Saigon

The Blade

The Bride with White Hair

The Case of the Cold Fish

Casino Raiders

Chicken and Duck Talk

A Chinese Odyssey I: Pandora's Box

Crime Story

The Day that Doesn't Exist

The Dead and the Deadly

Dream Lovers

Drunken Master

Duel to the Death

East is Red

Encounters of the Spooky Kind

Encounters of the Spooky Kind II

Farewell China

The Final Option

Final Victory

A Fishy Story

Fong Sai Yuk II

From Beijing with Love

Full Moon in New York

Gangs

God of Gamblers

Health Warning

Heaven Can't Wait

Hong Kong 1941

Iron Monkey

King of Chess

Legend of the Mountain

Love Among the Triad

Love Massacre

The Lovers

Miracles

A Moment of Romance

Now You See Love . . . Now You Don't

On the Run

Once a Thief

Once upon a Time in China

Once upon a Time in China III

One and a Half

Plain Jane to the Rescue

Princess Fragrance

Private Eye Blues

Queen of Temple Street

Red Rose, White Rose

Romance of Book and Sword

Saviour of the Soul

The Secret

Security Unlimited

Shanghai Blues

Swordsman

Temptation of a Monk

Teppanyaki

The Terracotta Warrior

To Be Number One

To Liv(e)

Twenty Something

We're Going to Eat You

Wicked City

Winners and Sinners

Zu: Warriors from the Magic Mountain

BARRY LONG

In terms of the sheer number of Hong Kong movies he has seen, not many *gweilos* can compete with Barry Long – a feat all the more impressive considering that he came to the genre fairly recently. Since attending a John Woo double bill in 1993, Long says he has barely let a day go by without watching at least one Hong Kong film, and his personal collection of videotapes exceeds six hundred titles. As assistant manager of the Kim's Video outlet on St. Marks Place in New York, Long built up the store's outsized sampling of Hong Kong videos, earning him write-ups in *The Village Voice* and *Time Out*, and a surprise visit by Michelle Yeoh, who was stunned by his knowledge of even her most obscure films. (The Kim's collection has badly dwindled since Long left the store in 1996.)

Long who grew up on a farm in Pennsylvania, and earned a BA degree in film production and cinema studies at New York University is currently film programmer for the Brooklyn Museum of Art, where he recently hosted a retrospective of the Hong Kong gangster film. He appears as an extra in Peter Chan's 1996 drama, *Comrades, Almost a Love Story.* and recently hosted a Hong Kong film series at the Brooklyn Museum of Art.

Most Highly Recommended

Ah Ying

"The antithesis of what most Westerners think of as a Hong Kong movie. Not only a superb social-realist film, but an engrossing one, with first-rate performances by a cast of relative unknowns."

All Night Long

Ashes of Time

"The artistic success of this film, to me at least, is a given, but what makes *Ashes of Time* truly stand out is the acting. Maggie Cheung and Brigitte Lin prove hands down that they are the best actresses working in Hong Kong, while Leslie Cheung gives his most restrained and subtle performance since *Rouge*. A film that cannot be fully appreciated on one viewing."

A Better Tomorrow III: Love and Death in Saigon

"Simply the best of the series. It has what John Woo's entries are lacking – honest emotion, and a strong female presence."

The Blade

"Tsui Hark, who reinvented the martial-arts genre in *Once upon a Time in China*, goes back to the grim violence and frantic cutting of his early, angry work to reinvent it yet again. Told from a woman's perspective, the male body becomes pure spectacle; with all the nude male flesh, *The Blade* gets my vote as the most homoerotic film to come from Hong Kong."

The Bride with White Hair

"The best genre elements come together to make something more than a genre film."

Bugis Street

"Forget *To Wong Foo* and *Priscilla: Queen of the Desert* – this is *the* drag-queen film of the 1990s. Not only do these lovely 'ladies' actually (God forbid) have sex, but they are presented as complex characters who use their wit and sarcasm as a means of survival in an unforgiving world."

Bullet in the Head

"The scene in which a severely beaten Jacky Cheung shows up at his friend's wedding and attempts a façade of normalcy is one of the most beautiful testaments to loyalty and friendship ever put on film."

By Hook or by Crook

"Sammo Hung and Karl Maka rework the *Lucky Stars* formula into one of the funniest – not to mention strangest – films I've ever seen."

Center Stage

Days of Being Wild

"If *As Tears Go By* was hampered by the constraints of genre, Wong Kar-wai's second film is all the better for simply leaving genre behind. Heartfelt and brilliant, not to mention having a dynamic soundtrack."

The Day the Sun Turned Cold

Drunken Master II

"When Jackie Chan is on, he is on! A great throwback to his

earlier martial-arts films, with set pieces that have yet to be topped."

The Eagle Shooting Heroes
"The type of film sadly lacking in Hollywood – a film with a wicked sense of humor directed at itself."

Encounters of the Spooky Kind

Fallen Angels
"A lot of critics have complained that this film is too similar to Wong Kar-wai's previous work – but so what?"

Forbidden City Cop
"Stephen Chiau is a brilliant comic, but what he often lacks is a director who can keep up with him; here, he is his own co-director, along with Vincent Kok. It also doesn't hurt that Chiau is paired with Carina Lau, with whom he has far more chemistry than with most of his leading ladies."

Gangs
"This should be required viewing for anyone who thinks Hong Kong movie violence is cool. Cold and clinical, the film has a near-documentary quality that will keep it in your memory probably longer than is comfortable."

Green Snake

The Heroic Trio
"One of the films that hooked me on Hong Kong cinema – a whole new level of pop art."

Hu-Du-Men

Once a Thief
"It's become a tedious cliché to refer to John Woo as a homoerotic director – but really, I couldn't tell if Leslie Cheung was in love with Chow Yun-fat or Cherie Chung until midway through the film."

Peking Opera Blues

Red to Kill

"Director Billy Tang has made some of the most offensive movies in film history (*Dr. Lamb*, *Run and Kill*), but he has truly outdone himself here – and God love him for it! By placing a rapist into the world of the mentally handicapped, Tang pushes all the buttons to make this an uncomfortable viewing experience for even the most jaded of horror fans; and he elicits such good performances, and films the carnage so stylishly, that the movie is almost hypnotic in its effect."

Rouge

Song of the Exile

"Ann Hui's best film deftly weaves together many of her familiar themes – the impossible situation of people who leave their homelands, the destructive effects of politics, and the act of grieving that must be gone though in order to get on with one's life."

Supercop

Swordsman II

"Bordering on expressionism, this film contains all the classic elements of a Tsui Hark Film Workshop production – crisp action choreography, an ensemble of A-list performers, a visual flair that is always eye-popping, and plenty of gender confusion."

To Liv(e)

"Evans Chan's first feature establishes him as the most intellectual of the current crop of Hong Kong directors."

Tricky Brains
"Stephen Chiau's funniest film."

Highly Recommended

92 Legendary La Rose Noire

All the Wrong Clues . . . For the Right Solution

All's Well, Ends Well

Autumn Moon

Awakening

The Barefooted Kid

The Big Heat

Boat People

Boys Are Easy

Burning Paradise

Chez 'n Ham

China Dragon

Chungking Express

Comrades, Almost a Love Story

The Dead and the Deadly

Deception

Dragon Inn

Dr. Wai in "The Scripture with No Words"

Encounters of the Spooky Kind II

Executioners

Fatal Encounter

Flirting Scholar

Flying Dagger

Fong Sai Yuk

Gunmen

He Ain't Heavy, He's My Father

High Risk

Holy Weapon

Love Among the Triad

Murder

My Heart Is that Eternal Rose

Naked Killer

Once upon a Time in China

Once upon a Time in China II

Once upon a Time in China IV

Once upon a Time in China V

Out of the Dark

Passion 1995

Plain Jane to the Rescue

Princess Fragrance

Private Eye Blues

The Private Eyes

Project S

Raining in the Mountain

Red Rose, White Rose

Royal Warriors

School on Fire

The Secret

Sexy and Dangerous

Shanghai Blues

Slave of the Sword

Soul

The Spooky Bunch

The Story of Woo Viet

Summer Snow

Super Mischieves

Top Banana Club

What Price Survival

Yes, Madam!

Recommended

All For the Winner

Always on My Mind

An Amorous Woman of the Tang Dynasty

Before Dawn

The Black Panther Warriors

The Bride with White Hair II

Bunman: The Untold Story

Burning Ambition

Butterfly and Sword

Butterfly Murders

The Case of the Cold Fish

Casino Raiders

A Chinese Ghost Story

Chinese Ghost Story II

Chinese Ghost Story III

The Chinese Ghostbuster

Crossings

Dangerous Encounter of the First Kind

Days of Being Dumb

The Day that Doesn't Exist

Dirty Ho

Dragons Forever

Dream Lovers

Dr. Lamb

East Is Red

Even Mountains Meet

The Final Judgement

Final Victory

Fist of Legend

Full Moon in New York

Full Throttle

Games Gamblers Play

God of Gamblers' Return

Hard-Boiled

Health Warning

Hong Kong 1941

Iron Monkey

It's a Wonderful Life

Kawashima Yoshiko

Lai Shi, China's Last Eunuch

Last Hurrah for Chivalry

Love, Guns and Glass

Love Massacre

Love in the Time of Twilight

The Magic Crane

New Tenant

Oh! My Three Guys

One of the Lucky Ones

Passion Unbounded

Pedicab Driver

People's Hero

Red Dust

Reincarnation of Golden Lotus

Retribution Sight Unseen

Romance of Book and Sword

Rose, Rose I Love You

Saviour of the Soul

Semi-Gods and Semi-Devils

Somebody up There Likes Me

Starry Is the Night

Swordsman

Tai Chi Master

To Live and Die in Tsimshatsui

Twenty Something

Twinkle, Twinkle Lucky Stars

Wing Chun

Zodiac Killers

RIC MEYERS

A prolific and prodigiously talented writer, Ric Meyers has published more books (and under more different *noms de plume*) than he can easily keep track of – espionage thrillers, science fiction, war novels, horror stories, and about a dozen non-fiction titles, including two Edgar-nominated books about television detectives. He is perhaps best known to Hong Kong movie fans as a regular columnist for *Inside Kung-Fu* magazine, and as the author of *Martial Arts Movies: From Bruce Lee to the Ninja* (Citadel Press: 1985), and co-author of *The Encyclopedia of Martial Arts Movies* (Scarecrow Press: 1995). He recently wrote the script for the 1997 Topps comic, *Jackie Chan as Spartan X*.

Born and raised in Connecticut, Meyers began his writing career at Atlas Comic Books, and had his eyes opened to the Hong Kong cinema as "comic books come to life" in 1979, when Larry Hama (who scripted Atlas's *Wolf the Barbarian*) took him to Chinatown to see Jackie Chan in *Drunken Master*. The movie is one of Meyers' three-star selections on the list that follows:

Most Highly Recommended

A Better Tomorrow

"John Woo establishes complex relationships and personalities with a superior knowledge of film language and the intensity of his personal vision. What could have been a standard gangster tale is elevated into a fever-dream on the nature of brotherhood, with roaring action set-pieces that galvanized Hong Kong audiences like nothing before."

A Better Tomorrow II

"A fun-house reflection on the original that manages to be both a satire and a homage. As such, it is at times almost more exhilarating, because we no longer have any real emotional investment in the characters' plagiarized personalities. We are free to be thrilled without worry, as dozens upon dozens of white-suited gunsels are mown down – falling out of closets in contorting waves like clowns tumbling out of circus Volkswagens."

The Bride with White Hair

"So foreign, yet so familiar. This fantasy epic elicits memories of some childhood story, yet its Asianness allows the *gweilo* viewer to admire even more its aggressive flights of frenzy. The story and the visuals are agonizingly beautiful, but what sends it to the top (and over) is its extraordinary Siamese-twin brother-and-sister villain. The sequel, while fun and fascinating in its own right, merely finishes the story without really adding anything necessary to it."

Bullet in the Head

"The first five minutes of Woo's masterpiece on the nature of brotherhood has more cinematic potency than many entire movies. Tsui Hark tried to undercut Woo with a rushed-out *Better Tomorrow III*, featuring the contractually straitjacketed Chow Yun-fat, but Woo's bleak, operatic version remains supreme. Meanwhile, Chow's absence is compensated for by Jacky Cheung's bold, brave performance as the 'title character,' Tony Leung's ability to communicate tragedy, and Waise Lee's wonderful way with the line, 'All I want is this box of gold. Is that so much to ask?'"

A Chinese Ghost Story

"Ching Siu-tung's splendid fantasy of a thousand-year-old unisex tree demon with a mile-long tongue, pimping a beautiful spirit for 'the big evil.' Sit back – you literally haven't seen anything like this before. For an audience weaned on such labored sword-and-sorcery exercises as *Krull*, *Willow*, and *Dragonheart*, *A Chinese Ghost Story* comes as a brain-blooming revelation."

Dragons Forever

"A martial-arts milestone, created as a swan song for the starring trio of Jackie Chan, Yuen Biao, and Sammo Hung. More challenging than the trio's previous team-ups in that they play antiheroes – a corrupt lawyer, a demented cat burglar, and a gun seller – who are redeemed; but all that is wedged in between many, many fights, none of which have been surpassed in speed or showmanship."

Drunken Master

"Seeing Jackie Chan at the height of his youthful power is enlightening, and he attacks stardom with far more verve than he attacks his enemies. The sequel, which was made sixteen years afterwards, has incredible martial arts and many amazing moments, but much of the spirited fun of the original has been lost."

God of Gamblers

"Chow Yun-fat loves acting so much that the audience becomes his paramour. In Wong Jing's blend of *Rain Man* and *The Cincinnati Kid*, Chow moves so effortlessly between playing a divinely lucky card player, a chocolate-loving retarded man, and a chocolate-loving retarded man who's pretending he's a divinely lucky card player, that anyone who knows anything about acting can only watch dumbstruck."

The Heroic Trio

"Quite simply, the best Marvel Comics movie that Marvel Comics never made. One superheroine (Anita Mui as Wonder Woman) and two super-antiheroines (Maggie Cheung as Thief Catcher and Michelle Yeoh as Invisible Girl) take on a powerful, ancient eunuch who's abducting babies. The movie's very absurdity works in its favor, as spandex-clad Asian beauties leap all over the screen – supported by wires, splendid visuals, and a swell performance by Anthony Wong, as a monosyllabic henchman who is not averse to eating his own hacked-off fingers."

The Killer

"An amoral cop hunts a moral assassin, allowing John Woo to choreograph a dance of death that reaches its height as the two characters tango around each other, their guns in each other's faces, while a woman the hitman accidentally blinded obliviously prepares tea for them. As if that, and the many thunderously exciting 'gun-fu' sequences aren't enough, Woo wraps it up with one of the greatest black-comic moments in movie history."

Mr. Vampire

"Another Asian eye-opener, which reminds audiences that the concept of the supernatural blood-sucker was created – like so many things – in China, and Bram Stoker only got his hands on it once it reached Europe. Producer Sammo Hung (who was largely responsible for making Chinese horror a valid subgenre) creates a new vampire mythos out of the *gyonshi* – hopping, blind, flesh-sniffing blood-quaffers, garbed in Chinese burial finery, who can be repelled with the right kind of rice, hurt by rooster-bloodied coins, rendered helpless by yellow prayer-parchment, and eliminated at the source by the proper use of 'feng shui.' The cast is winning, the comedy is plentiful, and there's a lovely subplot involving a lovelorn spirit who literally loses her head when her attempt to seduce a living hero is foiled by the Priest with One Eyebrow."

Once upon a Time in China II

"This hundredth Wong Fei-hung movie – the series given new life by director Tsui Hark and star Jet Li – works on all levels: action, emotion, romance, political subtext, and drama."

Peking Opera Blues

"What initially seems to be a tract on women's liberation set amid turn-of-the-century Chinese political intrigue becomes a soaring, romantic action-comedy, with loads of eye-popping color, French-farce-flavored set pieces, and high-octane cinematic imagination. (Being that this is a Hong Kong film, Tsui Hark also throws in torture and corpse manipulation.) So glorious a showcase for the talents of Brigitte Lin, Sally Yeh, and Cherie Chung, that their male co-stars fade away, both on screen and in memory."

Police Story

"Jackie Chan followed up his breakthrough *Project A* with this effort, which revolutionized the modern-day Hong Kong action film in many of the same ways that *Project A* revolutionized the historical costumer. Although the version edited for the Japanese market is five minutes longer and more emotionally valid, even the streamlined, dubbed version shown at the New York Film Festival is a satisfying, entertaining, complete film that stands head and shoulders above every Chan movie that has followed."

Project A

"In his youthful enthusiasm and willingness to change, Jackie Chan dragged the kung-fu film into the twentieth century, both literally and figuratively. Before *Project A*, almost every Hong Kong fight flick took place in a narrow historical period, with dialog limited to the likes of 'You must be tired of living'; but in Chan's vision, it was 1903, and he could challenge his audiences with what his characters said. Add to that what he and co-star Sammo Hung did with the fight scenes – weaving them inextricably with the plot, actually showing people hitting the ground (and painfully bouncing!), and creating a sustained, virtuoso mid-film chase worthy of Buster Keaton and Douglas Fairbanks."

Highly Recommended

Boat People

Center Stage

Dirty Ho

Drunken Master II

Duel to the Death

Fist of Legend

Flirting Scholar

God of Gamblers II

God of Gamblers' Return

Hard-Boiled

He's a Woman, She's a Man

Iron Monkey

King of Beggars

Naked Killer

Once upon a Time in China

Painted Faces

Police Story II

Project A II

Royal Tramp

Royal Tramp II

Swordsman II

Wheels on Meals

Yes, Madam!

Zu: Warriors from the Magic Mountain

Recommended

All for the Winner

All's Well, Ends Well

Armour of God

Au Revoir, Mon Amour

An Autumn's Tale

The Barefooted Kid

A Better Tomorrow III: Love and Death in Saigon

The Blade

The Bodyguard from Beijing

Bunman: The Untold Story

Burning Ambition

Butterfly Murders

C'est la Vie, Mon Cherie

Chicken and Duck Talk

A Chinese Ghost Story II

A Chinese Ghost Story III

A Chinese Odyssey I: Pandora's Box

A Chinese Odyssey II: Cinderella

Crazy Safari

Days of Being Wild

The Dead and the Deadly

Dr. Lamb

East is Red

Encounters of the Spooky Kind

Encounters of the Spooky Kind II

Fong Sai Yuk

Fong Sai Yuk II

From Beijing with Love

Full Contact

God of Gamblers III: Back to Shanghai

Gunmen

He Ain't Heavy, He's My Father

Heart of the Dragon

Kung Fu Cult Master

Last Hurrah for Chivalry

Love in a Fallen City

Love on Delivery

The Lovers

Once upon a Time in China III

Organized Crime and Triad Bureau

Pedicab Driver

Project S

Robotrix

Rock 'n Roll Cop

Saviour of the Soul

Security Unlimited

Sex and Zen

Story of Ricky

Supercop

The Sword

Swordsman

Tai Chi Master

Temptation of a Monk

Tiger Cage

Tiger on Beat

Twinkle, Twinkle Lucky Stars

We're Going to Eat You

Winners and Sinners

JIMMY NGAI (Ngai Siuyan)

Born and educated in Hong Kong, Jimmy Ngai studied English literature at Baptist College, and has been passionate about movies since he was a child. After years of writing film criticism for various publications, he was invited in 1994 to contribute a weekly column to the *Hong Kong Economic Daily*. He joined the Hong Kong Film Critics Society (of which Law Kar is also a member) when it was established the following year.

Ngai recently co-wrote with Stanley Kwan the screenplay for Kwan's forthcoming *Moon of Joy*. He is also the author of the 1995 book *Wong Kar-wai X 4*, an analysis of the director's first four movies. He wrote the English subtitles for Wong's *Days of Being Wild*, and has also written Chinese subtitles for Hollywood movies. His affinity for Wong Kar-wai, and Wong's partner at Jet Tone Production Co., the director Jeff Lau, is readily apparent in his selection of favorite films.

Most Highly Recommended

All for the Winner

"Jeff Lau plus Stephen Chiau – the dynamic duo that set the standard for *mo lai to* (a particular Hong Kong genre that dwells on the bizarre and inconsequential, achieving, at its best, a comic-tragic effect). A must for anybody who claims to have any interest in Hong Kong comedy."

As Tears Go By

"Wong Kar-wai's début remains a classic combination of style and commercialism. Much of what was to be seen in his later works can be traced back to this little gem."

Ashes of Time

"The most ambitious of Wong Kar-wai's films also happens to be his best to date. This is a work that grows on you – because its sentiment is wrapped up and buried deeply, *Ashes of Time* requires a certain willingness from the audience to appreciate its beauty."

A Chinese Odyssey, Parts I and II

"This reinterpretation of the Chinese classic *Monkey King* is so full of surprises that 'amazing' cannot begin to describe it. Unfortunately for English-speaking audiences, the movie is crabbed with shabby subtitles."

Chungking Express

Days of Being Wild

"The sense of purity in this movie exceeds that of all of Wong Kar-wai's other works."

Final Victory

Long Arm of the Law

"Probably the only Hong Kong 'macho' film that is as moving as it is violent."

Out of the Dark

"Panned by many critics, this is finest Jeff Lau/Stephen Chiau collaboration, a movie that works subtly on both a personal and political level (Hong Kong 1997). Lau's expertise at hitting an emotional chord at the least expected moments should not go unnoticed."

Highly Recommended

92 Legendary La Rose Noire

Autumn Moon
"The bathroom love scene in this movie has a beastly aspect seldom seen in any other film."

A Better Tomorrow

A Better Tomorrow II

Bullet in the Head

Dangerous Encounter of the First Kind
"A very raw, angry, and energetic Tsui Hark that was not to be seen again."

The Dead and the Deadly

The Eagle Shooting Heroes
"An underrated Jeff Lau movie that should have acquired the cult status of *92 Legendary La Rose Noire*."

Fallen Angels
"More like a Wong Kar-wai sampler than a standalone exercise. The monologues here, in particular, are obviously inferior to those of his previous work."

Hard-Boiled

Heroes Shed No Tears

Homecoming
"Yim Ho's best work."

Hong Kong 1941

The Killer

Love unto Waste

Mr. Vampire

Once a Thief
"John Woo relaxed and flamboyant, not to be seen anywhere else."

Private Eye Blues
"A small gem that defies classification."

Saviour of the Soul

The Secret
"Ann Hui's début film is arguably her best, but definitely her most creative."

The Spooky Bunch

We're Going to Eat You
"Tsui Hark's one and only film noir, from his more creative days."

Zu: Warriors from the Magic Mountain

Recommended

All's Well, Ends Well

An Amorous Woman of the Tang Dynasty

Boat People

Butterfly Murders

The Day the Sun Turned Cold

Drunken Master

Encounters of the Spooky Kind

Farewell China

From Beijing with Love

Full Moon in New York

Gangs

Love and the City

Painted Faces

Peking Opera Blues

People's Hero

Rouge

JOHN POWERS

After several years teaching at Georgetown University, John Powers began making his living as a journalist in the early 1980s. He is currently the film critic for *Vogue*, and for National Public Radio's "Fresh Air." Between 1985 and 1993, he was the film critic for *L.A. Weekly*. His articles have appeared in a variety of publications, including *Rolling Stone, New York, The Washington Post, Harper's, The Nation, Premiere, Us, Sight and Sound, American Film, Film Comment*, and *California* (for which he was the film critic from 1987 to 1989). In 1993, he and Vikram Juyanti made the documentary *I Am a Sex Addict* for the BBC; it played on the international film-festival circuit before being aired in the UK in the summer of 1994.

An Iowa native, Powers discovered the Hong Kong cinema at a screening of *A Better Tomorrow* at the 1987 Toronto Film Festival, where he was seated next to David Chute, then the film critic for the *Los Angeles Herald-Examiner*. The following year, Chute guest-edited a seminal special issue on Hong Kong movies for *Film Comment*, and Powers was the lead-off contributor. (Dave Kehr, meanwhile, weighed in with an article on Jackie Chan.) Powers quotes from his *Film Comment* article in some of the commentary below.

Most Highly Recommended

Autumn Moon

A Better Tomorrow
"This great gangster picture features the kind of iconic performances that are the genius of the movies. Simply by the way he eats street food in the opening scene, Chow Yun-fat tells us all we need to know about his character – his warmth, his cocksure

humor, and the careless *joie de vivre* that will get him in Dutch later on. It's an unforgettable piece of screen acting – the kind that people emulate when they walk onto the streets after the show."

Bullet in the Head

"Far richer and more moving than *The Deer Hunter* – to which it's an answer – this epic of friendship and war in 1960s Saigon has Woo's trademark delirious intensity. Of all his films, this is the one with the greatest sweep and passion."

Center Stage

A Chinese Ghost Story

Chungking Express

"One of contemporary cinemas's triumphant films. Wong Kar-wai's marvelous romantic comedy does for 1990s Hong Kong what the New Wave did for 1960s Paris. A triumph of lyricism, the movie makes us feel the tantalizing amphetamine rush of urban life, but also shows how the city's good cheer is shot through with wistfulness. For all his jokes (and they're amusing ones), Wong shows us a Hong Kong full of solitary souls who can't quite bridge the abyss separating their sunny public faces from their lonely private dreams; as openhearted as its characters, the movie smiles tenderly on those brave enough to keep risking their hearts."

Days of Being Wild

"Brilliant, gorgeous, and a tad obscure, this film proved that Wong Kar-wai had the stuff of a major international filmmaker. Even when it seems overly arty, it's utterly ravishing to watch. Wong is one of the rare Hong Kong directors to care about sheer beauty; no other director in the world graces the screen with so many exquisite-looking actors and actresses."

Eastern Condors

Fallen Angels

"Like Jean-Luc Godard, Wong Kar-wai sometimes has so many ideas that he doesn't know what to do with them all. While this movie is most striking for its stylistic razzmatazz, especially its use of wide-angle lenses, its finest moments tend to be small – a dead pig getting a rub-down, the haunting video diary of a dead father. A fine sadness pervades all of Wong's work, where human feeling is always attempting to make itself felt through modern bustle. Photographed by the great Christopher Doyle, the movie ends with the most thrilling final shot in 1990s cinema – a transcendent vision of skyscrapers in the sky."

The Killer

Lady in Black
"Although every shot seems to belong to a different movie and the subplots proliferate like scandalous tubers, Sun Chung's thriller is held together by the charisma of beautiful, somber Brigitte Lin, who gives the plot's inanity a gravity it doesn't deserve. A classic star turn by one of the world's greatest screen actresses."

Peking Opera Blues
"Sheer hyperkinetic pleasure – it makes Hollywood stunt films look simple-minded. Much of the movie's joy grows from our amazement that the actors are able to do this stuff – pull off those impossible acrobatics, engineer bedroom farce with split-second timing, or transform a rooftop climax into an inspired piece of pop-culture ballet."

Police Story
"One of the two or three best Chan films, this movie boasts Maggie Cheung, his sleekest female co-star, and contains the wittiest use of a shopping mall in motion-picture history."

Project A

Project A II
"A classic. With a closing stunt worthy of (borrowed from?) *Steamboat Bill, Jr.*, this movie makes it explicit that Chan has the grace of Buster Keaton, if not the metaphysical temperament."

Romance of Book and Sword

Rouge
"One of the best and most underrated films of the 80s. Stanley Kwan's funny, moving melodrama is steeped in the vanished glamor of Hong Kong's past – it's all ghosts and opium pipes and

brothels filled with beauties. Yet Kwan tempers this romanticism with an ironic portrait of a contemporary city where everybody's seemingly too busy for passion. At once a love story, a mystery, a yuppie comedy and a portrait of time's dark handwriting on Hong Kong culture, the movie offers the kind of smart, sensuous entertainment that Hollywood used to make and no longer can."

Shanghai Blues

The Sword

Highly Recommended

Aces Go Places

Ah Ying

Armour of God

Ashes of Time

As Tears Go By

A Chinese Ghost Story II

Comrades, Almost a Love Story

Hard-Boiled

Long Arm of the Law

Once upon a Time in China II

Passion 1995

Police Story II

The Spooky Bunch

Swordsman II

Zu: Warriors from the Magic Mountain

Recommended

Aces Go Places II

A Better Tomorrow III: Love and Death in Saigon

Boat People

Butterfly Murders

City on Fire

Crime Story

The Dead and the Deadly

Dream Lovers

Drunken Master

Duel to the Death

Farewell China

Full Moon in New York

Gangs

Green Snake

Moon Warriors

Mr. Vampire

Naked Killer

Once a Thief

Operation Condor

Painted Faces

People's Hero

Red Dust

Sex and Zen

Song of the Exile

Supercop

Tiger on Beat

Wheels on Meals

TONY RAYNS

Critic, journalist, filmmaker, teacher, and, since 1988, programmer of the Vancouver Film Festival, Tony Rayns has played a significant role in bringing Hong Kong films to audiences in the West. Born in Oxford, England, Rayns began programming films as a boy – he founded a film society at school in order to screen 16mm prints of movies by directors that intrigued him, from Fritz Lang to Roger Corman. He went on to Cambridge University, where he ran three film societies, and helped found a short-lived but influential magazine called *Cinema*.

Rayns's interest in Hong Kong cinema dates from the early 1970s, when *Time Out* asked him to review a Shaw Brothers series in London, and he became aware that Hong Kong films had English subtitles. (He has since learned to speak conversational Mandarin and Cantonese.) On subsequent trips to London's Chinatown, he saw numerous swordplay and kung-fu films, and began to write about them. In 1977, he was invited to the first Hong Kong International Film Festival, and met key figures in the emerging generation of new-wave directors, such as Patrick Tam, Ann Hui, Tsui Hark, and Yim Ho, who were still working in television. The following year, he traveled to China to acquire prints of movies for the world's first historical retrospective of the Chinese cinema, which was presented by the National Film Theatre in London in 1980.

Rayns has appeared as an extra in a number of Hong Kong productions (he played a launch captain opposite Chow Yun-fat's policeman in a Kirk Wong-directed episode of the TV series *The Man from Hong Kong*, for instance). He recently assisted Stanley Kwan on a documentary for the British Film Institute, *Yang ± Yin: Gender in Chinese Cinema*, which premièred at the Venice Film Festival; Rayns provided English subtitles for film clips featured in the documentary, and an English voice-over for the documentary itself. For Faber and Faber he wrote an essay about contemporary mainland Chinese cinema as an introduction to the screenplay of Chen Kaige's *King of The Children*.

Most Highly Recommended

Ah Ying

"Allen Fong invents the Chinese docudrama, asking a real-life family to act out its own domestic strains and crises. The style was rooted in the work he'd previously done for TV, but this film took the method to a much higher level. The character played by Peter Wang was based on the recently deceased Koh Wu, and the film was intended in part as a memorial to him."

An Amorous Woman of the Tang Dynasty

"Outstandingly original début feature by Eddie Fong, reading the gender confusions of the 1980s through what we know of Tang Dynasty morals and mores. As daring visually as it is thematically. Sadly, the production company was Shaw Brothers – which means that it's now impossible to see a good print."

Ashes of Time

"Everything that should have gone into *Days of Being Wild, Part II* found its way into this eccentric masterwork, along with most of Wong Kar-wai's ambiguous feelings about the *wuxia pian* [martial chivalry] genre, and the essential androgyny of Brigitte Lin."

Bullet in the Head

"The echoes of *Deer Hunter* are too strong for it to be a truly great film, but the rhapsodic opening forty minutes (based closely on John Woo's adolescent memories of Hong Kong in the late 1960s) are the equal of anything by Bertolucci and Storaro – and the best thing Woo has ever done."

Butterfly Murders

"The *wuxia pian* as a Borgesian conundrum, and as a reflection of the thinking of Hong Kong radicals in the 1970s."

Center Stage

"Not only another of Stanley Kwan's exquisite studies of the process of victimization, but also the most reasonable and humane account of the Shanghai film industry in the 1930s we are ever likely to have. It is founded on extremely detailed and careful research, and its deliberate rehabilitation of the reputation of director Fei Mu is a conscious affront to the Communist critics who have vilified him."

Chungking Express

"Some say that the excitement generated by the early Godard movies in the 1960s can never be recaptured or matched, because the cinema has changed too much. This film proves them wrong."

Dangerous Encounter of the First Kind

"Tsui's masterpiece – the most complete statement of his xenophobia, his fear of women, and his ambivalent feelings about Hong Kong."

Days of Being Wild

"Peerless evocation of the roots of 'Hong Kong identity,' which sees the archetypal Hong Kong protagonist as something between a gambler and a fatherless, mother-fixated playboy. Utterly original – nostalgia for the 1960s as future shock."

Health Warning

"Kirk Wong's most daring film, a deeply cynical take on the kung-fu genre crossed with dystopian sci-fi and an attitude toward sexual kinks straight out of an early Lou Reed song."

Kawashima Yoshiko

"Funnier if you take it as an all-out satire of Bertolucci's *Last Emperor*, but anyway a wonderfully subversive rereading of China's modern history. The scene in which Anita Mui plunges a hypodermic needle into Andy Lau's naked buttock may never be equalled."

The Killer

"The best Scorsese/Melville homage ever made."

Lai Shi, China's Last Eunuch

"Jacob Cheung meets the Sammo Hung roadshow in a minor classic of revisionist historiography. Also notable for marking the last occasion when it was possible to take Andy Lau seriously."

Nomad

"Wildly inconsistent (and not only because the producer added the ridiculous ending against Patrick Tam's wishes), but still the best account of Hong Kong's dawning 'Generation X,' and of Hong Kong kids' passion for all things Japanese. The only Patrick Tam

film to approach the level of achievement in his TV work of the
1970s."

The Private Eyes

"The best comedy ever made in Hong Kong."

Rouge

"Stanley Kwan turns a piece of opportunistic pulp fiction into an
elegiac meditation on the space between tradition and modernity –
and between meaning it and faking it."

Security Unlimited

"Slightly less achieved than *The Private Eyes*, this is nonetheless
another high point in Michael Hui's quest for the perfect Chinese
visual comedy."

The Spooky Bunch

"Brilliant horror-comedy about the hold of the past over the
present. Ann Hui's many good ideas included that of shooting it
hand-held, like documentary. It remains remarkably fresh and
inventive."

Sunless Days

"Shu Kei's documentary was the most reasoned and intelligent
response from any Hong Kong artist to the Tiananmen Square
Massacre."

Highly Recommended

As Tears Go By

"Blatant knock-off of *Mean Streets*, but it was already obvious
that Wong Kar-wai was going to be a major talent. Compared with
the films he scripted for (e.g.) Patrick Tam, this was a triumph of
rigor and originality."

Autumn Moon

Before Dawn

"Too ramshackle and chaotic to earn three stars, but still a
phenomenal extremist melodrama – and the first sustained account
of Hong Kong's gay subculture in the old, 'unliberated' days.
Clarence Fok's best film."

A Better Tomorrow

The Blade
"By far the most interesting of Tsui Hark's later films, not least for the overt homoeroticism. Pity they didn't spend a bit longer writing, shooting, and editing it; despite its qualities, it's as sloppily made and careless as Tsui's other recent work."

Boat People
"There's a major weakness in the central casting, but Ann Hui's vision of South Vietnam falling to the Communist North is both a great imaginative feat and a persuasive paranoid vision of Hong Kong's own possible fate."

Chicken and Duck Talk
"The last gasp of Michael Hui's once formidable talents."

A Chinese Odyssey, Parts I and II
"Best seen in the re-edited version which combines both parts and eliminates a lot of redundancy and repetition. It confirms Jeff Lau's talents as a latter-day Lau Kar-leung, and gives Stephen Chiau his best role."

Crime Story
"Kirk Wong accentuates the action in Jackie Chan's schtick, with literally explosive results."

The Day the Sun Turned Cold
"Yim Ho's most sincere film."

The Dead and the Deadly
"The *ne plus ultra* of Chinese black comedy."

Drunken Master II

Fallen Angels

Fong Sai Yuk
"Both stars for Josephine Siao, and half of one of them for the talented Corey Yuen."

Full Moon in New York
"There's something fundamentally spurious about the basic

concept (women from Hong Kong, Taiwan, and China meet in New York), but Kwan's film contains some of the most trenchant scenes of overseas Chinese life ever written and shot."

Hard-Boiled

Her Fatal Ways
"Alfred Cheung's wittiest comedy. Shame about the political cop-out in the final scenes."

Iceman Cometh
"After *Before Dawn*, the only film in Clarence Fok's lengthy filmography which hints at a talent worth pursuing. It makes funny and mildly subversive use of various genre conventions and stereotypes."

Love in a Fallen City
"Brave but probably doomed attempt to find a film form equivalent to Eileen Chang's prose."

Love unto Waste

The Magnificent Butcher
"Finely balanced between reverence and disrespect for tradition, this is a superior kung-fu film. Also notable for giving the late Kwan Tak-hing his last memorable appearance."

Miracles
"Jackie Chan does Capra, and just about gets away with it."

Once upon a Time in China

Painted Faces

Peking Opera Blues

Police Story

Private Eye Blues
"Eddie Fong finds the hidden qualities in Jacky Cheung."

Project A

Red Rose, White Rose
"Brave but probably doomed attempt to go beyond Eileen Chang's prose in visual terms."

Romance of Book and Sword, Parts I and II (Princess Fragrance)
"Grand-scale *wuxia* fiction in China locations."

The Secret
"Ann Hui's auspicious début. Founded on a commitment (inherited from her TV work) to bring Hong Kong's social realities to the screen – and thereby to criticize the studio-bound norms of the day – but it also delivers as an analysis of the power of superstition in Chinese society."

Song of the Exile
"Ann Hui's autobiography."

The Story of Woo Viet
"Doomed romance noir with a Tagalog accent."

Summer Snow
"The film which consolidated the comebacks of both Ann Hui and Josephine Siao."

Swordsman II

Temptation of a Monk

Recommended

92 Legendary La Rose Noire

All's Well, Ends Well

An Autumn's Tale

The Barefooted Kid

A Better Tomorrow II
"John Woo himself asked me not to see this film, and said it was 'the worst film ever made.' He was wrong, of course, but you can see that he made it under duress."

Bugis Street
"One star for the sexual and cinematic candor of its direct-to-camera monologues – and for its cheek in defying Singapore's censors."

Cageman

C'est la Vie, Mon Cherie

A Chinese Ghost Story
"Competent Sam Raimi rip-off, but also surprisingly close to the 1958 original directed by Li Hanxiang."

Dream Lovers
"One star for the sheer folly of its pretensions."

Drunken Master
"Atrociously directed, but its subversion of the myth of the young Wong Fei-hung deserves one star."

Duel to the Death

East Is Red

Encounters of the Spooky Kind

Farewell China

Final Victory
"The epitome of Patrick Tam's misogyny."

God of Gamblers

Gunmen
"Creditable knock-off of a Hollywood formula, and one of the few Film Workshop films not redirected or hijacked by Tsui Hark."

Heaven Can't Wait

The Heroic Trio
"Only for the hints of Lautreamont-esque perversity."

Homecoming

Hong Kong 1941

Last Hurrah for Chivalry

Long Arm of the Law

Love Among the Triad

Love and the City

Magnificent Warriors

Moon Warriors

Mr. Vampire

New Legend of Shaolin
"Not as good as the old ones, but still . . . ."

Once a Thief

Once upon a Time in China III

Organized Crime and Triad Bureau

Pedicab Driver

People's Hero

Plain Jane to the Rescue

Police Confidential

Police Story II

Red Dust

Reincarnation of Golden Lotus

Rock 'n Roll Cop

Saviour of the Soul
"Quite good of its kind, but those who profess to love it have never seen Chu Yuan's series of adaptations from the novels of Gu Long."

Shanghai Blues

Soul
"Shu Kei tries to transplant Cassavetes' *Gloria* to Hong Kong and

Macao with mixed results, but he has the wit to put Hou Hsiao-hsien in a white suit and have him blowing sax in a cemetery."

The Sword
"Disappointingly ordinary after Tam's previous achievements for TV."

Swordsman
"Despite the credits, nothing to do with the veteran King Hu."

The Terracotta Warrior

We're Going to Eat You
"Failed black comedy, notable for its fudged political satire."

The Wicked City
"One star for setting its climax on top of the new Bank of China tower – although the idea was ripped off from the Black Panther comic strip."

Witch from Nepal

Zu: Warriors from the Magic Mountain

Not Recommended

All the Wrong Clues . . . For the Right Solution
"Foundation-stone of Tsui's attempt to reinvent himself as a family entertainer. The edge found in all his previous work is utterly erased."

Armour of God
"Did it make sense to try to sell Jackie Chan to the rest of the world by putting him in an Indiana Jones rip-off?"

Cherry Blossoms
"Disowned by Eddie Fong (it was taken out of his hands), but anyway a textbook example of Hong Kong cinema's perennial ineptitude in representing Japan and Japanese culture on screen."

Gangs
"Quintessential phony Hong Kong sociology."

Green Snake
  "Tsui Hark's nadir, and Maggie Cheung's most undignified
screen moments."

He's a Woman, She's a Man
  "Quintessential phony Hong Kong sexual liberalism."

BARBARA SCHARRES

Director of the Film Center at the School of the Art Institute of
Chicago since 1988, Barbara Scharres is well known to Hong Kong
film enthusiasts as a leading scholar, historian, and critic. Every
year as director, Scharres has programmed a Hong Kong festival at
the Film Center, including retrospectives of Chow Yun-fat (1990),
Jackie Chan (1991), and Michael Hui (1992), at which those stars
each were present to speak to the audience. Scharres recently
lectured at Yale on how the Hong Kong cinema has dealt with the
approach of 1997, and wrote the liner notes for the Criterion laser-
disk edition of John Woo's *Hard-Boiled*. (She also appears as an
extra in Woo's *Once a Thief*.) Her commentary has appeared in the
*Chicago Reader, Variety, American Cinematographer, Film Com-
ment,* and *The Independent*.

Scharres was born in Canada – to parents who, she says, loved
the theater but disdained movies – and grew up in Chicago. Her
passion for films was unleashed when *Lawrence of Arabia* opened;
"I fell madly in love with Peter O'Toole, and saw it five times," she
recalls. As a junior at St. Xavier's, a Catholic college in Chicago,
she persuaded the school to create an independent study course in
film-making so that she could produce student films for credit.
Upon graduating, she worked as a projectionist, and earned an
MFA degree in film-making and painting from the Art Institute of
Chicago. She was hired part-time at the Art Institute's Film Center
in 1974, went full-time the following year, and, over the next
decade and a half, rose to director. She credits David Overbey of
the Toronto Film Festival for sparking her interest in Hong Kong
movies; a 1986 screening of Tsui Hark's *Shanghai Blues* made an
especially strong impression.

Most Highly Recommended

A Better Tomorrow

"The film that declared John Woo's artistic maturity, featuring the passionate male bonding, intricately choreographed metaphoric gunplay, and theme of loyalty betrayed that would become his trademarks. Legendary, career-altering performances by Chow Yun-fat, Ti Lung, and Leslie Cheung."

Bullet in the Head

"The riskiest, most challenging Woo film to date. Total appreciation calls for a degree of emotional identification that may not come easily to some Westerners (particularly male)."

Chicken and Duck Talk

"A brilliant performance by comic genius and satirist Michael Hui, highlighting his favorite theme of a Hong Kong Everyman facing change and cultural erosion."

A Chinese Ghost Story

"The quintessential merger of the traditional Chinese ghost story with the Hong Kong pop sensibility. The film's endearingly comic romance, pathos, and gross-out special effects stand the test of time."

Dream Lovers

"An audacious combining of genres gives Chow Yun-fat the chance to play comedy, tragedy, and everything in between, in a movie with something for everybody."

Drunken Master

"Jackie Chan coming into his own as a comic master – a performance to be treasured forever."

Drunken Master II

Eastern Condors

"Sammo Hung's short-lived, rip-roaring bid for hunk status (to impress his co-starring girlfriend) is the best realized of the films he's directed."

Fong Sai Yuk

"A brilliant, multifaceted comeback performance by veteran actress Josephine Siao."

From Riches to Rags

Games Gamblers Play

Gunmen

"Kirk Wong's best early film, although the hand of producer Tsui Hark can't be denied in the elegance of the action sequences and the overall historical romanticism."

Hard-Boiled

"The film became Woo's calling card in the West while providing closure on his career in Hong Kong. For once his spectacular action seems to signify a state of endless purgatory rather than the consummation of passion."

The Killer

"Woo's ode to Chow Yun-fat, showcasing his nobility, decency, and simmering sexuality as no other director can. The best performance of Danny Lee's career."

King of Chess

"Disowned by co-director Yim Ho, the film is nonetheless a credit to him and Tsui Hark, growing richer with multiple viewings. One of the best films addressing the uncertainty of 1997 and the pain of the Chinese diaspora."

Miracles

"Jackie Chan makes a rare acknowledgment of his own mortality by experimenting with a higher drama quotient and some lovely sleight-of-hand in place of major stunts – the result is electrifying."

Once upon a Time in China II

"The best of the cycle for its emotional resonance. The stunts and fights are thrilling, but Tsui Hark's concluding ode to Chinese freedom will send shivers down your spine."

Painted Faces

"It may not be historically accurate (according to Jackie Chan), but this romanticized fictional view of the childhood of Chan, Sammo Hung, and Yuen Biao is perfectly balanced between joy and pain, nostalgia and yearning. Truly great performances by all the kids, and by Sammo Hung as his own former master."

Peking Opera Blues

"One of Tsui Hark's best. Everything works – the triple-pronged plot, the historical setting, the madcap comedy, and the cast chemistry."

People's Hero

"Ti Lung has never given a better and more sustained performance, demonstrating how fully he had made the transition from over-the-hill action star to character actor. Sad to say, he is no longer considered leading-man material in Hong Kong."

Police Story

"A perfect time capsule – Jackie Chan simultaneously at the height of his physical and creative prowess. Great performance, great stunts, great heart."

Police Story II

"I prefer Part I, but it's still pretty great."

The Private Eyes

"Michael Hui perfects his mean-spirited comic persona in this film and delivers one of Hong Kong's first social satires for the screen."

Project A

"The film that earned Jackie Chan the comparisons to Buster Keaton and Charlie Chaplin. The comic imagination of a lifetime is packed into one work that deserves a very high place in film history."

Project A II

"It's great and many people prefer it, but for me Part I has the edge."

Rouge

"Marvelously entertaining as a ghost story, especially due to Anita Mui's elegantly creepy performance, but also one of the most intelligently scripted of the films consciously foreshadowing 1997."

Security Unlimited

"The best ensemble piece starring the three Hui brothers."

Shanghai Blues

"Tsui Hark moved in a new direction with this film, and it transformed his future work."

Swordsman

"The film that re-launched the period-action movie in Hong Kong, and still one of the best of the genre. The chemistry between Sam Hui and Cecilia Yip, and the song 'Hero of Heroes,' are among its most memorable aspects."

Highly Recommended

An Autumn's Tale

A Better Tomorrow II

A Better Tomorrow III: Love and Death in Saigon

Boat People

Center Stage

A Chinese Ghost Story II

Chungking Express

City on Fire

Dangerous Encounter of the First Kind

Days of Being Wild

The Day the Sun Turned Cold

Dragon Inn

Dragons Forever

Father and Son

Fong Sai Yuk II

Full Contact

God of Gamblers

Her Fatal Ways

Hong Kong 1941

Iron Monkey

Killer's Romance

Last Hurrah for Chivalry

Love in the Time of Twilight

Loving You

Money Crazy

Mr. Vampire

Now You See Love . . . Now You Don't

Once a Thief

Once upon a Time in China

Operation Condor

Queen of Temple Street

Rumble in the Bronx

The Spooky Bunch

Summer Snow

Supercop

Teppanyaki

Tiger on Beat

Treasure Hunt

Twin Dragons

Wheels on Meals

Winners and Sinners

Zu: Warriors from the Magic Mountain

Recommended

92 Legendary La Rose Noire

Aces Go Places

Aces Go Places II

Aces Go Places III: Our Man from Bond Street

Ah Ying

All for the Winner

Armour of God

Arrest the Restless

As Tears Go By

Ashes of Time

Au Revoir, Mon Amour

Autumn Moon

The Barefooted Kid

The Big Heat

The Bodyguard from Beijing

The Bride with White Hair

Burning Paradise

Butterfly Murders

Cageman

The Case of the Cold Fish

C'est la Vie, Mon Cherie

A Chinese Ghost Story III

Crime Story

Dragon from Russia

The Eagle Shooting Heroes

East Is Red

Executioners

Final Option

First Strike

A Fishy Story

Fist of Legend

Flirting Scholar

From Beijing with Love

Full Moon in New York

Gangs

God of Gamblers II

God of Gamblers III: Back to Shanghai

God of Gamblers' Return

Green Snake

Gun-N-Rose

He Ain't Heavy, He's My Father

He's a Woman, She's a Man

Heaven Can't Wait

Heroes Shed No Tears

The Heroic Trio

High Risk

Iceman Cometh

Island of Fire

Kawashima Yoshiko

King of Beggars

Kung Fu Cult Master

Last Hero in China

Long Arm of the Law

Lord of East China Sea

Love and the City

Love in a Fallen City

The Lovers

Love unto Waste

My Father Is a Hero

New Legend of Shaolin

Once upon a Time in China III

Once upon a Time in China IV

Once upon a Time in China V

Peace Hotel

Pedicab Driver

Plain Jane to the Rescue

Prison on Fire

Prison on Fire II

Project S

Red Dust

Red Rose, White Rose

Reincarnation of Golden Lotus

Rock 'n Roll Cop

Roof with a View

Romance of Book and Sword

Rose, Rose I Love You

Royal Tramp

Saviour of the Soul

School on Fire

Sex and Zen

Somebody up There Likes Me

Song of the Exile

The Story of Woo Viet

Swordsman II

Tai Chi Master

Temptation of a Monk

The Terracotta Warrior

Thunderbolt

To Be Number One

To Liv(e)

To Live and Die in Tsimshatsui

Tricky Brains

Twinkle, Twinkle Lucky Stars

The Wicked City

Wild Search

Wing Chun

Witch from Nepal

Wonder Seven

Not Recommended
("These are all, in my opinion, horrible.")

All's Well, Ends Well

An Amorous Woman of the Tang Dynasty

Black Cat

Black Cat II: The Assassination of President Yeltsin

Holy Weapon

Crazy Safari

Dr. Lamb

The Eighth Happiness

Farewell China

Remains of a Woman

Robotrix

The Magic Crane

Royal Tramp II

The Bride with White Hair II

Naked Killer

Night Caller

CHUCK STEPHENS

Chuck Stephens is the film critic for the *San Francisco Bay Guardian*, and a freelance contributor to *Film Comment* and *The Village Voice*. Born in Nashville and raised in Baltimore, Stephens developed an interest in obscure cinema as a boy; at eleven, he made "imitation Hammer horror films" with a Super-8 camera, and acted all the parts. He got his BFA in film-making at the University of Maryland, where he studied with the experimental animator Stan VanDerBeek, then moved to Manhattan to take graduate courses at New York University. (Barry Long was a classmate.)

Stephens discovered Hong Kong films during his time in New York; he saw *A Better Tomorrow* in Chinatown, and *Peking Opera Blues* at the Film Forum. "The combination of exotica and hyperbole in the Hong Kong cinema turned me on," he recalls. "I also liked the pervasive sense of hopelessness – that the main figure of identification is often allowed to die at the end of the film, and die horribly."

Stephens is currently at work on a critical biography of Jack Webb.

Most Highly Recommended

Ashes of Time

A Better Tomorrow

Bullet in the Head

Center Stage

Dangerous Encounter of the First Kind
"Tsui's greatest, weirdest film, a true psychotronic wonder – call it 'Puking Opera Blues.' School kids plant bombs for kicks and run afoul of American arms traders; a psychotic chick pushes pins through the head of a mouse; no one survives intact. Political allegory or drive-in delight? You decide."

Days of Being Wild
"A clock-watching meditation on invented memories, missed opportunities, and misanthropic Mom-ism, Wong Kar-wai's intensely moody masterpiece put the director – and his cinematographer, Christopher Doyle – on the world-cinema map. Detractors have nattered that the film's loose ends – especially Tony Leung Chiu-wai's fleeting, cryptic appearance – belittle its formal coherence, when in fact they seem precisely the point. Nowhere else in Hong Kong film-making do visual glory and narrative invention – not to

mention Xavier Cugat and Rebecca Pan – find this sort of emotional alchemy."

Dragons Forever

"Goofy, irresistible clubhouse comedy in the old Buena Vista mode: imagine Jackie Chan as Dean Jones, Sammo Hung as Tim Conway, and Yuen Biao as Don Knotts."

Fallen Angels

"Wide screen wizardry abounds in this love-addled 'sequel' to *Chungking Express*. See Takeshi Kaneshiro ride a butchered hog! See Leon Lai attempt to emote! Watch Michelle Reis snarl her fishnet stockings! Whimsical and erotic, heartrending and finally full of hope. What *Days of Being Wild* did for Mom, this one does for Pop."

Full Contact

"Ringo Lam's particle-accelerator action flick features unforget-tably cheese-whiz villains and choice subtitling – such as when Chow Yun-fat glances at Bonnie Fu's lap and announces that he's seen a 'vomiting crab.'"

The Killer

Rouge

Highly Recommended

92 Legendary La Rose Noire

As Tears Go By

A Better Tomorrow II

"Painting the world exit-wound red, this film confirms that in Hell, there are no dry-cleaners."

A Better Tomorrow III: Love and Death in Saigon

The Blue Jean Monster

"*The Killer's* villain Shing Fui-on – 'Big Sillyhead' to his fans – stars as an undead police detective; Amy Yip's prime assets get a gory going over; demented, George Romero-esque sick trip/comedy."

Chungking Express

Hard-Boiled

My Heart Is that Eternal Rose
"Terrific slo-mo mayhem from the underrated Patrick Tam, Wong Kar-wai's one-time mentor and all-round demented film-maker. Shot by the brilliant Christopher Doyle, it's Joey Wong's best film, and a breakthrough for the young Tony Leung Chiu-wai."

Nomad
"Patrick Tam's berserk, forgotten mindblower mixes political zealotry with teen angst, and forges a *Beyond the Valley of the Dolls* for Hong Kong's ideological malaise; plenty of taboo-busting sex scenes featuring a very young Leslie Cheung."

On the Run
"Yuen Biao tries to run, but doesn't get far; as Hong Kong film maven Tod Booth says, 'Whatever happened to the good old days of Hong Kong cinema, when the heroes always died?'"

Peking Opera Blues

People's Hero
"Tough-as-nails rewrite of *Dog Day Afternoon*, with the forever-fraught Ti Lung, and without the sex change."

Red Rose, White Rose

Saviour of the Soul

Recommended

Dr. Lamb
"A Category III exploitationer guaranteed either to clear the room, or lodge eternally in the crevices of the viewer's lizard brain."

The Eagle Shooting Heroes

East Is Red

Haunted Cop Shop II
"Goofy comedy from Jeff Lau (Wong Kar-wai's partner at Jet

Tone Productions) featuring a very funny riff on Chow Yun-fat's famous guns-in-the-potted-plant scene from *A Better Tomorrow*."

The Heroic Trio

"A cartoon with millennial frosting, worth a visit just for its tinkling, end-of-an-era theme-song: 'London Bridge is falling down . . . .'"